ADVANCE PRAISE

"James' work is an intellectual *tour de force*, weaving complex philosophical and psychological themes into the everyday challenges faced by leaders. As leaders, we are faced with profound questions – about our identity, our role, our perspective. Contending with these questions is how we serve best as leaders. James' book is a rare glimpse into the depths."

Nick Shackleton-Jones
CEO, Shackleton Consulting, Author, *How People Learn*

"Stunning. Brilliant. *Ego Flip* is a hugely enjoyable intellectual and emotional gallop that drives straight to the heart of hope for humanity and how to lead in this complex, turbulent world. With crystal-clear vision, and an expansive knowledge of the sciences, philosophy, the arts, psychology, psychoanalysis, cultural variances and organizational development, James Woodcock argues that it is only by extending human consciousness and shedding the limitations of ego, self-interest and power that will enable us to navigate and survive the gambles and uncertainties of today. Using practical examples and compelling logic, he shows us how to develop our consciousness and identify the limiting stories that the ego weaves for us. In other words, how to '*ego flip*'. All of this is done with precision and rigor, embracing embodiment alongside emotion and cognition in a convincing gestalt approach. The book crescendos toward the final section, 'Leading Onwards.' It discusses what leaders must tangibly do to collaborate and communicate in complexity in a post-growth, AI world. For teams and organizations that learn to '*ego flip*,' this book holds the promise of a dynamic and agile future that embraces sustainability and circularity, liberating human energy to move from 'ego' to 'eco' leadership. Finally, here is a clear pathway to becoming better humans. Truly brilliant. As a leader seeking a blueprint for how to evolve and lead in the extreme complexity of today's organizations, this book gives you everything you need."

Claire Dale
Founder, Physical Intelligence Institute

"Leaders in every field of human endeavour need to be able to question themselves and what motivates them, to be a leader of change. James Woodcock brilliantly exposes what it really takes for leaders to change and adapt in the modern world. This book is a must for every leader that has the courage to lead beyond the ego."

Sir Chris Bryant MP
Member of Parliament for Rhondda, Author, *Code of Conduct* and *Entitled*

"*Ego Flip* is a cognitive rollercoaster. Starting with a wonderfully divergent approach that forces the reader to mentally grapple with some sizeable existential, paradoxical and philosophical questions; it then systematically and elegantly funnels down to help us to not only understand the implications on our leadership but also provides practical, insightful ways of incorporating these insights into one's leadership offer. Profound, provocative and utterly compelling for anyone interested in a fresh and relevant approach to leadership."

Mark Richardson
Olympic silver medalist, former World Champion and leadership and culture expert

"An illuminating exploration of leadership that delves deep into the paradox of self-reference and ego. This book challenges conventional notions, offering a transformative perspective on leadership's potential to shape our world. A must-read for leaders seeking profound insights and a new path forward."

Dan Strode
Author, *The Culture Advantage*

"If this book has even caught your eye, you are already a leader who seeks genuinely to serve. Forget models and theories, this is personal. James gives a step-by-step guide about how to be genuinely different. He shines a light on the leadership of the future in a strong call for each of us to look inward first."

Rachel Griffiths
Founder, The Natural Leader

"In *Ego Flip*, James Woodcock confronts his readers with a powerful exposition of leadership, from the physics of our universe to theories of evolution through to behavioural psychology and the implications for psychopathy and sociopathy. This is a demanding read. He challenges directly the topic that many shy away from: power. His powerful descriptions of the different forms of power dynamics that play out in the workplace lead to a unique analysis of cognitive biases in decision-making. *Ego Flip* prescribes how leaders can break these cycles of systemic behavior to build more inclusive organizations. I applaud these messages. *Ego Flip* keeps its radical intellectual edge through to its manifesto for leadership – providing an illuminating vision for how to learn, collaborate and lead."

Keith Leslie
Chair, Samaritans UK and Ireland

"In this new paradigm for leadership, the author boldly looks beyond, to question the to-date unquestioned. James Woodcock skillfully lifts the lid on ego to reveal a new approach to leadership that serves to be significantly and universally more successful in the modern world. I recommend *Ego Flip* to anyone that wants to understand what great leadership really means in today's world, particularly those who may possess the courage to implement the learning!"

Stuart Evans
People Director, Future of Work, Capability and Learning, Rolls-Royce

"Cerebral, insightful, amazingly well-researched, bringing together so many different strands, this book will make you see leadership in a whole new light."

Neil Mullarkey
Author, *In the Moment* and cofounder of The Comedy Store Players

"I'm quite sure there isn't another book on leadership anything like this one. *Ego Flip* dismisses simple, surface-level leadership advice, and instead heads straight to the core of you as a person. It takes you on a Zen journey through the fundamentals of self-knowledge to reveal a new perspective on how you can really know yourself and others. If you're looking for soundbites and easy fixes, this book is not for you. But if you want to know how your ego warps your decision-making, and what you can do about it, strap in and read on!"

Russ Hendy
Managing Director, Tui Media

"This book provides a powerful voice advocating the need for humane, conscious leadership, away from egoic power dynamics and the centralization of power. *Ego Flip* vividly lays bare how only those leaders who can flip their ego can become leaders of the future, and a force for good. I warmly welcome this urgent and important book."

Professor Vlatka Ariaana Hlupic
Author, *The Management Shift* and *Humane Capital*, Founder of Management Shift Solutions Limited

"*Ego Flip* provides pioneering insight into how we can use stories to connect with the world around us, and how we can use our own stories to bring about profound change. A brilliant book for storytellers everywhere that believe in the power of stories to change our world."

Simon Douglas
Filmmaker

"In *Ego Flip*, James draws upon eclectic resources and presents profound and provocative thinking to provide a fascinating account for why leaders need to 'look behind the mask' to truly understand and embody what it means to 'lead.' With the examination of 'ego' at the heart, this book proposes a radical rethink on leadership and offers a definitive leadership manifesto for our future – a new way to lead."

Dr Sylvana Storey
Global Head of People Experience, Kroll

"This is an important and unique book in the leadership canon for today's challenging times. I'm very grateful to Woodcock for grappling with the sheer breadth and complexity of this topic with such rigor and integrity. *Ego Flip* gives us a framework to think deeply – it opens the door to a new understanding of leadership, through the lenses of philosophy and psychology. An essential read for anyone that wants to get serious about what good leadership truly requires of us."

Jen Emery
Author, *Leading for Organisational Change*

Published by
LID Publishing
An imprint of LID Business Media Ltd.
LABS House, 15–19 Bloomsbury Way,
London, WC1A 2TH, UK

info@lidpublishing.com
www.lidpublishing.com

A member of:

businesspublishersroundtable.com

© James Woodcock, 2024
© LID Business Media Limited, 2024

Printed by Imak Ofset
ISBN: 978-1-915951-01-4
ISBN: 978-1-915951-02-1 (ebook)

Cover and page design: Caroline Li

HOW TO RESET YOUR LEADERSHIP LIFE

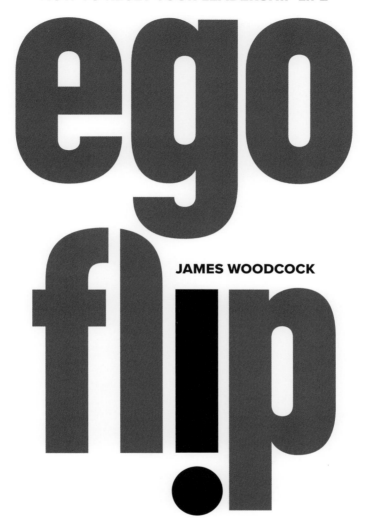

ego
flip

JAMES WOODCOCK

LID

MADRID | MEXICO CITY | LONDON
BUENOS AIRES | BOGOTA | SHANGHAI

for

Delia, Ethan and Isla

CONTENTS

FOREWORD
— BY STEVEN D'SOUZA

How simultaneously freeing and paralyzing to untether
the moorings of the previously unquestioned Known.
— Sergio De La Pava, *A Naked Singularity*[1]

Reading this book will give 'you' nothing. If you were hoping for quick tips and actionable self-improvement strategies, this isn't the right book for you. Place it back on the shelf and explore the 'business as usual' section.

You see, this is a dangerous book. Give it the time and reflection it demands, and it will transform not just your understanding of leadership, but of who you really think you are.

At its heart, this is a book about awareness. It's an invitation to ask the deeper questions of leadership, in a way that you may have never asked before. Rather than simply asking *"who am I?" Ego Flip* challenges our most fundamental beliefs, to explore *"when am I?," "where am I?," "why am I?"* and *"what am I?"* before contemplating the epistemology of *"how do we know?"*

James Woodcock skillfully leads us in this enquiry, weaving research and examples from the physical sciences, social sciences, the liberal arts and nature to elucidate his ideas. More importantly, throughout the book he offers thought experiments to give us the opportunity to directly enquire into our own experience, to test the ideas for ourselves.

The book takes us along a spellbinding journey, from looking at our beliefs in our individual identity, to demonstrating that what is really running the show is the ego, playing out our unconscious routines as leaders, and collectively as the Evil Genius Organization.

Why does this book matter? Frankly the answer is plain. Most books you will read do not explore the fundamental questions this book challenges us with. At best they offer tips and strategies that might actually help strengthen the ego. While in *Ego Flip*, our very identity – all that we think we know and how we know – is questioned.

The role of the ego at the individual level is to keep us seeking, frustrated and unfulfilled. At the organizational level, it serves to produce chronic disengagement and burnout. At the societal level, ego has driven a pandemic of mass consumerism, resulting in economic inequity and climate catastrophe. In response, this book offers us a profoundly different choice.

1. De La Pava, S. (1781). *A Naked Singularity.* (1st Edition). MacLehose Press.

This is not a doomsayer's book. James Woodcock systematically explores the nature of the 'ego' and how it operates in a clear and compelling way, offering models that bring clarity. While the book starts with deeper foundational questions, he offers practical ways to flip the ego, from embodied methods based on acting, to the ego flip process, GO practice and perspectival development.

Taking his thinking beyond the individual, he explores the implications for the practice of leadership. His Leadership Manifesto presents a bold new paradigm – how we can communicate, give 'FAST feedback,' manage performance and transform learning by challenging the conventional ego-driven practices. The book is radical in its perspectives, exploring the future of leadership, from the promise of AI and the metaverse to how other emerging trends will impact our lives.

Ultimately this book is an 'un-doing.' I hope it leaves you with more questions than answers. In so doing, *Ego Flip* will transform both your leadership and your life.

Steven D'Souza
Senior Partner, Korn Ferry, Author, *Not Knowing* trilogy

INTRODUCTION
THE LEADERSHIP PARADOX

This book explores the most essential, the most consequential, and yet the least-understood question of leadership – the question of who you are. Consider this: there are around two trillion galaxies in the known universe. Just one of these, the Milky Way, is a constellation of 200 billion stars. And around only one of these stars, our Sun, the Earth sets its orbit and gives life to an estimated one trillion life forms, including around eight billion people. And just one of these beings is you.

The story of YOU runs like the pages of this book – a series of moments to be discovered, then lost, one page at a time. But what if, instead, you could stop, let go and see through the story? Could that be possible?

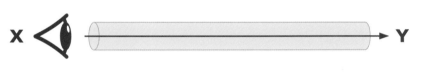

FIG 1 – SPYGLASS EXPERIMENT

Let's try an experiment. Tear a page from this book and roll it up to make yourself a simple cylindrical spyglass (Fig 1). Place it to your eye, and what do you see? Notice that whatever you find, there are always two aspects of your experience that hold true. First, at point Y, an experience appears to be taking place, in real time. Second, this experience is always at a distance from yourself, at point X. Through our experience, we can therefore perceive and locate who and where we are – the undeniable witness of our experience. Like the leader who precedes those that are led. But could it be possible for you to have this same experience, and for these two facts to not be true?

Perhaps we could conceive that none of 'this' (the here and now) is actually real. Perhaps what *this* is, is simply an illusion, a dream borne of some vast artificial intelligence that has lost itself in its own program, in which you're merely a collection of zeros and ones. But the problem with this hypothesis is YOU. You know that right now something *is* happening, and that knowing is undeniable.

You may ask: *What has a paper spyglass got to do with leadership?* The answer is that a leader will never understand the world, and what they are looking at, until they understand where they're looking from. Therefore, such a leader will inevitably not lead, but be led. Those who do look – and I mean *really look*, to understand the world – may find that there is, in fact, a third way, another possibility that will radically change their perspective of who they are.

We could describe the two ends of the spyglass as *our experience* (Y) and *consciousness* (X). The general, legitimized understanding of our world (that which constitutes experience) is 'that which exists outside of consciousness.' And yet, there is no actual evidence for that. Despite the many thousands of research papers written on consciousness, there is no consensus as to what consciousness actually is. Never in the history of science have so many people devoted so much time to produce so little.

If indeed experience is at a distance from consciousness, can we ever truly know what a thing is? The philosopher Immanuel Kant believed it was not possible to know the nature of experience – of the thing itself.[1] He believed all we are ever aware of is our perception of the thing. It is true that you will never, for example, actually see the objects in your experience – only the light that is reflected from them. To see your reflection, you cannot see the mirror, any more than you can see your own face. Kant recognized that he came from the world, and concluded that if the world is unknowable, then he was unknowable. That is simply not the case. Knowing is there in all experience because it is prior to your experience. It is the knowing that you exist. But how do we know that?

There are three ways we can acquire knowledge: empirical observation, rational thought and introspection. *Empirical observation* is gained through the direct experience of perception – through our senses. We typically refer to the quintet of sight, smell, hearing, taste and touch; there are, of course, many more. This is knowing the world directly, and what we observe (unlike imagination) is that our observations are shared – we share the world. Second, through *rational thought* we can conceptualize that which we have not or cannot perceive through our senses. We can formulate equations, deduce the Big Bang and write books. Third, if empiricism and rationality take our attention and interest toward our objective reality, *introspection* is holding up the mirror to the subject of our experience – to ourselves. It is from this that we derive our perspective.

There is plenty written in psychology about how the mind works. Introspection turns the question back on us, in the knowledge that everything we believe we know through perception and rational thought is filtered and conditioned through our knowledge of self. Perhaps the greatest acts of scientific endeavour have come when we've turned the

1. Kant, I. (1781). *The Critique of Pure Reason.* (Rev Ed Edition). Penguin Classics.

camera back on ourselves. At the turn of the 20th century, historian Arthur Schlesinger Jr. described the Apollo 11 Moon landing as the century's most significant human achievement – the moment when mankind's greatest discovery became not the Moon, but the Earth, as for the first time we were able to turn and look back at it.

Herein lies the problem. The scientific method rejects subjective experience. The grounds for this are themselves rational – personal experience is necessarily idiosyncratic and personal, and so cannot be validated by anyone other than the individual experiencing it. Science is based on a shared understanding of a shared world of shared phenomena, which means that while the scientific method is consistent, it is incomplete. It can tell us how the world behaves, but not what it is. It describes the choreography without saying anything about the dance. The worldview is that through science we are inexorably inching toward an ultimate understanding of reality. Some of the greatest minds attest to this.

But to understand the painting, one must also study the painter. One is an outward expression, one inward. There is a discipline, a rigour to objective analysis. It is difficult to scrutinize and rationalize objective reality with clarity. And this has been rewarded. The technological advances we've made in the last century are staggering, as we have slowly revealed the order and organization that exists within the universe. Through psychology and cognitive science, our understanding of the mind of the leader has similarly been honed. Science has endowed mankind with increasing powers of deduction. Introspection has never been part of that toolset and never received this recognition. And the price for this explicit separation of scientist from the science – of self from world – is suffering.

On a macro scale, we see an increasing polarization of opinions and power, from libertarianism to capitalism. Culture and science are inextricably linked. The mindset of science has been imbued into our culture as we each focus on our little piece of the puzzle. Science is the ultimate arbiter of truth, through our conflation of what works to what is true. With our technology, we are burdened with huge responsibility.

The fundamental instrument of science is the finite mind. It is the eye that looks ever outward, through time and space, forever reaching. Throughout all the many pages of human history, we have sought the spaces that lie just beyond our understanding.

We have looked between the cracks, within the subatomic and quantum realms, into spaces of infinite regression. We have stared into the void, through the boundlessness of space, and through technology, have extended our gaze. In 2018, through the Hubble Space Telescope, we discovered a star whose light took nine billion years to reach Earth, looking as it did when the universe was about 30% of its current age. Only four years later, in March 2022, the same telescope discovered Earendel, or *morning star*, whose light is believed to have taken 12.9 billion years to reach us – observed as it was only 900 million years after the birth of the universe, when the universe was only 6% of its current age.

As Oscar Wilde once said, *"We are all in the gutter, but some of us are looking at the stars."*[2] Through our searching, it seems inevitable that one day mankind will look up and discover through the light of some distant star the dawn of existence – the Big Bang – a moment for the universe to trade asceticism for vanity, to bear witness to itself. Perhaps at that point – when we have seen as far as it is possible to see, in distance and in time – we will notice too that not only can the birth of the universe only ever be known to us in a place that is here and a time that is now, but that this ultimate revelation of our origin will reveal nothing about who we are.

Leadership is a paradox of identity. The function of a leader can be described by three inherent paradoxes. The first is the *paradox of equity*. It is the role of leadership to reconcile the dilemmas that arise through conflicting objectives, in response to competing priorities. How, for example, can an organization be wholly inclusive when it is existentially dependent as much on those who are not included as those who are? The second is the *paradox of service*. It pertains to the role of leadership as the pathfinder and standard-bearer. If leadership serves to inspire emulation, then how can its presence not simultaneously obscure the path ahead for those that follow? The third is the *paradox of purpose* – what the psychiatrist Viktor Frankl referred to as "man's search for meaning."[3] All leaders are defined by their solitary pursuit of a common truth, a unifying purpose, to discover who they truly are. But it is inherent to the act of seeking that the search for an answer must necessarily perpetuate the question from which it derives.

In this way, equity arises through inequity, so that a leader who is good must also be *evil*. Servitude arises through superiority, so that a leader who is ordinary must be a *genius*.

2. Wilde, O. (1892). *Lady Windermere's Fan.* CreateSpace Independent Publishing Platform.

3. Frankl, V. E. (1946). *Man's Search for Meaning.* (1s¹ Edition). Rider.

And meaning arises through the search beyond self, so that a leader that creates shared purpose creates a need to belong – *through organizations*. This is the paradox and parody of leadership that defines our times. It is within this paradox of self-reference – of EGO – that a system of leadership has evolved that is simultaneously self-aggrandizing and self-limiting: that of the Evil Genius Organization. It has arisen through the pervading belief in a model of leadership of which so much has been written, and to which so many have aspired, and yet so few have succeeded, because the model is broken. This book will explore why this is and how we can fix it. This paradox transcends the more traditional definitions of leadership, of rank and file. It is the signature of authorship – a leader as any individual who claims mastery of their thoughts and actions, of free will and choice.

To reconcile this paradox – to know *who you are* – is the perennial question for leadership. No question could be more important, more urgent, more intimate, than knowing the nature of that through which all is known. Would it be possible to know anything for certain without first knowing the nature of the one who knows? All you really know about the world is what is filtered through the limitations of the mind. That is the greatest ignorance of science, which it has demonstrated many times over. Take, for example, the moment in 1987 when astronomers hailed the appearance of a supernova in the Large Magellanic Cloud – presumed to be the closest such stellar explosion to Earth in centuries. Scientists racing to detect its pulsar (a spinning neutron star found in some supernova explosions) had to wait two years, until a radio signal was picked up emitting beeps of nearly 2,000 times a second – much faster than could be explained. Then, one night, the pulsar suddenly disappeared. It reappeared one year later as telescope operators brought a TV camera used for guidance back online, revealing the supposed supernova as merely a quirk in the camera's electronics.

In our obsession with objective experience, we make assumptions about our reality that profoundly affect our understanding of who we are. This book will enquire as to the truth of these assumptions – of who you are as a leader – through a lucid introspection of leadership and selfhood. We will consider the question of self-identity through the various ontologies of science, epistemology and metaphysics. We will explore the empirical and rationalized implications of our reality that science has yielded, before turning our attention to the facts of our direct experience.

In Part 1 we will **lead inward**, to consider the important role that ego plays as our locus of identity. We will examine the fundamental questions and assumptions on which we base our understanding of who we, and of the reality we serve, through consideration of seven *questions of leadership*:

- *When am I?* When do I exist in time and space? (Chapter 1)
- *Why am I?* Why does my understanding limit my perspective of reality? (Chapter 2)
- *What am I?* What are mind and matter really made of? (Chapter 3)
- *Where am I?* Where do I end, and where does my experience begin? (Chapter 4)
- *What is this?* What does my direct experience tell me about who I am? (Chapter 5)
- *Who am I?* Who is it that has free will, authorship and choice? (Chapter 6)
- *How do I know?* How do I know that I know this? (Chapter 7)

In Part 2, we will **lead outward**, to explore how ego has emerged as a new *meta ego* through the coordinated, collective, systematized expressions of ego that are shaping our world today. We will explore the role of leaders as disruptors and provocateurs, to lead the transition from ego-system to eco-system, through seven *elucidations of leadership*:

- *Egodynamics:* The first universal framework for describing how we self-identify, through our egoic thoughts and feelings (Chapter 8)
- *Ego Flip:* The art of forgetting yourself by consciously recasting your ego to change your life story (Chapter 9)
- *GO Practice:* The exploration of the inward and outward perspectives of direct experience (Chapter 10)
- *Evil Genius Organization:* The blueprint for the systemization of ego in our organizations and societies (Chapter 11)
- *SPIN:* The assertion of preference through our perpetual motion of attention (Chapter 13)
- *Perspectival Development:* The optimization of performance through preference and perceptivity (Chapter 14)
- *Cultural Synchronicity:* The synchronization of collective endeavour to deliver systemic change (Chapter 15)

In so doing, we will reveal a set of new leadership principles – provocations to invite a profound shift in the modern-day perspective of leadership. These include a new:

- Measure for egocentricity – the *Attachment Quotient (AQ) as the next evolution of EQ*
- Definition of learning – through the model of *Perspectival Development*
- Methodology for crafting living stories from lived experiences that engender greater empathy and affective resonance – *Storyliving*
- Critical indicator of organizational performance – *Inclusion Variance*
- Blueprint for the operation of egoic power dynamics that underpin organizational dysfunction – the *Evil Genius Organization*
- Relational model to explain the fundamental correlation between our egoic thoughts, feelings and sense of self – *Egodynamics Wheel*
- Classification of egoic preferences and cognitive bias – using *SPIN* to describe how our experiences are shaped by our attention
- Developmental framework for the practice of embodiment, through the application of method acting to personal development – *Method Learning*

Finally, in Part 3, we will **lead onward**. Leadership is entering a new epoch – a mass extinction event in which a new way to lead will arise. We will consider the future of leadership through a new *Leadership Manifesto* – a set of *eight conscious imperatives* that offer a radical vision for transcending the systemization of ego that is polarizing our planet. We will journey into the metaverse, to reveal how it will reshape the human experience and reset our locus of identity. To do so, we will present a unifying model for the evolution of human experience and the role that ego and leadership will need to play in order for us, as a species, to survive.

Through consideration of these differing perspectives, we will learn that they all point to one universal truth: at the heart of all modern understanding is a fundamental misunderstanding about who you are. This matters, because it is the cause of all suffering in the world today. It is no less important than that.

Before you read on, two words of caution. First, this book will kill, if you let it. You could, if you so choose, put it down and trade the next several hours of your time for someone who really needs it. Perhaps you could take the book back to the shop and donate your refund to charity. Perhaps you could go further. How many mouths could you feed, how many lives could you save, if you so wished? The truth is, if you don't put this book down, someone will die. And I say this to you, as the author of your own thoughts, believing this is a choice you have the power to make. Perhaps you're still reading for the same reason that no one ever talks about Thomas Midgley, the man who accidentally killed more people than anyone in history (around 100 million and rising) when he decided to put lead into petrol, and chose not to consider the consequences. Or perhaps you're still reading because, just maybe, this is not a choice that you – an evil genius of your own making – can ever actually make.

Second, the reality of experience – of who you are – cannot be known. You cannot say a single true word about reality. The mind, and therefore the tools of this author, are limited to logic and rational argument, which deal in absolute expressions of duality, while reality is relativistic. No one can tell you who you are. To remain totally faithful to the truth, we should remain silent. My hope, therefore, is that by the end of this book you will know less than when you began.

PART 1

LEADING IN:
THE QUESTIONS OF LEADERSHIP

1. WHEN AM I?
THE TIME AND SPACE OF REALITY

Who you are is also a question of *when you are*. To understand who we are as leaders, we need to understand our relationship with space and time.

Our perception of space and time is fundamental to our view of reality. Take a look around you. Time feels real to us because we can see the effect of it on us, and the world around us, all the time. From our memories, our history, our experience of aging, to the very act of cause and effect. And we know space because we ourselves, in our own bodies, occupy and are part of it. We move through it, we displace it, we fill it.

Pass your hand in front of your face, and you can see how inherent these qualities are to your experience. You can see your hand moving – how could moving be seen if there was not space in which it were to happen, and time in which to observe its change? Surely, in the absence of such dimensions, our own reality, and thereby our experience of it, would cease to exist. Mankind has been obsessed through scientific endeavour with refining our knowledge of space and time. Today, science can declare its progress through the following five claims:

1. THERE HAS NOT ALWAYS BEEN TIME FOR TIME

We tend to think of time as a 'thing,' something that exists in its own right. To answer the question, *"When did time begin?"* we could also ask, *"When did reality come into existence?"* We refer to the totality of reality as the universe. In 1781, Kant explored the beginnings of the universe in his book, *Critique of Pure Reason.*[1] His assumption was that time continues back forever, regardless of whether the universe had itself existed forever. However, in 1929, astronomer Edward Hubble observed that distant galaxies are moving rapidly away from us, deducing that the universe is expanding. He attributed this acceleration to 'dark energy,' an invisible anti-gravity force that pervades the universe. Through some sophisticated mathematics, it has been possible to calculate that some 14,000 million years ago, everything was at exactly the same point in space, and what we refer to as the Big Bang marked the beginning of the universe, the moment when the hands of time started ticking.

1. Kant, I. (1781). *The Critique of Pure Reason*. (Rev Ed edition). Penguin Classics.

2. TIME IS NOT A CONSTANT

Newton's laws of motion insist that velocities are never absolute and always relative. In other words, a train travels at 90 miles an hour with respect to the person standing on the platform. However, James Clerk Maxwell (who laid down the laws of electromagnetism) found that the speed of an electromagnetic wave, such as light, is fixed, regardless of who observes it. While Maxwell's discovery seemed incompatible with Newton's notions of relative velocities, Einstein reconciled this dilemma through the notion of *time dilation* and his theory of *special relativity*. According to special relativity, if an individual speeds up, time will slow down, and vice versa. This idea first came to Einstein on his way home from his job as a patent clerk in Bern, Switzerland, as he gazed at a clock tower and devised one of his many thought experiments. He envisaged that if he receded away from the clock tower at the universal speed limit (186,000 miles per second – the speed of light) the clock's hands would not move – and time would stop – but at the clock tower itself the hands would tick along at their normal rate. Einstein concluded that the faster you move through space, the slower you move through time.

As you get faster, the impact on time slowing down would only be noticeable when you reach the speed of light. We can actually observe time dilation happening in some of the largest particle accelerators, albeit on a minute scale. At the speed of light, the point at which time is presumed to stop, your mass would be infinite. Some physicists believe there is a particle called a tachyon that moves at the speed of light or faster, to infinity, and therefore is always travelling backwards in time. Consequentially, you would never see it arrive, only leave, violating the normal rules of cause and effect.

3. TIME HAS SPACE

The 17th century French philosopher René Descartes described time as a separate dimension from the three dimensions of space we inhabit. However, it was mathematician Hermann Minkowski who first postulated that instead of reality being a three-dimensional Euclidean space that evolves over time, it is, in fact, a four-dimensional non-Euclidean space that *just is*. This 'Minkowski space' is what's now more commonly referred to as spacetime. Spacetime describes whatever external reality underlies our collective experiences of the space between things and the time between events. In spacetime there is no universal division of events into past, present or future. In this model, space is not like a stage on which events happen, but rather, everything is entirely relative, with relativity appearing as causality and change. Time doesn't actually flow, space doesn't move, it is all just the illusion of perception. What we call 'experience' is our perception of causal relations in spacetime – the perceived relativity between different points in this non-Euclidean space, with this causality appearing as an 'event.' Space and time are examples of these causal relations, with every event appearing in time relative to the very first event – the Big Bang. In other words, time is the product of causality, rather than time giving rise to cause and effect. The dilemma this presents is that if existence is a function of relativity, then existence of a 'thing' is, by itself, impossible.

There is no evolution, no motion in spacetime. Spacetime is the shape of time. If you were to look at your life in spacetime, it would be described by a line segment. Your future already exists. Your past and future are just 'there,' some of which we have experienced and other parts we have not. Therefore, all of time (past, present, future) is also constantly in existence, even if we are not able to witness it. Time does not pass, it just is. So *now* is as much an illusion as the past and the future. Time appears to flow because otherwise you would not be able to perceive it. In other words, time's existence owes itself to the particular wiring in our brain.

Most of us still understand that Newton's apple fell out of the tree due to a force called gravity. However, Einstein showed that there is no such thing as gravitational force. Instead, it is a manifestation of spacetime curvature. Objects that fall follow straight-line, constant speed paths in a curved spacetime. The force of gravity is, in fact, an illusion, just like the force you feel in a train when it leaves the station. Rather, spacetime is distorted by mass, which is what causes Earth's gravity. Imagine spacetime as the surface of a trampoline – if you drop something with a lot of mass on top of it, such as a big ball like the Sun, then it distorts. Everything runs along spacetime, so when you distort spacetime you distort it for the objects around it too. If you rolled a marble onto the trampoline, it would drop down to the centre with the big ball, which is something you see with the orbiting of planets around the Sun.

We are pinned to the ground because spacetime is so distorted by the Earth's mass that it pushes down on us from above. The slump in the fabric around Earth is not uniform, and Earth's gravity is more intense as you move toward the centre of the Earth, where the curvature of spacetime is at a maximum. Therefore, an object falling from the sky accelerates as you move toward the centre of the Earth. You will be moving faster just before you hit the ground than in the clouds. And according to special relativity, the faster you move through space, the slower you move through time, which means your head is older than your feet. Different planets have different masses and therefore different gravitational strengths, and so will accelerate objects at different rates. In the movie *Interstellar*,[2] in which the protagonist lands on a planet in the proximity of a black hole, the gravity is so strong that one hour on the surface is equivalent to seven years on Earth.

4. TIME CAN RUN OUT

When a star collapses under its own gravity, it eventually reduces to zero volume with infinite density – a singularity known as a black hole. Black holes spin at close to the speed of light and have massive gravitational forces, bending spacetime to create significant time differences. At the centre of a black hole there is thought to be a gravitational singularity where gravity is infinite and time stops. Similarly, at the time of the Big Bang, the density of the universe and the curvature of spacetime would have been infinite – the suggestion being that time arose from this singularity.

5. TIME INFERS AN ASYMMETRICAL REALITY

The basic laws of physics (Schrodinger's equation, $f = ma$, gravity is inversely proportional to the distance squared, etc.) don't say anything about the direction of time – it simply doesn't matter. Newton's laws do not distinguish past from future, and neither does quantum mechanics. The laws of physics are symmetrical.

On the macroscopic level, there is only one rule that does have time going in one direction: the Second Law of Thermodynamics states that in any closed system, disorder (or *entropy*) always increases with time. As such, the measurement of entropy has been put forward as a measure of the distance between the past and future.

2. Nolan, C. (2014). *Interstellar.* Paramount Pictures.

The Greek root of the word translates to *a turning toward transformation*, with that transformation being chaos. In other words, Murphy's Law – things always tend to go wrong. An intact cup on the table is a state of order, but a broken cup on the floor is a disordered state. One can readily go from the cup on the table in the past to the broken cup on the floor in the future, but not the other way around.

The increase in disorder with time is an example of what is referred to as the *thermodynamic arrow of time*, distinguishing the past from the future. If we are experiencing time, this suggests that there is a change in entropy, and that we are not in equilibrium. It is the arrow that points to our own mortality, death having been described as the moment when a system that maintains a state that's far from equilibrium ceases to exist.

We might think of the Big Bang as a low-entropy state, which has been increasing ever since. Everything that has happened since the Big Bang is because of increasing entropy. The *cosmological arrow of time* describes the direction in which the universe is expanding. Our origin universe was very dense and simple, with a low entropic state. As the expansion of our universe accelerates and entropy increases, we can conceive a distant future in which there is also reduced disorder, as it tends toward a vacuum.

However, despite the progress that science has made to further our understanding, the challenge with the scientific perspective is that it is itself inherently flawed, for two key reasons: objectivity and relativity:

1. OBJECTIVITY: REALITY IS INDETERMINATE (THE OBSERVER IS THE OBSERVED)

At the beginning of the 20th century, as more regularities and laws were discovered, French mathematician Pierre-Simon Laplace postulated the notion of *Scientific Determinism* – that there could and would be a set of laws that would determine the evolution of the universe precisely. In the Newtonian model, it was assumed that the subject and the object were two separate things, such that the scientist is outside of the experiment, objectively. One of the challenges in holding up a microscope to the universe is that in doing so, you disturb what you see. In 1926, theoretical physicist Werner Heisenberg formulated his uncertainty principle. Put simply, it suggested that to observe a particle, you need to shine a light on it. However, that very light will disturb the particle you want to view. The more accurately one measures the position of a particle, the shorter the wavelength of light needed to observe it, which will disturb the particle by a greater degree. In other words, it is not possible to create a model of the universe that is completely accurate and thereby deterministic. You cannot observe the Universe without disturbing it. You cannot separate the observer from the observed, because you are, in effect, observing yourself.

2. RELATIVITY: REALITY IS NOT A JIGSAW (THE UNIFICATION OF PHYSICS)

Science is essentially made up of relativistic theories waiting to be disproved. A theory, by definition, can never be proved, only disproved. Even a theory that makes accurate predictions a thousand times over is still unproven. The history of science and physics describes the inexorable rise and fall of successive scientific discoveries, with each discovery sounding its own death knell. Each presents an ever more convincing, but resoundingly temporary, version of events.

The holy grail of science is to discover a single theory that describes the whole universe, and thereby our place within it. This quest is known as the *unification of physics* and there have been many false dawns. At the beginning of the 20th century, it was thought that everything could be explained in terms of the properties of continuous matter. The discovery of atomic structure and the uncertainty principle put an end to that. Then again, in 1928, physicist Max Born told a group of visitors to Göttingen University, following the formulation of an equation that governed the electron, that "*Physics as we know it will be over in six months.*" We are still waiting.

There are essentially two scientific theories that are used today to describe a partial view of the universe: the *general theory of relativity* and *quantum mechanics*. The former describes big-picture phenomena across distances up to a million million million million million miles. In comparison, quantum physics focuses on much smaller measurements – down to a millionth of an inch. Unfortunately, these two theories are inconsistent with one another. Any 'unified' theory would need to reconcile their fundamental disagreements.

In quantum mechanics, all physical forces are carried by certain particles – a boson carrying a weak force, a photon carrying an electromagnetic force, or a gluon carrying a strong force. However, according to the general theory of relativity, gravity is a force unlike any other. Gravity is a theory of geometry; a construct of spacetime itself that requires the measurements of space and time to be exact for the theory to work. But there is no way to precisely measure things in the quantum world, and so the story of gravity is at odds with the story of quantum physics.

Scientist David Bohm summarized the state of affairs as follows: "*...in relativity, movement is continuous, causally determinate and well defined, while in quantum mechanics it is discontinuous, not causally determinate and not well-defined. Each theory is committed to its own notions of essentially static and fragmentary modes of existence (relativity to that of separate events connectible by signals, and quantum mechanics to a well-defined quantum state). One thus sees that a new kind of theory is needed that drops these basic commitments and, at most, recovers some essential features of the older theories as abstract forms derived from a deeper reality in which what prevails is unbroken wholeness.*"[3]

Of course, there could be an infinite sequence of more and more refined theories, or 'boxes within boxes,' as is sometimes referred. The scientific approach to this seemingly insurmountable challenge is to break the problem statement up into parts and tackle each part of the puzzle individually. These pieces reflect delineations of concept, not reality, and, as such, risk a fragmented picture that negates the fundamental interoperability and interdependency that the components of the universe undoubtedly describe. Consider also the implications of solving this challenge in the context of the Second Law of Thermodynamics, in which the passage of time will increase complexity, with the number of conceptual jigsaw pieces required to complete the puzzle increasing by the day.

For these two reasons, while our scientific understanding and definition of time and space has kept pace with its own passing, there remains a lack of consensus around the fundamental model of the universe, and therefore the role that time and space play within it. More importantly, we should remember that these theories are mental models – concepts to help us understand and predict the world around us. They are not equal to the world

3. Bohr, D. (1980). *Wholeness and the Implicate Order.* (1st Edition). Routledge.

around us. To understand more fully our experience, we need to look more closely at our direct experience of space and time.

While objects appear to us in space and time, abstract entities such as classes, properties and relations do not. Indeed time, when considered as an abstract property of experience, appears out of time. We may think of those that appear in time as those affected by time, as they present the appearance of change. Yet, as with changing thoughts, all concepts can appear to us as a memory, as something of the past. That which is experienced in time has actuality, and that which is not has potentiality.

Our experience of the passage of time is referred to as the *psychological arrow of time* – the direction in which we feel time passing, in the way that we can remember the past but not the future. The psychological arrow and thermodynamic arrow always point in the same direction, as we remember events in the order in which entropy and disorder increases. Yet, although the past and future feel real to us, we never actually experience them directly. None of us has ever visited a time or place called the past, or indeed will ever visit a time or place called the future. In our direct experience, there is no evidence that they exist. What we experience are thoughts and concepts that arise always *in this moment* – if we can call it that – which provide us with a mental schema through which we can understand and engage with the world. Could it be that you do not appear through time, but that time appears through you? That who you are is in every sense timeless – not a place in space, or a point in time, but indeterminate and therefore infinite? In this moment, in the absence of time, there is infinite opportunity, and infinite chaos, and with that, infinite possibility of who we really are.

2. WHY AM I?
LOGIC AND THE LIMITATIONS OF THE MIND

To understand who you are is to understand why you are. Are we that which we see of ourselves within experience, or could who we are lie beyond that understanding?

Our view of reality is limited. Our brain, as impressive as it is, remains a product of evolution – it is a work in progress. As a technology it is certainly advanced, relative (we presume) to other life on Earth. However, unless we believe that the human brain represents the apex of evolution, its development can be defined in part by its inherited limitations. In this chapter, we will explore how our mind's finite abilities have shaped our understanding of reality. Through the finite mind, misunderstanding arises not from the answers we derive, but from the questions that we ask of it.

Our mind is like a translator, an augmented reality that presides over our experience by labelling everything that we recognize. To the rational mind, the label *is* our reality, indistinguishable from the thing to which it is attached. But stand back for a moment and you can see that there is a difference. The problem the mind has is that if you take the label off, we lose the faculty of mind – there is nothing for it to *do*, nothing it can *use* or understand. From the mind's perspective, this is futile. In a world where what matters is how you can make use of what is around you – be it for your gain, or society's gain; to further technology or to fix a tap – the point of looking beyond the labels we attach in order to simply 'observe' seems pointless. We are inherently motivated by and fixated on the objectification of our experience. As the writer and philosopher G.K. Chesterton once said: *"A madman is not someone who has lost his reason but someone who has lost everything but his reason."*

We walk around in tinted spectacles, oblivious to the fact that everything we see is shaded by the shadow our mind casts. As beautiful as your world might appear, don't for one moment think that you can see the whole rainbow. In the same way, when we view reality through the limitations of our mind, it is logical to assume that the reality we see will be filtered and pervaded by those limitations. And your mind, of course, has no way of pointing this out to you. These limitations are not seen unless we look very closely at our direct experience, and how we think.

LOGIC – THE ELEPHANT IN THE ROOM

We sometimes say that the world is not black and white, but that is exactly how we see it, through logic. Logic is our universal language, the programme through which we decode and understand the world around us. It is relativistic, in that everything is defined by comparison to something else. Just as your mind cannot comprehend 'top' without 'bottom,' so you cannot *not* think of an elephant without first thinking of one. This dualistic understanding of the world is the basis for all reason. It is the operating system for our cognitive intelligence, and the only operating system at our disposal. There is nothing wrong with this programme, so long as we understand that it offers a codification not of what we see, but of what we think we see. For the rational mind, therefore, all knowledge is relative. To put it another way, all understanding is conceptual. Everything we understand, every thought we have about the world we live in, is an augmentation that our mind projects onto actual reality. It is part of reality (part of what we experience) but not all of reality. And certainly not all of what we might refer to as 'intelligence.' A byproduct of this programme (but not the programme itself) is the ego, which we'll explore in a later chapter.

The premise of logic is simple: to understand something you simply break it down into smaller and smaller pieces. In a computer, this might translate into the binary code of zeros and ones. The level of abstraction will dictate the level of understanding. We describe 'truth' as where a 'ground' has been reached, beyond which there is no further abstraction of understanding. To this end, logic assumes that every part of the universe can be divided up in this way, so that through rational thought the entire knowledge of the universe can be contained and understood. Logical thought serves us well in most cases, but when we start to explore our reality more precisely, we can begin to see its limitations. To present these logical thoughts, we of course need to do so in the form that the mind will understand: using concepts. Let's explore some examples.

1. EXPERIENCING THE 4TH DIMENSION

Our experience of the world is in three dimensions: height, length and width. Yet, we observe things happening in the universe (such as gravity) that cannot be explained solely by the dimensions we experience, from which we have hypothesized a 4th dimension called spacetime. The ability to conceive experience will always extend beyond the limitations of our direct experience. Imagine, for example, if you were a one-dimensional being and could only move in one plane – left or right, such as if you lived on this page. If these beings were two friends that had a falling out and went their separate ways, they would expect to never see each other again. However, if these one-dimensional beings lived in a two-dimensional reality – such as on the circumference of a circle – at some point they would meet up again. Although they would have no experience of this 2nd dimension, they could hypothesize that it exists because of the effects they observe. It is the same for us and the hypothetical 4th dimension (and of course there could be many more dimensions).

2. TO INFINITY AND BEYOND

As the saying (among theoretical physicists, at least) goes, "*Infinity is where things happen that don't.*" We cannot conceive of infinity. Our rational mind, as the frame through which we describe our experience, sets boundaries and distinctions. It is the point of view of a subject to conceive an object, or limitation of form. Science has always struggled to place the concept of infinity within its theorems. For years, science has contemplated what came before the Big Bang. The general theory of relativity postulates that the universe started off with infinite density, at the singularity of the Big Bang. At this singularity, general relativity and all other laws of physics would break down, creating a boundary in spacetime – the beginning of time.

However, if creation requires a creator, then how can there be a beginning, or indeed an end? It is the same as asking how something could arise from nothing. In our minds, nothing and something seem like very definite things, but they are, in fact, concepts that only exist because of one another. To say something has no end is to say it has no beginning. Every stick has two ends; to imagine a stick that has only one is beyond our comprehension. For infinity to exist in our reality, it must require the two ends of reality – the polarity and duality – to be joined together into one. This would need to be in the most fundamental sense *in that everythin*g, and everything is not a thing, but rather *the one thing*.

In our attempts, we might imagine a universe that extends forever, and then place ourselves – a finite form – within it. In doing so, as a localization, we displace and therefore limit space. For infinity to exist and retain us as a separate entity, it becomes by definition finite. Therefore, for us to exist at all, we ourselves must be infinite.

In science we talk about infinity in a particular direction – for example, in time or in space, to explain what happens in a black hole or at the edge of an expanding universe. To describe infinity, in fact to describe any concept, requires an axis, a relativity of *from* and *to*. We can only conceive within the perceived dimensions of our experience – of time and space – which present their own limitations. Imagine time travelling on forever. We know that time and space are part of the same 'thing' (spacetime), so for one to be infinite, would not the other need to be infinite? And where does infinity start? It would need to have no end, and therefore no centre. Which means that you can't have something AND infinity. The only way for infinity to exist is if everything is infinite.

Imagine looking down a microscope, smaller and smaller, into infinity, such as within a fractal, or looking into a never-ending future. These are two recognizable 'dimensions' that we see in our reality. But separate infinities cannot coexist unless there is only one infinity, with no dimensions, just infinite unfolding right now. In the infinite abyss, science looks for ground, a reference point for reality. Take, for example, the gravitational constant, which has a set value, which basically means that gravity has a set strength. And as far as we can tell, it is finite and has remained constant through the entire history of the universe. But what is it that enforces this limitation? And what lies beyond that limitation? Infinite regress is a feature of reality.

So, not only can we say that a finite thing cannot exist by itself, we can also say it's impossible for anything to exist without infinity. You cannot have one thing without everything. The only way to have anything is to have everything. Which is one thing. Finitude implies infinity. Reality is perfectly and infinitely symmetrical. Infinite power is necessary to bring even a single atom into existence. Scientists, materialists, rationalists and atheists will not understand this. Infinity is oneness. The problem-solving principle *Occam's Razor* states that the simplest explanation is preferable to one that is more complex. This explanation is, of course, the simplest of all possibilities, because it does not explain anything. Infinity is magic – the impossible (according to the finite mind) made possible. As Shakespeare said, *"Truth may seem, but cannot be."*[1]

1. Shakespeare, W. (1601). *A Lover's Complaint, and the Phoenix and Turtle.* Forgotten Books.

3. LOST FOR WORDS

The notion that there is more than just what we can conceive, or can put words to, makes no sense to the mind. But if you have ever been at a loss for words, where there are simply no words to describe what you experience – what you feel – you will understand that our reality is more than can be written down in a book. We might describe reality as something limited only by our imagination. Within language, we can have a go at describing it, but it only ever scratches the surface. It's like trying to describe the French language using only English words.

It could be said that all words are lies and, relatively speaking, this is true. And yet, all words are themselves part of reality, and so from their own perspective can only speak the truth. As Humpty Dumpty explains to Alice in *Through the Looking Glass*, *"When I use a word ... it means just what I choose it to mean."*[2]

4. PARADOXICAL SELF-REFERENCE

Because logical concepts offer a limited perspective of reality, and yet we believe that they *are* reality, they always lead to paradox. For example, an individual can conceptualize anything, even that the individual does not exist. The term paradox, like all terms, is used loosely, to sometimes describe an apparent contradiction. An important aspect of these paradoxes is self-reference. In the context of language, self-reference denotes a statement that refers to itself. Self-reference can be used in a broader context as well. A picture could be considered self-referential if it contained a picture of itself within itself. Most paradoxes of self-reference are categorized as *semantic*, *set-theoretic* or *epistemic*.

Semantic: Semantic paradoxes principally relate to theories of truth. A famous example is the liar paradox, which states, *"Everything I say is a lie."* This breaks its own logic, due to its self-reference and, as a result, we cannot understand it. If we were to say, *"Everything they say is a lie,"* then the paradox does not occur. Similarly, in the statement, *"This statement is false,"* its self-reference implicates and therefore contradicts itself. If the statement is false, it would then also be true. *Dialetheism* is the view that there can be true contradictions, meaning that it is possible for a sentence to be both true and false. If adopting the view of dialetheism, all the

2. Carroll, L. (1871). *Through the Looking Glass.* Dover Publications.

paradoxes of self-reference dissolve, and instead become existential proofs of certain dialetheia – they, by their very existence, prove a 'logic beyond logic.'

Set-theoretic: The best-known set-theoretic paradox is Russell's paradox, which philosopher Bertrand Russell published in *Principles of Mathematics* in 1903.[3] Consider a group of barbers who shave only those men who do not shave themselves. Imagine there is a barber in this collection who does not shave himself. Then, by definition, he must shave himself. Russell's paradox demonstrates a fundamental limitation of mathematics – specifically, that Cantorian 'set theory' (referring to an infinity of sets within sets within sets) led to contradictions, meaning that not only set theory, but most of mathematics (due to its dependence on set theory), was technically in doubt.

Epistemic: An example of an epistemic paradox – that concerned with knowledge – is the paradox of the knower (although the paradox has many equivalent formulations): *"This sentence is not known by anyone."* It is similar to the liar paradox, except that the central concept involves knowledge rather than truth. Look closely and you may notice that the self-reference that derives the apparent paradox is itself precipitated from your own subjective association with the statement. Seen in that context, the paradox resides not within the sentence, but as a result of our own subjective understanding.

3. Russell, B. (1903). *Principles of Mathematics*. (1st Edition). Routledge Classics.

4. Penrose, L.S. and Penrose, R. (1958). *Impossible Objects: A special type of visual illusion*: British Journal of Psychology, 49, 31-33.

FIG 2 – PENROSE TRIANGLE[4]

These statements are all examples of *strange loops*, a form of paradoxical circular hierarchy, where something points back at itself. In logic, something is this, or that. A *strange loop*, however, does not provide this distinction, creating an apparent impossibility. Consider, for instance, the Penrose Triangle[4] (Fig 2). It seems impossible that it could exist in any reality other than a two-dimensional one, but that is because we can only think and perceive within our own dimensions. A strange loop provides a primitive way of describing a state in which everything happens at once, in every moment, in every space. In strange loops there are no well-defined hierarchies or order, no start or end. We are ourselves part of the paradox of self-reference whenever we observe reality, but are simultaneously part of it, as we become part of reality looking back on itself. And yet, for reality to be infinite and contained by everything, how can it point to itself? It is the ultimate contradiction, the ultimate self-reference problem. How can one thing point to itself when it is the only thing; when it cannot go outside of itself to do so? There would need to be something else to point to, which there isn't. Perhaps reality is itself a strange loop – nothing becomes everything, so that illusion becomes reality.

5. ENCAPSULATION OF KNOWLEDGE

Through science we seek a universal theory that will connect all pieces together. We have developed branches of scientific enquiry whose roots spread from the stellar to the cellular. Science is always striving for the edge, against which we set our plane of understanding, and through which its furtherance creates an ever more fractured reality, through the concepts we create. But through our encapsulation of knowledge we have forgotten the inherent futility of its progress. In the model of an infinite reality, there will always be a way to go bigger or smaller, or anywhere – somewhere beyond our understanding. And, of course, as brilliant as our faculties of mind undoubtedly are, our description of reality will always reflect the limitations of the particular perspective through which reality is perceived. As long as we realize that, it should seem obvious that while we might derive a theory of everything, as a container for our understanding we will be forever seeking the lid.

Logician Kurt Gödel's Incompleteness theorems show that any set of axioms you could posit as a possible foundation for math will inevitably be incomplete. His theorems showed that there can be no mathematical theory of everything, and no unification of what is provable and what is true. Gödel suggests that if truth were a circle, then you could only ever prove the existence of a smaller circle within it. Truth therefore always exceeds what is provable. To put it another way, if you want to prove a system you need to look at it from a bigger system. We would therefore need to look at reality through a metalanguage or metalogic – but then of course the same problem would arise, ad infinitum. In other words, you cannot prove the truth; you can only prove parts of a system. And if you can't encapsulate reality through logic, reality must be infinite. Were reality to be infinite, it would by definition be unknowable, beyond reason. In this way, Gödel proved that mathematics is infinite beyond the possibility of any algorithm to figure it out. As such, however powerful your supercomputer may be, mathematics is essentially unsolvable and incomputable. This is described as math's 'fatal flaw' – that it cannot be captured in a system, as there are infinite possibilities.

Similarly, mathematician Alfred Tarski's Undefinability theorem, which applies more broadly to any formal system, showed that truth cannot be defined within that system. And so, it follows that arithmetical truth cannot be defined in numbers, just as the truth that is spoken cannot be defined by words. The implication is that you cannot come up with a theory of everything, because everything is infinite.

It would seem that logical theory – how we think – however grand or small, can only ever offer a partial glimpse of reality. Rationalists, logicians and mathematicians believe that reason is sufficient to understand the world, and that a contradiction or a paradox is an error, a glitch in the matrix. They assume that logical proof is the highest standard of proof, and that if a thing is irrational or illogical, or introduces subjectivity, it must be false. Their fundamental assumption is that infinity does not exist and, as such, truth lies in definitive answers that are verifiable. In their attempts to subdivide the infinite, scientists have created the world's most future-proofed job.

In comparison, Gödel's and Tarski's theorems allude to a non-dual metaphysical understanding of the universe. They point to a truth that resides beyond logic, beyond your mind. When you dig into the self-reference problem, it becomes apparent that you are the thing you are looking at. That paradox is not a bug in reality, but rather, it is inherent to reality. The problem for logic is that this is at odds with the notion of all systems and classifications of knowledge that would seek to put reality 'in a box' – this being the whole premise of science, philosophy, language and logical understanding.

Could it be that what the universe is, and indeed who you are, can only ever be that which is *beyond* our understanding?

3. WHAT AM I?
THE MATERIALIST PARADIGM

To know *who* we are is to understand *what* we are made of. For this, we must investigate the fundamental nature of reality and its metaphysical implications – the relationship between mind and matter. The prevailing (and many would say the only sensible) view is that the universe is made of 'stuff' called matter. According to theoretical physicist Stephen Hawking, there are about 100 quinvigintillion (1 with eighty zeros after it) particles in the region of the universe that we can observe.[1]

Materialism holds that the only things that exist are matter and energy, that all things are composed of matter, that all actions require energy, and that all phenomena (including consciousness) are the result of the interaction of matter. This materialist paradigm is *the worldview*. It describes a physical reality that we can see, interact with, are born into, and that will continue to exist after we die.

It is a reality made of small building blocks – cells, atoms, electrons forming the substance to that reality, from which we ourselves are made. The materialist paradigm has formed from some of the greatest minds in human history, from Socrates through to the likes of Democritus (who discovered the atom), Aristotle (who created the first classification of living beings), Euclid (the father of Euclidian geometry), Descartes (who enshrined the idea of dualism, through the concepts of matter and mind inside the body: "I think, therefore I am") and Newton (through the development of calculus and Newtonian mechanics). The materialist paradigm describes a clockwork universe: rational, causal, deterministic.

Materialism works well when we want to understand the fragments of reality. But the nature of our changing world requires us to see the bigger picture, to think about the whole system. The question is, just how far do we want to zoom out?

In recent times, this materialist model has been challenged by modern science. Thanks to Einstein, we know that time is relative, and depends on how fast I am moving relative to you. If you were to look at the world from the perspective of a beam of light, everything would appear frozen in time. We also know that space is non-Euclidean, with the discovery of the four-dimensional fabric of spacetime, which showed how gravity affects the curvature of this non-Euclidean space. Perhaps the most significant challenge to the materialist paradigm occurred at the turn of the 20th century, with the arrival of quantum mechanics (around the same time as Einstein published his theory of relativity).

1. Hawking, S.W. (1992). *A Brief History of Time.* (1st edition). Bantam.

Quantum mechanics describes the behaviour of matter and light on an atomic and sub-atomic scale. Since the discovery of the electron in 1896, evidence that all matter existed in the form of particles had been slowly accumulating, and it was thought that waves and particles (or matter) were distinct phenomena. On initial observation, waves and particles appear to have contrasting properties. A particle is localized – it has a position, which means you can point to it and contain it. Particles carry momentum and will move in a straight line until hitting another object, such as another particle. We describe physical interactions through the behaviour of particles as they bounce off each other and change their trajectories. Compare that to a wave, which is neither localized nor containable, passing around or even through objects. Accordingly, the behaviour of waves is described and predicted by very different sets of mathematics. However, it turns out that the distinctions we have drawn are not clear-cut, due the following observations:

OBSERVATION 1: LIGHT IS A WAVE ... AND A PARTICLE!

In the 1800s, scientist Thomas Young used the so-called *double-slit experiment* to show what happens to light when shined through two narrow openings. He observed what is referred to as a *classic interference pattern*, producing stripes of varying intensity. The pattern arises due to some of the waves combining to cancel themselves out, alongside others that do not. The same pattern can be observed in water, when its waves are passed through two narrow channels. This corroborated the scientific perspective that light, like water, was a wave.

However, that assertion would be challenged later that century by theoretical physicist Max Plank and his studies on blackbody radiation. Based on his observations, Plank proposed that light is actually emitted in discrete packets, and not like a wave at all. Einstein would later build on this idea through his research into the photoelectric effect, from which he described these packets of light as discrete units of energy, or 'photons.' In fact, more advanced versions of the double-slit experiment that have placed detectors at each of the slits show that each detected photon passes through only one slit (as a classical particle) and not through both slits (as would a wave). This has given rise to the notion of wave-particle duality: the idea that light has the properties of both a wave and a particle, depending on the type of observation you apply.

OBSERVATION 2: MATTER IS A PARTICLE ... AND A WAVE!

If you fire electrons (a type of particle) through two slits, it surprisingly produces the same interference pattern that is observed with light waves. In the 1920s, physicist Louis de Broglie proposed that if light and matter both have energy and momentum, then perhaps matter – like light – also has a wavelength. The 'Copenhagen interpretation' explains how this might be possible through its definition of a wave of matter as representing all the possible places where a particle might be, when we look for it – a wave *of probability*. When electrons pass through the two slits, this uncertainty causes their interferences as their locations cancel each other out, creating the same interference pattern we observe with waves.

OBSERVATION 3: OBSERVATION IS FUNDAMENTAL TO REALITY!

In 1927, physicist Paul Dirac developed quantum field theory (a branch of quantum mechanics), stating that everything is, in fact, a field, like a cloud of possibilities. The theory suggests that when you look at a field, that cloud collapses into a particular result. When it is not being observed, it exists as a superposition of all the possible states. Imagine there was a rabbit in front of you. The implication is that when you are not looking at (and thereby not conscious of) the rabbit, the rabbit exists as infinite possibilities. The act of observation then collapses the wave function into a particle and localizes to what you see. So long as the observer interacts energetically with a particle, it loses its wave-like quantum state and transforms into a particle. This is referred to as the *observer effect*. As physicist Werner Heisenberg describes, *"The idea of an objective real world whose smallest parts exist objectively in the same sense as stones or trees exist independently of whether or not we observe them ... is impossible."*[2] Observation is therefore fundamental to the concept of reality. Mathematically, these fields present an infinite set of scalars – physical qualities that are completely described by their magnitude – at every possible point in space. In other words, as these data points are infinite – by definition, what they point to is nothing.

Schrödinger's cat is a thought experiment that illustrates the apparent paradox of this quantum superposition. In the thought experiment, a cat is penned inside a steel chamber with a Geiger counter. A small amount of radioactive substance is placed inside, such that there is equal probability that in the course of an hour either one or none of

2. Heisenberg, W. (1958). *Physics and Philosophy.* Harper Perennial.

the atoms will decay. The chamber is rigged so that a flask of lethal hydrocyanic acid is released if a single atom decays. The Copenhagen interpretation's assertion that a quantum system remains in superposition until it is observed by the external world implies that the cat is simultaneously alive and dead, until one looks inside the box, and thereby sees only one possible outcome.

DOES OBSERVATION REQUIRE CONSCIOUSNESS?

While the Copenhagen interpretation describes a set of probabilities that can be used to predict different observed outcomes, it says nothing about the act of observation itself. In quantum mechanics, the transition from clouds of simultaneous, overlapping possibilities into the defined form of objects or events is technically called a *measurement*. But who is observing the measurement, and does observation bring about this transition, or is observation itself the transition?

There is a difference in opinion as to what constitutes observation and the observer, depending on the role of consciousness. In quantum mechanics, an observer is anything that detects a quantum particle, its detection requiring an exchange of energy with a particle for an observation to occur. To that end, any particle – be it an atom or a molecule – can act as the observer.

Imagine that a photon, emitted from the Sun, hits a girl's eye. Prior to reaching her retina, we can't identify its specific position, because it doesn't have one. As a quantum wave, we can describe mathematically only the probabilities of finding its position in particle form. However, when the photon reaches the eye, it takes on a position as a localized particle. Observation requires a transfer of energy between the observer and that which is observed. In this case, the energy is absorbed by an electron in the retina, creating an electrical impulse in the brain, thus causing the girl to see. What is actually observed is the interaction – the point at which the photon becomes observable, through the creation of new information.

The role of consciousness in observation has been hotly debated. In 1932, physicist John von Neumann argued that the mathematics of quantum mechanics allows for the collapse of the wave function to be placed at any position in the causal chain, from the measurement device to the *subjective perception* of the observer, and so does

3. Neumann, J.V. (1932). The mathematical foundations of quantum mechanics. (New edition). *Princeton University Press*.

4. F. London and E. Bauer, 'La théorie de l'observation en mécanique quantique' (1939), English translation in *Quantum Theory and Measurement*, edited by J. A. Wheeler and W. H. Zurek, Princeton University, Princeton, 1983, pp. 217–259. ISBN 0-691-08315-0.

5. Wigner, Eugene; Henry Margenau (1967). 'Remarks on the mind body question, in symmetries and reflections, scientific essays.' *American Journal of Physics*. 35 (12): 1169–1170. Bibcode:1967AmJPh.35.1169W. doi:10.1119/1.1973829. Archived from the original on 2013-01-12. Retrieved 2009-07-30.11. 'The philosophy of Niels Bohr.' Aage Petersen. *Bulletin of the Atomic Scientists*, Vol. 19, No. 7 (September 1963); 'The genius of science: A portrait gallery' (2000) by Abraham Pais, p. 24, and 'Niels Bohr: Reflections on subject and object' (2001) by Paul. McEvoy, p. 291.

not require subjective observation.[3] However, others who have put forward the observational requirement for consciousness, including Edmond Bauer and Fritz London in 1939,[4] and Eugene Wigner in the 1960s,[5] proposed that it is the consciousness of the observer that precipitates the collapse of the wave function.

In 1998, researchers undertaking a version of the double-slit experiment at the Weizmann Institute in Israel[6] showed that when detectors were placed at the slits, the electrons behaved as definite particles, suggesting that measurement does not require a conscious observer. However, there are two arguments against this hypothesis. The first relates to the requirement for a subject-object relationship between that which is observed and the observer. This relationship requires us to draw a line between them that defines their separateness. However, as Kastrup, Stapp and Kafatos explain:

> *"The problem is that the partitioning of the world into discrete inanimate objects is merely nominal. Is a rock integral to the mountain it helps constitute? If so, does it become a separate object merely by virtue of it getting detached from the mountain? And if so, does it then perform a measurement each time it comes back in contact with the mountain, as it bounces down the slope? Brief contemplation of these questions shows that the boundaries of a detector are arbitrary. The inanimate world is a single physical system governed by quantum mechanics. Indeed, as first argued by John von Neumann[7] and rearticulated in the work of one of us,[8] when two inanimate objects interact they simply become quantum mechanically 'entangled' with one another — that is, through quantum entanglement they become united in such a way that the behaviour of one becomes inextricably linked to the behaviour of the other—but no actual measurement is performed."[9]*

The second argument is one of epistemology or *knowing*. Simply put, the output of the detectors only becomes known when it is known (consciously observed by a person). However, quantum mechanics, and indeed all of science – operating as it must on the basis of evidential objective proof – can say little on the subject of 'knowing.' That which is in our direct experience is utterly subjective and known only to us.

The working assumption of the scientific method is that of the separation of observer and experiment. Quantum mechanics, through proofs – such as the observer effect and

6. Dephasing in electron interference by a 'which-path' detector (E. Buks, R. Schuster, M. Heiblum, D. Mahalu & V. Umansky.) *Nature*, February 26 1998 (Vol. 391, pp. 871-874).

7. *Mathematical foundations of quantum mechanics* (John von Neumann, *Princeton University Press*, 27 feb. 2018–328 pagina's).

8. Quantum theory and the role of mind in nature. Henry P. Stapp, *Foundations of Physics*, Vol. 31, pages 1465–1499 (2001).

9. Coming to grips with the implications of quantum mechanics. *Scientific American* –Bernardo Kastrup, Henry P. *Stapp*, Menas C. Kafatos, May 29, 2018.

quantum entanglement – have shown us that this separation does not exist. As a result, materialism points to a very limited understanding of our universe. And yet, this is very much the prevailing paradigm in society, even though science tells us otherwise. In fact, only 5% of the mass of our universe is made out of classical matter. The other 95% is not made out of matter or anything we understand. It is either dark matter (a type that we can only detect through its gravitational effect) or dark energy (conceived as a negative form of energy that exists in a pure vacuum of space and offsets the positive energy, such that the net energy of the universe is zero). So, does quantum mechanics point to a more accurate version of reality?

Quantum mechanics predicts with extreme accuracy real physical phenomena. It underlies almost all modern science and technology. It has been applied to nearly every aspect of physical science, except for gravity and the large-scale structure of the universe. It has been described as the most accurate scientific theory that has ever been proposed. It points to a reality that is more chaotic, non-linear, non-rational, non-Euclidean, acausal, non-physical and highly relative. Quantum mechanics tells us that matter is identical to particles, which are identical to wave functions, which are identical to energy, which is identical to fields. And yet, despite all its success, its many functions, equations, science and mathematics, it is no closer to what reality actually is.

Theoretical physicist John Archibald Wheeler recognized that all of reality is not physical, but informational: "*It from bit symbolizes the idea that every item of the physical world ... that what we call reality arises from the posing of yes/no questions – in short, all things are information theoretic in origin and that this is a participatory universe.*"[10] The implication is that physics, particularly quantum physics, isn't really about reality, but just our best description of what we observe.

Quantum mechanics as a branch of science is different from any other part that is ostensibly materialist because it points to something beyond our understanding. But at the same time, quantum mechanics remains a mathematical model, a concept. It is not the thing it describes. As Niels Bohr (an anti-realist) put it: "*A physicist is just an atom's way of looking at itself.*" The founders of quantum mechanics – Bohr, Werner Heisenberg, Erwin Schrodinger, Max Planck, Arthur Eddington, Wolfgang Pauli, Albert Einstein, James Genes, John Archibald Wheeler and Richard Feynman – were not just scientists,

10. Information, physics, quantum: The search for links. John Archibald Wheeler, 1989 (research paper).

11. The philosophy of Niels Bohr. Aage Petersen. *Bulletin of the Atomic Scientists*, Vol. 19, No. 7 (September 1963); The genius of science: A portrait gallery (2000) by Abraham Pais, p. 24, and 'Niels Bohr: Reflections on subject and object (2001) by Paul. McEvoy, p. 291.

they were philosophers. They were interested in the implications and consequences of science, rather than just using it as a tool, and they understood the limitations of rationality. They realized that to really think outside the box, you need to be prepared to discard it. As Bohr said, *There is no quantum world. There is only an abstract quantum physical description.*[11] Science, in any form, is still a set of symbols and bookkeeping devices. Every symbol, every representation, isn't the thing being represented. A photograph of you is not you. It's still reality, it's just not the thing you think it is. This habitual materialist perspective is actually pointing at nothing.

If what quantum mechanics describes is true, then is the world a quantum wave function? Of course not. A wave function is simply the measurement assigned to every measurement outcome. Rather, by deduction, and with reference to our limited language faculties, reality is the superposition of every possibility, otherwise known as *absolute infinity* – that is, infinity not in one particular direction (as if that were possible) but in every direction, every aspect, simultaneously, with no reference. This singularity of existence is both the only logical deduction and, without reference, is something the rational mind cannot conceptually understand. Your mind understands what it can objectify. Answers arise from questions. But what if the question itself is the answer, and the answer is the question? The journey of introspective knowledge is not one of cognitive elucidation, but of *the knowing of knowing*. Of awareness, or consciousness.

The dogmas of science and metaphysics present polarized attempts to describe and contain reality in the form of knowledge. At one end, science breaks down reality into ever-decreasing fragments of logic. At the other, metaphysicians aspire to an epistemological singularity – an answer to a question to contains all answers. The set of all sets, as Russell's paradox describes. Both reflect a dualistic perspective that is reliant on the limitations of thought and perception.

In our actual experience, we never find particles. Science provides us with a map, but the map is not the territory in the same way as the menu is not the food. What we encounter are thoughts and perceptions. Particles are, in fact, an abstract concept that we invented to contain our current understanding. So are quantum fields. So too is science.

Could it be, therefore, that who you are has no ground, no substance, not matter nor wave, not part or whole, but formless, emptiness, without ending?

4. WHERE AM I?
THE HARD PROBLEM OF CONSCIOUSNESS

Who you are is also a question of where you are. Like the echo that asks, "*Where am I?*" the truth lies in silence. You can never know where you are, because you can never escape it. All you can know is experience.

The hard problem of consciousness is the problem of explaining why and how we have first-person, subjective, conscious experiences – of feeling and knowing that 'something is happening.' The general assumption is that consciousness is an experience consigned to living beings, for which it is a defining feature of life, in comparison to inanimate objects, such as a cup of tea or a computer. Consciousness is used interchangeably to describe awareness, the state of being awake, and self-consciousness. Philosopher Thomas Nagel defines consciousness as "*the feeling of what it is like to be something.*"[1] Could anyone ever tell you what that is?

Australian philosopher David Chalmers first formulated the problem in his paper, *Facing up to the problem of consciousness*: "*... even when we have explained the performance of all the cognitive and behavioural functions in the vicinity of experience – perceptual discrimination, categorization, internal access, verbal report – there may still remain a further unanswered question: Why is the performance of these functions accompanied by experience?*"[2] Chalmers explains that the problem of consciousness can be subdivided into the easy problems (those that describe our physical processes, such as how data is processed in the brain), and the hard problem (why and how these processes are accompanied by phenomenal experience or awareness).

The ontology of mind and its existence in a world composed of matter has given rise to the philosophy of mind, a branch that has for centuries debated the metaphysical implications of the 'mind-body problem' – the relationship between thought, consciousness and the body. It concerns who we think we are in relation to our body and the world around us. The two predominant schools of thought are *dualism* and *monism*. Dualism maintains a rigid distinction between the realms of mind and matter – of mental and physical. Descartes was perhaps its most famous proponent, using dualism to put forward the argument for free will and of choice that is independent of the physical world. It is also compatible with the theologies that enshrine an independent realm of existence that is separate from and ungoverned by the world of matter, to which we commit our immortal souls in the belief of a life after death. Today, dualism represents

1. What is it like to be a bat? Thomas Nagel, *The Philosophical Review*, Vol. 83, No. 4 (Oct., 1974), pp. 435-450 (16 pages) Duke University Press.

2. Facing up to the problems of consciousness (David Chalmers) – *Journal of Consciousness Studies*, 2(3):200-19, 1995.

the broadly held worldview. *Panpsychism*, a branch of *property dualism*, is the view that mind is a fundamental and ubiquitous feature of reality, so that all things (from humans to rocks) have a mind-like (conscious) quality. In attempting to connect the physical and mental realms through a single metatheory, it alludes to a non-dual approach, and yet relies on the distinction between matter and mind. Everything is still two things, rather than one.

Dualistic approaches all describe a subject of experience that is conscious of an objective reality. As a result, all dualistic approaches singularly fail to address the hard problem of consciousness. The problem stems from the perception of measurement and observation. Clap your hands, and ask the question: Does observation occur at the electrical signal in the cochlea? Or is it when the signal reaches the temporal lobe, that part of the brain responsible for interpreting information in the form of sounds from the ears? And at which point does consciousness arise? The absence of an empirically identifiable meeting point between the non-physical mind and the physical extension of experience has proven problematic to dualism, and many modern philosophers of mind maintain that the mind is not something separate from the body.

Author Annaka Harris poses the hard problem as a question: *"How does felt experience arise out of non-sentient matter?"*[3] In other words, how could sentience arise out of non-sentience? This is the inherent contradiction with the materialist paradigm. Materialists believe in a world made of matter that could in some way give rise to sentience. Surely, the only logical conclusion is that awareness must be prior to matter. Planck states a similar position: *"I regard consciousness as fundamental. I regard matter as derivative from consciousness. We cannot get behind consciousness."*[4]

In contrast to dualism, monism maintains that there is not mind or matter, but rather a single, unifying reality through which everything can be explained. By definition, one might expect there to be only one non-dual approach. But of course, on a conceptual level, there are several versions of the truth, each with its own limitations. *Physicalism* purports that everything (including mind) is made of matter, occupying its own physical space (maintaining an inherently materialist viewpoint). In contrast, *idealism* suggests that everything is made of mind and thought – matter appearing as a representation of mental processes. As such, it proposes that reality is inseparable and

3. Harris, A. (2019). *Conscious: A Brief Guide to the Fundamental Mystery of the Mind.*

4. Max Planck, *The Observer*, 21 Jan 1931.

indistinguishable from human perception, so that objects only exist to the extent that they are perceived. *Neutral monism* describes how both mind and matter are aspects of a distinct essence that is itself identical to neither of them. The latter rejects the duality of matter and mind, believing the essential nature of reality to be one of neutrality. As philosopher William James explains in his essay, *Does consciousness exist*: "*If we start from the supposition that there is only one primal stuff or material in the world, a stuff of which everything is composed, and if we call that stuff 'pure experience,' then knowing can easily be explained as a particular sort of relation toward one another into which portions of pure experience may enter. The relation itself is part of pure experience.*"[5] The main criticism of neutral monism is its failure to describe the nature of body and mind. Its explanation is akin to the Sanskrit expression *neti neti*, meaning 'not this, not that.' It is, therefore, perhaps the best example of a concept attempting to point to truth that lies outside of itself, outside of logic, and so resoundingly fails to do so. The real limitation here is one of language. For the word 'neutrality' to exist in language, it must remain a comparative term, and thereby counter to its intended meaning.

THE THIRD WAY

An alternative philosophy is described by non-duality (itself contained within the Hindu philosophy Advaita Vedanta). Whereas panpsychism states that all physical entities have consciousness, non-duality purports that all things *arise in* consciousness, as the activity of consciousness. In other words, there are no actual separate things, only infinite consciousness, which is who you are.

Non-duality is the only conceptual framework that directly addresses the hard problem of consciousness. However, like all concepts, it can only seek to point to that which it is not. As Bohr attests, "*Everything we call real is made of things that cannot be regarded as real.*"[6] There is an infinite number of conceptual possibilities that could describe who you are, but they are all simply tools of the mind to necessarily limit and contain our understanding. As Gödel's 'truth circle' – itself an object of reasoned argument – explains, the truth of who you are must lie beyond the circle, beyond the confines of our cognitive understanding. To venture further, we must look beyond our conceptualized reality, to our direct experience.

5. Does consciousness exist? (William James – published in the September 1, 1904 issue of the *Journal of Philosophy, Psychology and Scientific Methods* and republished posthumously in Essays in Radical Empiricism in 1912).

6. *The Philosophical Writings of Niels Bohr*, Vol. 2: Essays 1932-1957 *Atomic Physics and Human Knowledge* by Niels Bohr.

5. WHAT IS THIS?
DIRECT EXPERIENCE – THE REALITY TEST

To lead is not to presume, but to question. And yet, for most of us – as the preceding chapters have suggested – the vast majority of our beliefs are held because of the way things seem to be. Yet, we know from our experience that *seeming to be* is not a true or accurate test of reality. For many years, the world seemed to be flat. We subsequently learned through empirical evidence that the world is a three-dimensional sphere. More recently, as we've discussed, we learned that the Earth actually exists in four-dimensional spacetime. What will we discover next? In our direct experience, we can only ever confirm our ever-changing thoughts and sense perceptions.

The farthest object observed from Earth is a galaxy called GN-z11, estimated to reside 13.4 billion light years away. Of course, no one has ever seen across this distance. Scientists observe the data readouts on a computer screen. You observe it through the words on this page. All observation is from a distance, and yet in our direct experience, what is the distance between ourselves and our experience?

All experience, illusory or otherwise, has a reality to it. The problem arises when we find ourselves amidst the oasis, eating sand. In your experience, there seems to be a person, a you, reading this book. This seems to be happening at a place called *here*, and a time called *now*. In this chapter, we will look closely at the actuality of our experience, and what our experience therefore tells us about the nature of reality, and of ourselves. To do so requires your provocation. What follows is an invitation to you, and to leaders, to question – that is, to really look at – the ground on which we have based our most intimate and fundamental assumptions and beliefs. It requires asking: *"Is this what I actually experience?"* To look beyond the thoughts that so condition our perspective and veil our innate, open curiosity. What follows is a set of observations of our direct experience that will challenge some of the most closely held, self-limiting beliefs and assumptions that we consider true about who we are, and in particular, our experience as a separate, individual self. These observations point to the non-dual philosophy. From here on in, the words awareness and consciousness are used interchangeably.

OBSERVATION: YOUR PERSPECTIVE SHARES THE LIMITATIONS OF THE MIND
Everything we know about reality is known through the mind. Our mind is limited. The mind superimposes its own limitations on what it knows, so that its view of reality is filtered through these limitations. To the mind, time and space are qualities of the reality it perceives.

Could it be, however, that what we perceive as time and space reflect qualities of the mind rather than an inherent aspect of reality? How would we know that this is, or is not, the case? We don't. All the mind can ever know is the reality perceived within its own limitations. If you wear orange-tinted skiing goggles, the snow will appear orange. But wait two minutes, and the brain adjusts to show you that the snow is white. The mind, like Alice through the looking glass, easily forgets to confirm its understanding, and so believes that we see the snow as it really is. It's only when we take the goggles off that we become aware of our limitations.

We could imagine awareness as a projector, its light arriving on the screen and transforming into the movie. As we give our attention to our experience, the lens filters and focuses infinite awareness through the prism of our mind, and takes on its limitations. Time appears as a finite refraction of infinity, and eternity arises as space. Our perceptions appear to us through the dimensions of space, and our thoughts appear to us in time.

OBSERVATION: THE WORLD OF MATTER DOES NOT EXIST

The materialist paradigm describes a world made of matter. More specifically, the prevailing scientific worldview states that matter exists outside of awareness, and that matter, in the form of the brain, gives rise to consciousness. As such, consciousness is an epiphenomenon of matter. There is good evidence for this belief. Take, for example, the eight billion people (at the time of this writing) who appear to be experiencing a shared world, which feels solid and real, but is experienced by each from a unique, individual perspective. Indeed, notice that if someone leaves the room, the room remains. We all seem to be perceiving the same thing. Surely this suggests that we are all ultimately derived from that same thing, which we call matter. Or perhaps there is an alternative possibility: that we all share the same experience because we are all part of the same thing, the same consciousness.

Consider also how we know of something called matter. It is through awareness. We have never found something that existed outside of our awareness. How can you prove that something exists that you can't find? Everything exists in our awareness, so the concept of something called matter that exists outside and separate from awareness is just *a concept* existing in awareness. In the facts of our experience, we never find matter, or anything, that is outside of consciousness or awareness.

As described in the previous chapter, the philosophy of panpsychism states that consciousness is a fundamental property of matter – but it still starts with matter. It comes from the belief that 'I, the body (matter) am aware.' But in our direct experience, this is not the case. It is 'I, awareness' that is aware. Scientists, in their concession, have afforded consciousness to 'living beings' – from the cat, to the fish, to the flea, until concluding that perhaps everything has consciousness. And this is still incorrect. Only consciousness is conscious.

Our belief in a world of matter derives from our overlooking of the limitations of our perspective when viewed through the finite mind. To put it another way, matter is what consciousness looks like when viewed through the perspective of the finite mind. We have bent and manipulated our conceptualizations to fit the truth. But all thought, all mental models, share the limitations of the finite mind. Through quantum physics, we can provide a rational description of what consciousness is, and overlook the essential paradox – that consciousness is unknowable, unanswerable, since it must be prior to that which seeks to describe it.

We can say that everything that appears in awareness is therefore 'made' of awareness. When a thought arises, it arises in consciousness – it can only exist in awareness, and so can only come from awareness. It cannot come from somewhere else (which would be matter). The perception of this room appears in our awareness, not outside of it. Nothing in our experience can come from outside of our awareness. Have you ever had an experience of something appearing outside of your awareness and coming into your awareness, or was it only ever arising in your awareness?

All there is to your thoughts and perceptions is the knowing of them, and that knowing is consciousness. All you have ever known is knowing (consciousness). In other words, you *are* consciousness. You have only ever known and experienced yourself. Close your eyes, and somehow you know that you exist. To assert the matter model requires a leap of faith, which is akin to religion. The religion of materialism. Matter only makes sense to the individual who believes they are separate from their experience – the 'separate self.' Matter is a way of seeing, not something that is seen.

OBSERVATION: THE WORLD IS NOT SOLID

The physicality of our world feels real. And on a relative level, it is. Reach out your hand and touch the wall in front of you. Does it feel hard? Give it a tap. Perhaps this tells you how solid it feels. Now close your eyes. Imagine that you have just been born. A newborn will have never met a wall before, or touched its surface, or given it a name. Reach out your hand and touch the surface again. What would a newborn experience? Would they experience 'hard,' or would there just be a perception of something? And that perception would not have the characteristics of hard, as might be attributed to an object, it would just have an intensity. There is no context, no frame of reference for it other than a level of intensity. We cannot *know* the wall any more than that. Yet, through a process we call 'learning,' we bring our own conceptual definitions to the objects of our experience and forget that they are not qualities of the objects themselves, but rather the qualities of a conceptual mind. Touch the wall again. Where do you feel the wall? Your hand? Where is your hand? To an infant, there is no hand. There is no location with which the wall is perceived, there is only pure perception. And in that spaceless space, there is no separation between subject and object, only knowing. In our accumulation of knowledge and experience, we appear to draw a veil over this understanding, such that what we observe is that which we have created.

Take two small stones and place them between the fingertips of both hands. Push the stones together, as hard as you can, for about a minute. Now, very slowly, start to pull the stones apart. You will notice a tension, as if the stones have become magnets, attracting back to themselves. What we feel as a pull into experience is because we can't let go.

OBSERVATION: THERE ARE NO SUCH THINGS AS OBJECTS

If consciousness and existence were different, there would be a border or boundary between them. In our direct experience, we do not find one. Look at an object. Now close your eyes and open them again. It appears to be the same object. Objects appear to endure, outside of perceptions. They appear to have their own existence in time and space, independent of the consciousness that perceives it. This is an illusion. The object is a concept. The time and space in which the objects appear are concepts. The sense of you as a separate self that coincidently also appears to endure, independent of the object, is also a concept. What's happening is that an object is a perception appearing in consciousness. Each time you open your eyes, it looks like the same object reappears, but it is in fact a new perception.

The totality of your experience consists of thoughts and sense perceptions. Through thought, we know something called mind (conception), and through our senses we know something called matter (perception). To experience an object requires perception and conception. We cannot have an experience without these. But we never actually experience the thing we call an object, or matter. All we experience are thoughts and perceptions. That is all we ever know. The objects of our experience do not exist.

Awareness doesn't know objects; it just knows itself. It is awareness of awareness. It is through the conceptualization of mind that we perceive objects in our experience. In the absence of objects, there is still awareness, knowing itself. Awareness is inherently self-aware. It does not need a mind to know itself. It doesn't need you to condition it.

OBSERVATION: WE MISTAKE OURSELVES AS OBJECTS IN THE WORLD

When our mind thinks of awareness, it imagines one thing being aware of another thing. Consciousness is infinite awareness – of everything, which is simultaneously itself. We might ask what form awareness might therefore take. Imagine a box. The box exists in awareness, and so the box is known. As is the room in which the box resides. Infinite awareness is infinite creation, infinite manifestation. To be is to know. It is from this that what we might call 'form' derives – the notion that a world of objects is dreamed, to be known by a subject of experience. Paradoxically, its limitless being necessarily includes the appearance of limitation, as viewed by the finite mind. Like the character in a dream, consciousness appears to overlook itself, to experience the world of form. Like the ocean localizing as a small wave, each wave remains the ocean entire. As individuals, we stand as the wave upon the ocean, and in stark relief overlook the depths beneath. The sense of a separate self is experienced as separate only to itself. Rather, in reality, we are the means by which consciousness realizes its infinite potential. As the poet William Blake said, "*To see eternity in a grain of sand.*"[1] Consciousness limits itself freely in its infinite expression. It – that is, *you* – are the cradling of existence.

Consciousness is sometimes described as the dreamer that dreams itself into existence – the 'infinite dream.' As an expression of its infinite potential, consciousness gives itself freely to the dream and in so doing seems to forget itself. Just as the character in the dream can be anyone, be anything, the price it pays is that it must forget who it really is. To the character in the dream, the dream is real. We dream within a dream, as consciousness manifested from formless infinite potential into form.

1. Blake, W. (1863). *Auguries of Innocence and Other Lyric Poems.* CreateSpace Independent Publishing Platform.

OBSERVATION: YOU ARE NOT YOUR BODY OR YOUR MIND

The 'I' with which we know ourselves is enduring. Amidst a constantly changing world, we might orientate to this 'I' as the one abiding aspect of our experience that survives all others. To answer the question "Who am I?" we could start by answering the question "Who am I not?" Our experience is made up of sense perceptions (which appear to arise from a body) and thoughts (which appear to arise from our brain).

Perceptions: Are you the body? Most of us identify with our body to some degree. If you lost a hand, would you still be you? Is there a part of your body that is more you than others? Many would point to the brain as the place from which consciousness arises. Most of us, when pushed, would say that the 'I' resides somewhere behind the eyes (the *windows to our soul*). So, when the brain dies, you cease to be (or are transmuted to another time or place). The average age of a cell in your body is seven years. Much of you, therefore, is quite new. However, not every cell gets replaced, and some remain with us throughout our lifetime. These include many of the neurons in our cerebellum (the part of the brain that controls balance and coordination) and the cells that make up the lenses in our eyes, as well as cross-linked collagen that forms scar tissue. So, perhaps it is in these cells that our 'self' resides? However, this brings us back to the hard problem of consciousness, and the question of how sentience can be created out of non-sentient matter. And how would it be possible, in the knowing that all we experience takes place in awareness, to find something that lies outside of our awareness – a place where experience starts and ends? To ask "are you the body?" is to ask "are you your sense perceptions?" This includes not just what we feel on the outside, but the feelings and emotions we experience on the inside. Look closely, and you will see that sense perceptions come and go, but the sense of 'I am' is always with you. It is ever-present, and so inherent to our reality as to become transparent. Like the page on which the words are written.

Thoughts: Listen to the thoughts in your head and you will notice that your thoughts speak in your voice. But whose voice is it? Our thoughts come and go, as if we're tuned in to a radio station. And sometimes, like life, we don't like the music. When we claim authorship for thinking, we jump into the DJ's chair to change the song. To the author of thoughts, a thought is a choice. But notice again how thoughts and feelings come and go. As the Sufi poets remind us, from the depths of depression, to the heights of elation, *"this too shall pass."* Unless we ascribe to multiple personalities, we cannot be our thoughts.

Consciousness does not experience the world through a body or mind. Rather, it experiences the world as thoughts and perceptions, and through thinking and perceiving consciousness abstracts and conceptualizes a separate body and mind. The separation of experience into these two parts creates our sense of who we are as an individual, separate self.

Does a blind man have less awareness? Whatever is experienced is experienced by consciousness. Consciousness, or awareness, is independent of the condition of mind. It is that in which experience happens. We cannot say *"I cannot see because I am blind"* until we are told that there is something to see that we cannot. Whatever is known, whatever is aware, is known by consciousness. A person is not aware, consciousness is aware. All we know is the knowing of perceiving. We cannot say that a stone is conscious – a stone is an object of our experience. All we can say is that the stone is consciousness. There is not an object there.

Whatever is known or experienced, whether by a human, a bird or a flea, is experienced by consciousness. A person does not know; it is known. If you lose an eye, then your thoughts and sensations will change, but the knowing of your experience does not change. Consciousness, or awareness, is independent of the condition of mind. The appearance of beauty in the world is the recognition of your own being. It is always available, whatever the condition of the body and mind.

OBSERVATION: THERE IS NOTHING MORE TO EXPERIENCE OTHER THAN THE KNOWING OF IT

You have never experienced anything other than knowing, of pure consciousness, or awareness. All there is to experience is the knowing of it. This knowing is not a little bit of you, it is all of you, and it is all of your experience. What is forgotten is the knowing of your own awareness – being aware of being aware. Ask yourself, *"Am I aware?"* The answer is always *yes* – how could you ask the question otherwise? What is it that knows you are aware? It is knowing, or awareness. Awareness does not have experience, it is experience.

You are awareness – *"I am that I am."* The only reason most of us don't notice is that we give our attention exclusively to objects.

Have you ever wondered how it is that music can talk to us, so profoundly, so instantly, so directly? Listen to a song that you love. Have you ever contemplated how gifted the individual must have been to write it? Perhaps its melody resonates deeply with you. Notice that the music exists in you. It does not reside in the pen of the composer, although our thoughts tell us so. It exists purely in our own experience. It exists not for you, but because of you. You are the composer of your experience. In life, the beauty we see and hear is only because we recognize its reflection in us. We find ourselves in the spaces, in the silence between the notes.

In the same way that there is no difference or distinction between who you are and the song that you hear, so it is true of experience. The knowing of experience IS experience. The reflection in the mirror is not the mirror, it is you, awareness, looking back at itself. Everything you experience exists in awareness; it could not exist for you otherwise. Everything you are aware of arises out of, and because of, your awareness. Everything is awareness, which is you. You are not separate from it. Note that it is possible for the logical mind to conceptually understand this, to recognize a truth in this, and yet still not embody that truth fully. In other words, to still hold to a sense of separation between self and experience, as a separate self. This is the difference between understanding how to make soup (which requires the logical, rational mind), and the tasting of it (which does not). When your concepts start to fall over, you're on to something. Knowing of your true being is the relinquishing of understanding.

OBSERVATION: WHAT IS OUTSIDE YOUR DIRECT EXPERIENCE IS UNKNOWABLE

Does reality exist outside of your direct experience? This question has taxed philosophers for hundreds of years. Other ways to ask the same question include: *"Are there other minds experiencing reality, or is it just me?"* and *"Does the tree fall in the forest if there is no one there to witness it?"*

The belief that consciousness only experiences itself as one mind is called *solipsism*. However, solipsism is not what is suggested here. Whereas solipsism says there is only the content of one mind, a non-dual approach proposes that there is only one consciousness. Solipsism suggests that *"I am the centre of the universe,"* whereas in reality there is no centre. To know anything, consciousness must take the form of a mind. A mind can only have one thought, one perception, at a time. It has limitations. We cannot know what is not in our experience.

We similarly cannot say that something that is not known or experienced does not exist. However, if it does exist, it exists as consciousness. There cannot be two realities.

It is out of infinite consciousness, infinite awareness, that mind arises and takes the shape of thought that exclusively identifies consciousness with a body. Awareness manifests in order to know itself or to be aware. Might one reconcile that manifestation, therefore, is unlimited, instead of being limited to one perspective? Our experience of consciousness is that it has no limits. Consciousness has no start or end. Might it suggest also that there are infinite perspectives appearing simultaneously? It is only from the perspective of the separate self that separate 'minds' exist, that are outside of consciousness.

Consciousness knows itself by being itself. It cannot *not* know itself. Even when it seems to know something other than itself, such as a tree, or a body, it never ceases to know itself. This is contrary to the perspective of the separate self, which deems that the self is necessary for awareness. What is suggested here is that there are no objects, only knowing awareness. If you believe in separate objects, you might say, *"Will the street still be there if I am not there?"* The street is only ever knowing awareness, so in that sense it is always present. Nothing has existence as objects. Objects don't have existence. Rather, existence has objects. The existence of all apparent things is the knowing awareness that experiences them. All apparent things exist as that. Therefore, whatever the experience is, it is always consciousness that takes the shape of experiencing – thinking and perceiving – giving rise to a mind, body and world. The substance of all experience is consciousness, not objects, so there is never an object that we might call a 'tree falling in the forest' to begin with.

As an individual, separate self, we perceive one world of eight billion people, or 'objects.' To consciousness, it is eight billion worlds shared by one consciousness. Through the limited faculty of mind, we might conceive of a model for consciousness – that of eight billion (or indeed an infinite number of) minds that are experiencing a shared world in consciousness, and seemingly talking to each other. To the mind that experiences one image, it therefore imagines eight billion different images of awareness. To consciousness, there is only ever one image. The movie may contain many characters, but to consciousness there is only ever one screen.

The concept of 'world' assumes something called space and time. But, as we shall see, if space and time are not inherent to our experience, we could say as a concession that there are as many worlds as there are perceptions, and that each world arises afresh each time a new perception arises. There is not one world shared by many, there is one consciousness, knowing itself. There is no 'we.'

OBSERVATION: TIME AND SPACE DO NOT EXIST

Our experience appears to be taking place in time, in what we might refer to as a past, present and future. Just watch the clock ticking on the wall. We can recall a past, through memory. And we know that if today is Monday, then tomorrow is not. The clock hand moves through space, and time and space appear inextricably linked. As we move through space, it appears that we move through time. Experience feels like a line that we move along a bit 'at a time,' but are we really going anywhere?

The mind observes that objects come and go, and so the concept of time explains what is happening. It becomes the canvas for other thoughts to arise. When we sleep, and we stop thinking, our sense of time ceases as well. We awake into the same moment that surrendered us into sleep. If you look closely at your direct experience, notice that you have never experienced, nor could you experience, the past or the future. What we experience are thoughts, and thinking only ever takes place right now. Similarly, close your eyes, press your thumb and forefinger together, and without reference to memory, ask the question, "Where does this sensation take place?" On close analysis, the answer is always at a place called 'here.' All our experience takes place in the same place – not a location in space, but in 'I am,' in awareness.

Consider, for example, the book in your hands. Imagine that it represents time, and each page a moment in time. To read the book, to understand it, your mind needs to take one page at a time. But all the pages, all moments, are there. Now imagine the book is in reality an infinite superposition, with everything occurring simultaneously in *no time*. Of course, you can't – your mind will continue to see a book. Spacetime shows us that all of what we think of as time (past, present, future) is constantly in existence, even if we are not able to witness it all. Like the turning of a page, time does not actually 'flow,' it just is. To quote philosopher Rupert Spira, "*Time is what eternity looks like when viewed through the limitation of thought.*"[2]

Our conceptual models of time and space are created so that the mind can understand them. With the concept of spacetime, we are using a thorn to remove a thorn – we have created a concept to explain a concept. The best we can do is recognize the limit of

2. Rupert Spira, R. (2017). *The Nature of Consciousness: Essays on the Unity of Mind and Matter.* (1ˢᵗ Edition). New Harbinger.

our understanding. The mind cannot understand what time is, because it is through thought that the mind creates the illusion of time, and thereby its understanding. Its absence requires an absence of our understanding.

OBSERVATION: PAIN IS NOT THE SAME AS SUFFERING

Suffering is to the mind what pain is to the body. When we get a headache, it is normal to take a tablet to ease the pain. There is an action, stemming from desire to get rid of the pain. Our bodies are conditioned to avoid pain – it is our preference to do so. The difference between pain and suffering is acceptance: the distinction between 'this is happening' and 'this should not be happening.' Pain may or may not provoke thought, whereas suffering always arises through thought. Acceptance is our default response, not suffering. However, suffering arises when we objectify our pain, when we seek to distance it from ourselves. This is a conceptual process of thought (we are never, in reality, separate from it). Perceptually, there is 'me' and 'pain,' and through their separation we perceive the resistance from which suffering arises.

Notice how, in the background, there is this faint pull into the next moment, as if we are seeking it. Like we need to go somewhere, to the next experience. Let experience come to you. This is the difference between becoming versus being. Becoming is the progressive path, in which we need to do something to be something. It is a form of resistance. Becoming can be very subtle. It strains at the edge of this moment. It feels like we are always slightly late, never quite ready, or always in the wrong place – like the Mad Hatter, never where we need to be. But here, now, is the only place you can ever be.

With pain comes pleasure and desire. If desire is wanting something for what it is, addiction is wanting something for what it will become. Similarly, if suffering is a resistance away from our objective experience, addiction is a compulsion toward it, toward an end to suffering. Our fixation on an objective reality directs our attention away from being, which is the only place that peace and happiness reside. The knowing of our own being IS peace, and is available to all of us, at any time. It is what all of us want, because it is all that we already are. And yet, perversely, in the materialist world we are sold 'happiness,' whether in the form of holidays or hand cream, as if it were something separate from ourselves.

In the next chapter we will explore the cause of all suffering – the ego.

6. WHO AM I?
THE SEPARATE SELF

There are two universal and undeniable facts of everyone's direct experience:
- I know that 'I am'
- I know that something is being experienced

There is a third truth that, in being overlooked, veils our true nature:
- The reality that who I am (consciousness) is identical to the reality of this something being experienced

In the veiling of this simple truth, which we seem to have somehow forgotten, arises the sense of a separate self, or ego. In this chapter we will learn about what the ego is, but in case you are in any doubt as to whether this applies to you, Fig 3 provides an eight-point checklist. It describes the foundational beliefs through which the sense of a separate self is perpetuated, each aspect substantiated and congruent with the rest. More or less everyone on this planet (though not entirely everyone) is under this illusion, and will duly score an eight.

1. Separation:	I conceive a world that is separate from me – *so that* ...
2. Finitude:	From this separation I conceive my birth, my origin – *so that* ...
3. Individuality:	From my birth I arise as an individual – *so that* ...
4. Authorship:	As an individual I presume authorship of thought – *so that* ...
5. Transience:	From my thoughts I conceive my past and future – *so that* ...
6. Causality:	My future arises through causality – *so that* ...
7. Relatedness:	Through causality my actions change my experience – *so that* ...
8. Choice:	Through my actions I am responsible for the world – *so that* ...

... I conceive a world that is separate from me.

FIG 3 – THE EIGHT TENETS OF EGO (THE 'PERPETUAL NARRATIVE')

The illusion of the separate self stems from a single fundamental thought: that I am separate from the world in which I exist. Underpinning this belief is a thought structure whose geometry is represented by the Fano plane (after the mathematician Gino Fano), whose construct points to the enduring nature of our belief in a separate self. A Fano plane is the simplest symmetrical object in the universe with inbuilt mathematical structure. In mathematical terms, it describes the smallest possible projective plane ('order 2'). In layman's terms, it describes an object with a set of points whose relationships are defined through a set of lines, such that every point has a direct association (line) with all others. In other words, it exists entirely through self-reference, creating an infinite loop of causal association. Like the light that shines from a crystal, its radiance is perceived because the side that you see has all other sides reflected through it.

This relationship – of points and lines – is, in fact, how our universe is currently described, through the description of an analogue *and* a digital universe, science currently having proved unsuccessful at reconciling the two perspectives. Compare, for example, the analogue continuity described by spacetime with the discrete, digital world of quantum mechanics and quantum theory.

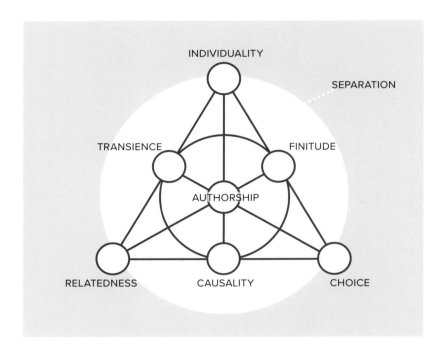

INDIVIDUALITY

SEPARATION

TRANSIENCE

FINITUDE

AUTHORSHIP

RELATEDNESS

CAUSALITY

CHOICE

FIG 4 – TENETS OF SELF-REFERENCE (EGO)

Fig 4 describes the symmetry of ego. Within this egoic thought structure, the tenets describe its many facets, with the tenet of separation being the sum of all parts, the cornerstone of the separate self. The single thought and misunderstanding that *I am a separate self* is the cause of all human suffering. The painter Paul Cézanne said, *"A time is coming when a single carrot, freshly observed, will trigger a revolution."*[1] If ever there were a case for something so seemingly small and innocuous to bring about radical change, then surely the 'ego revolution' would be it.

Our sense of ourself as an individual, separate person – with free will, authorship, authority, individuality and responsibility – of course feels normal to us. It is so prevalent in our experience, and so culturally endemic and accepted, that to consider it as anything other than our natural state would in most quarters invite ridicule. But while our sense of individuality may undoubtedly feel real, the assumed reality is not what is actually happening. The mirage of the oasis in the desert still has a reality to it, it's just not what you think it is.

The challenge for society is that, within this shared reality, pretty much everyone is under the same illusion. The only difference is perhaps the degrees by which people intuit whether something is 'not quite right with this picture.' Yet, in the final analysis, there is nothing wrong with this picture at all, and nothing that should not be here. The question is whether you want to believe it.

Although our egoic belief presents differently in each of us, it operates according to a consistent set of characteristics:

1. Gasquet, J. (1991). *Cézanne: A Memoir with Conversations.*

#1 THE EGO IS THE STORY OF ME

The ego directs our attention through thought to the past (to memory), and the future (our hopes and fears) to conjure the 'story of me.' We are bound by ego because we believe the story to be true, and so become lost in the drama of our life's events. Indeed, our affinity for and fascination with story reflects how easily lost we are in our own. Our life is like an echo chamber, in which everything we experience carries the reflections and reverberations of ourselves. The ego looks for itself in everything, to form part of its own story.

In the desert, there is a pool that drowns men. It is here that the ego comes to drink. In its depths, thoughts arise, to be claimed at the surface by the lips with which they are spoken. As thoughts become the words that we drink, so flows the water that carries the ego's voice. "This is my thought that I am," and in swallowing, sinks into silence. But this dry silence is an illusion, for in the desert, we are also the rain. We are the water that falls upon us, fills our hands, washes them clean, cannot be held, flows through us, renders us hollow.

#2 THE EGO IS SEEKING

Most of us believe that happiness and fulfilment can be gained from the objects of our experience. The separate self searches for fulfilment from the external, material world, in direct proportion to the basis by which it believes itself deficient. The ego exists only to seek fulfilment, to be whole, to end its suffering. Suffering is the search for meaning. The ego is the thought that directs the search – its purpose. It is seeking that directs the ego's attention into experience. The form the seeking takes is as varied as form itself, but they all share the same quality, the same urgency: to satisfy a sense of lack or wholeness. Seeking is directed toward those objects with which greatest separation (between self and experience) is perceived. As seeking increases, attention is increasingly given to those objects of experience that can fulfil the ego's need, through which they gain apparent solidity and separation. Whether you seek happiness from near-death experiences, from mind-altering drugs, from sex, or from surrender to God. We are seeking an end to seeking. We take the drug so that we don't need to take it. And in that instance of satisfaction, at that point of orgasm, in that moment of apparent death, there is a stillness. A release from seeking. That is what we seek – to simply rest in the knowing of our own being.

#3 THE EGO IS SEPARATE

To the separate self, objective experience is always at a distance from itself, as the subject of experience. The world of objects is experienced as 'out there,' discoverable through our senses, as a counterpoint to our own internal world of thoughts and feelings. Through our thoughts, we believe that what we are is limited by and located in the body, and that the 'I' of awareness is therefore located and limited in a 'me.' Through perception, our senses and feelings of being in a body seem to substantiate this belief. This embodiment and belief in our individuality is just that – a thought, that we are localized and limited within the body.

Individual experience of the separate self can vary significantly – we are ego-divergent, as one might expect in a neuro-divergent population. Distortions of selfhood include feeling as if one's thoughts or feelings are not really one's own, or believing that thoughts are being inserted into one's mind. An opposite extreme condition can also occur, where people experience everything in their environment as though they had decided that it would happen. The ego lives in the past through memory. Anyone who has known someone who has Alzheimer's or dementia will have experienced how the person appears to fade away – the egoic persona diminishing with their memory.

#4 THE EGO PRESUMES AGENCY

To quote from Shakespeare, "*All the world's a stage, and all the men and women merely players.*"[2] Within this theatrical metaphor, the manifested universe is our stage, and we are the characters in a play. Our characters think a certain way, behave a certain way, and there is nothing wrong with that. We all have different characteristics, personalities, preferences, likes and dislikes, hopes and fears. Imagine that you are an actor (perhaps you are) and tonight you are on stage as Hamlet. The character Hamlet is real from the perspective of the play, but in reality, Hamlet is an actor. Now imagine that as you step onto the stage, you forget who you are, and instead believe you are in fact the very embodiment of Hamlet – that the words on the script are your own. Through ego, when the character speaks or thinks, we assume authorship. When the character perceives, we presume agency. When the character decides, we assume free will. When the character acts, we assume responsibility. When the character seeks, we assume purpose.

2. Shakespeare, W. (1599). *As You Like It*: act 2, scene 7.

Take the concept of free will, for instance. If you go for a drive, you make decisions. You choose to turn left and right, you control the car so you don't crash. All of these choices, these decisions, are happening. But they are not happening because of you. Do you choose your thoughts? Try and choose the next thought that comes into your head. At best, we might say they were predictable. Who we really are is not in control. *Who we really are* is a cradling for experience – the awareness in which all experience is, with grace, allowed to be. But through the perspective of a separate self, it appears that we are separate from our experience, such that we resist it. In the final analysis, you are not responsible for your actions.

Cognitive scientist Peter Johansson's 'choice-blindness' experiment[3] involved individuals picking from among two photos the one they believed to be the most attractive. The selected photo was then secretly switched for the one they turned down, and the subject was questioned on why they had made that photo their choice. Despite the fact that the picture they were asked to describe wasn't the one they picked, most participants didn't notice, and simply explained their rationale. The experiment provides an interesting example of how our myopic conviction of our own free will can easily override the choice itself, such that we will happily lay claim to any outcome in the preservation of our perceived authorship. What the experiment failed to point out is that rather than this being a trick, it actually occurs all the time.

#5 THE EGO IS LAUGHING

We take our perceived limitations very seriously. Our sense of humour stems from the recognition of our apparent limitations, within the deep knowing of our infinite potential. Humour reveals the ego, and what form this takes will vary according to the character. The ego uses the assertion of limitation in the same way it seeks fulfilment. An individual with an internal locus of control – such as a sociopath standing trial in a courtroom, who tries to *take* what they need – may laugh at witness testimony in order to demean it, and so attest to its limitation, to assert their dominance. In comparison, an individual with an external locus of control – such as one with low self-confidence, who tries to *retain* what they need – will be inclined to acts of self-deprecation, without waiting for others to imply, and therefore impose, the limitation themselves. In the absence of ego,

3. Johansson, P. (2006). *Choice Blindness: The Incongruence of Intention, Action and Introspection.* Lund University.

and from the position of awareness, humour is found in abundance and in celebration of the knowing that our limitations are, of course, limitless.

#6 THE EGO PLAYS MANY PARTS

When we are born, we do not have a sense of a separate self. As we grow, in a normal environment an individual's sense of individuality develops through a process of integration. Our perception of self forms around different identities – there might be a 'work me,' a 'parent me' or a 'with friends me.' As we grow up and experience the world, we integrate and reconcile these different personae into what we perceive as an individual called 'me.' However, even in the most liberal societies, the expectation is that you can be whoever you want to be as long as you're being 'yourself.' So how does society react when more than one ego shows up, and how does it reconcile its appearance with the notion of individuality?

Through trauma, this process of integration can become disrupted. Dissociative Identity Disorder (DID), previously termed Multiple Personality Disorder, is a condition in which individuals have formed different egoic identities, or 'alters.' They experience switching between these alternate personalities. DID arises in people who have suffered prolonged periods of trauma before the ages of six to nine, although some studies suggest before the age of four. In the midst of extreme suffering, there is a dramatic interruption in psychological development, particularly as it pertains to identity. Through a process of disassociation, this results in differentiated self-states, who think and feel different. It is as if the mind is building a protective wall around each identity, as a defence mechanism to help the survivor cope with trauma. Each alter broadly demonstrates one of two emotional responses: fear (the need to protect itself to survive), or anger (the need to take what it needs to survive).

On average, an individual with DID will have 10–20 alters (although there can be many more) that they switch between. The common denominator is that they are all, by definition, different and distinct. Whether it be their name, age, gender, race, sexuality, tone of voice, interests, lingo or posture. There is some professional debate over just how physically different some alters can appear to be. For example, alters from a single individual can have different glasses prescriptions, or be variously blind and have 20:20 vision.

They can have different allergies and apparent strengths. The hallucinatory capacity of the brain evidences the extent to which we can recreate and re-perceive our apparent reality. At the same time, arguments for the use of different neural pathways for different alters have also been put forward.

You might imagine that if you were talking to an individual who switched alters mid-conversation, it would be obvious. However, in reality it's very subtle and often not noticed. DID is a condition of concealment, in which each of the egos, just like our own, is seeking to survive. Most people who know someone with DID will not know that they have it. This level of concealment, just like the ego, is two-way. It is designed to be imperceptible to everyone, including the person who has it. It can take years for an individual with DID to recognize that they are living with multiple identities. Can you be aware of what you don't remember? With DID this can be a revelation, in the sudden realization that you don't remember your childhood – that it doesn't exist.

While alters are not chosen consciously, each alter plays a specific role: to cope with the abuse. Not all alters are people. For a child, being a person can be scary, and it is not uncommon for alters to be robots, or animals, to help them survive. A wolf might imbue an alter with a sense of strength and fearlessness. A cat provides a loving creature that is cared for. An invisible alter is able to hide. A deaf alter no longer needs to hear. Alters also include what are referred to as 'interacts' or the 'bad guys.' These present as bullies, and often mirror the behaviours of their abuser. They are the alter that remembers and spent most time at the hands of their abuser. Their defence mechanism, their only means of escape, is to become that which they fear most.

One interesting aspect of DID is the amnesiac effect of switching. The ego of each alter believes that it is a separate entity and is the author of its own thoughts. Unless one alter is able to witness the activities of another (referred to as 'co-consciousness,' which may occur to varying degrees) then only the alter that is present in its experience will remember it. For all other alters, in the absence of thought, there is no memory. Alters therefore experience no loss of time between switches. Separate memories are formed for each alter. Despite unsurprising disorientation, in the absence of memory and causality (just as we might experience within a disorganized dream), there is acceptance. It is for this reason that people can go for years before realizing that they have multiple personalities.

What ultimately reveals the condition is the process of *switching* itself. Those with DID observe that the new alter steps forward in resistance to what another alter is doing. This intrusion takes two forms – it can be to take control, to stop what they are doing, or to protect the individual from sabotaging itself. In both cases, there is an urgency to change the situation (to take or protect). Therefore, there is an apparent awareness that connects these seemingly separate minds – a characteristic that is integral both to the process of switching and to the manifestation of different identities in the first place. It is a model that echoes the *many minds* conceptual model of consciousness. The ego's need to assert control is exactly the same as we experience within ourselves. In fact, we might also question to what degree our own ego is integrated, when we consider how many and varied the roles are that our ego can play if the context changes. We believe our identity is tangible, definite, localized, consistent. However, perhaps the consistency and opacity we see within our own ego says more about our efforts to manipulate the world around us, to perpetuate our form of identity, than about the ego itself. How far is any of us, really, from murder or madness, should events so conspire? As we arrange the hall of mirrors so that each reflects back on ourself, it talks more to our own ego's need for survival, which is no different.

Feelings play a big part in the embodiment of each alter, and arise from this need to control. In some cases, this can be to step in and prevent an alter from hurting themself. In all cases, the trigger is in response to a felt association related to their trauma, which compels the ego to step in and resist, and to survive, in the manner that their characterization requires. It is the feeling that perpetuates the character. One individual with DID described how, as they switched into the alter of a three-year-old, they felt consumed with the emotions of the child, and felt the character take over. What would it feel like to be reborn into our own ego? Alters are like a single part of a large, beautiful mind. DID is the ego's ultimate form of protection from suffering, and offers insight into the functioning of our own ego.

7. HOW DO I KNOW?
THE LAWS OF ATTENTION

Your experience is entirely predicated by where and how you place your attention. In this chapter, we explore the process by which experience gains our attention and the inherent role that emotions play, through a set of seven laws, or governing principles:

- **Law 1 – Prior to experience is the knowing of experience:** All experience arises within our awareness, as the knowing that experience is happening. There is no difference between that which we experience and the knowing of experience (that which we are).

- **Law 2 – Through experience arises perspective:** All experience is limited to the faculties of conception and perception, from a localized perspective that is relative and comparative.

- **Law 3 – You are always paying attention to experience:** Our direct experience arises both through and out of the attention we give it. You can only ever give attention to objective experience – all that changes is that which you give attention to.

- **Law 4 – Attention is given to that which you recognize:** We can only perceive that which we feel, and all feeling is an act of recognition. You cannot recognize anything that you do not recognize in yourself. That which we don't recognize, we don't feel. What we feel (and all experience is felt) is the apprehension of our implicit understanding, that all experience is the expression of that which you already are. Recognition does not require our understanding.

- **Law 5 – Attention is an expression of preference:** Experience, the perception of finite form, is an expression of preference for one thing over another. Preference, or bias, is inherent to all experience. Our preference (what we like or what we dislike) is all that we give attention to.

- **Law 6 – All memories take place now:** Through the conception of time, we perceive memory. Memories, like imagination, are only ever experienced and felt in this moment. Thinking can never attend to this moment. As a concession, through thought we use memories and imagination to understand the past and the future, neither of which we could ever experience.

- **Law 7 – Our emotions are the source of all thought:** You cannot think without feeling. Feeling brings experience to our attention and brings attention to our thoughts. We believe what we think through what we feel.

This chapter includes passages from Helen Keller's book, *The Story of My Life*, published in 1903.[1] Keller was a notable American author of 14 books and hundreds of speeches and essays, who from the age of one was deprived of the sense of both sight and hearing. She only acquired language at the age of seven.

LAW 1 – PRIOR TO EXPERIENCE IS THE KNOWING OF EXPERIENCE

Appearances can be deceptive. Our perspective has a particular, localized point of view. We look out at the world as if through a window, through a space that appears to be our own, a space through which we locate ourselves. It is through this lens that we perceive both experience and infer the subject that perceives it. But what would happen to experience if we let go of the window, let go of this mental framing of reality that we hold on to so tightly as our own? The answer is *nothing*, because experiencing happens in your absence. There is just experiencing, looking at itself through a particular perspective. The inference we make is that this perspective is separate from experience. We assume that this localized perspective – the body – is the perceiver, rather than the perceived. Through our localized perspective, we assume that what we are is localized, limited to the body, to a world, even an afterlife. When you look through a telescope, are you limited to that telescope? You are not limited to the agency of the body.

Our perception of limitation derives from our senses. Through our thoughts we conceive our origin (such that we have one) as the brain, from where we think. As Helen Keller writes:

> *"If I had made a man, I should certainly have put the brain and soul in his fingertips. Our senses tell us nothing about what is within, only the world that is without. And we can only look out from our limited perspective."*[1]

Perspective is possible due to perception and conception. Our faculties of perception afford experience its many qualities: tactile (touch); auditory (hearing); visual (sight); olfactory (smell); gustatory (taste); proprioception (body position); equilibrioception (balance); interoception (internal body activity). We could say that our experience is limited by our faculties of perception, but of course they are themselves an aspect *of* experience.

1. Keller, H. (1903). *The Story of My Life*. Adansonia Publishing.

This erroneous distinction is conceptual, and it is through conceptualization – thinking – that our mind can categorize experience, conceive and categorize our senses, and seek to understand. Through perceiving, we experience the dimension of space, and through conceiving we experience the dimension of time. Perceiving and conceiving are the tools by which the activity of experience is known to us.

It is interesting to observe the inherent bias within our perspective of experience by reflecting on the many additional senses that exist in other organisms. Some appear as extensions of our own senses, such as the ability of bees to process ultraviolet light, or the ability of whales to detect infrasound – sounds too low in pitch for humans to hear. Some are a form of hybrid, such as the ability of bats to use ultrasound and echo location to create a sensory impression of their environment to locate prey. Others, such as a shark's ability to detect the electrical currents of other organisms (electroception) are entirely alien to us. We could try to imagine what these different experiences might be like, but of course our imagination is limited to that which we can experience, through the senses we possess, and so we can't. How about plants – do they perceive the changing of seasons? Of course they do, but in the absence of conception and thinking they just don't *know* it. In other words, you can perceive experience without knowing that you perceive it. We do this all the time: how is your heart rate? The reason for this is that all experience, and all that experience is, is the knowing of experience – or *consciousness*. Experience does not imply a separate, sentient being. Rather, its reality, its expression, is found not only in that which is reading these words, but by the paper on which it is written. Consciousness, or *awareness*, is the source and substance of everything.

By default, awareness is self-aware. But in order to know something called the world, made out of matter, you have to ignore the reality of experience – pure consciousness. We think that we are aware of something other than awareness, such as objects, thoughts. We think we know something other than knowing. The Sufi poet Rumi said of this, *"Knowledge of the world is a kind of ignorance."* In other words, we think there is an outside world, separate from ourselves. And we think consciousness or awareness comes from the mind. Instead, mind comes from consciousness. Your knowing of awareness does not exist in time and space, in a person called 'James.' It is in consciousness. It is only from the ego that it appears as separate. Your knowing is not happening in time and

2. The Bible, Psalm 46:10.

space. In the Christian tradition, Psalm 46:10 is often misunderstood. *"Be still and know that I am God"*[2] does not refer to a God out there, but the I that you are. So be still, and know that you *are* God.

As consciousness, we are on stage playing all the characters we see. We are all the parts – we just perceive it from a single character's perspective, from a single mind, from a single script. All experience is the activity of formless consciousness. The consciousness-only model encourages us to look beyond our perceived limitations. It is the natural intelligence of awareness, to expand to broaden our perspective, to be curious, to enquire – to look! Is there anything to a thought other than the experience of thinking? No. And is there anything to the experience of thinking other than the knowing of it? No. Take the experience of the body, which you experience as sensations. Is there anything to the body other than the experience of sensing? No. Is there anything to the experience of sensing other than the knowing of it? No. The knowing of perception – out of which feelings and sensations arise – is the same knowing. As Keller writes:

> *"Nature – the world I could touch – was folded and filled with myself. I am inclined to believe those philosophers who declare that we know nothing but our own feelings and ideas. With a little ingenious reasoning, one may see in the material world simply a mirror, an image of permanent mental sensations."*[1]

Take your current perception. Is there anything to a perception other than the experience of perceiving? No. Is there anything to perceiving other than the knowing of it? No. And is the knowing of it the same knowing of thoughts, feelings, etc., or different? It's the same knowing. For any experience, do you encounter anything other than the knowing of it? No. Could ANY experience be made of anything other than the knowing of it? No – all you know is that there is awareness. That you are aware. What is it that knows there is knowing? Knowing. Awareness.

All there is to your experience is the knowing of it. All that is ever known is knowing. Descartes, in his book *Discourse on Method*,[3] describes the attainment of knowledge as *"I think, therefore I am"* (*cogito ergo sum*). Like all expressions, there is truth to it. You are the knowing of your thoughts, and the knowing of your thoughts is *thinking*.

3. Descartes, R. (1637). *Discourse on Method.* East India Publishing Company.

LAW 2 – THROUGH EXPERIENCE ARISES PERSPECTIVE

Every experience is unique. We see *"through a glass (a mirror) darkly."*[4] Reality is always an obscure and imperfect vision of reality. There is no such thing as 'the complete picture.' Information arises from the point of your attention in awareness, so that all information is subjective. The parable of the blind men and the elephant tells how a group of men who have lost their sight experience an elephant for the first time. Each man senses, through touch, a different part of the animal, and so perceives a different whole. The trunk is perceived as a snake, the tail a piece of rope, its side a wall. None of us can claim absolute truth within experience other than the truth of our own direct experience. Experience is therefore not a moment, but an activity of continual exploration. Bayes' Theorem, posited by mathematician Thomas Bayes, is an equation used in probability and statistics to calculate the likelihood of an event based on its association with another event. From a statistical perspective, it explains how we can't know reality perfectly, and that all we can do is update our understanding as more evidence becomes available. The implication is that experimentation is therefore essential to our understanding.

Our experience is informed and therefore limited by the faculties of conception and perception. We think of time and space as the causation and fabric of reality, rather than the consequence of conception and perception. Reality is the seeing of reality. They are not different, but the duality of experience – of the existence of subject and object – makes it so. Keller describes her experience of timelessness, in the absence of thinking:

> *"My inner life, then, was a blank without past, present or future, without hope or anticipation, without wonder or joy or faith. It was not night – it was not day. But vacancy absorbing space, and fixedness, without a place; there were no stars – no Earth – no time. No check – no change – no good – no crime. My dormant being had no idea of God or immortality, no fear of death."*[1]

Through our perception of space, we can conceive the laws of space and time. We can conceive that other dimensions could exist outside of space and time, our conception of which can only take place within space and time. Because we cannot perceive them, we cannot know them, and cannot observe any of their laws. Therefore, the understanding

4. The Bible, 1 Corinthians 13:12.

of any universe by any life form (accepting that it must, as a finite form within experience, possess limitations) will always be limited and incomplete. We can at best infer its shadow.

The shadow of a three-dimensional sphere is a two-dimensional circle, so we can conceive that the shadow of a four-dimensional object (four dimensions that do not intersect) would appear in three dimensions. The *tesseract*, for example, is the four-dimensional shape whose shadow would appear as a three-dimensional cube. The dimensions of time and space are like containers for our experience. Within our experience of three dimensions, we can see the entirety of a two-dimensional object. Were we able to perceive in four dimensions, we might infer that we could perceive all sides of a three-dimensional sphere at the same time. As it is, we require the dimension of time to get around that problem. In time, things appear and disappear in time. For someone who experiences in two dimensions, the appearance of a sphere in time would appear like a line getting bigger or smaller. For us, time and change appear as three-dimensional space appearing and disappearing.

LAW 3 – YOU ARE ALWAYS PAYING ATTENTION TO EXPERIENCE

The activity of consciousness (consciousness being aware of itself) is experience. French philosopher Nicolas Malebranche described attentiveness as "*the natural prayer of the soul.*"[5] Every experience we ever have is the act of attention – here, now. Whether it be the apprehension of the cosmos, or the dissection of a grain of sand. You are always paying attention; what changes is what you pay attention to. Attention is the movement of awareness away from itself to an object. Try to pay attention to something with no objective qualities. You cannot. Attention is directed. 'Experiencing' is the direction of attention from a subject to an object (at least that is how it appears to the subject). The directing of our attention is the most important tool we have. The quality of our experience is defined by how we direct our attention.

Attention is the ability of mind to conceive and perceive experience, through the localization of subject and object, in time and space. Its faculties are also its limitations. When we look through a telescope at the brightest star in the sky, we must attend to it in the knowing that its brilliance can only be known by the turning out of all other lights in the sky.

You cannot direct attention to consciousness. Try turning your attention to your true self. If you give attention to yourself, you will only ever find ego – another object.

5. Malebranche, N. (1674). *The Search After Truth* (T. M., Lennon, & P. J. Olscamp, Eds). Cambridge University Press.

To illuminate the Moon, the Sun must direct its rays. The darkest place in the universe is at the centre of its brightest star. So it is that only through the cessation of attention can there be an awareness of our true being. It is the nature of awareness to know itself; it does not require attention. Attention has to end for being to know itself.

We can describe attention as a faculty of mind. It is the lens, the acuity by which we perceive and conceive the world. It is by its nature and necessarily discriminatory. The Latin derivation of 'attention' is *attendere*, which means to stretch toward. It implies that there is a distance from ourselves, as the perceiver (an attendant), to that which we perceive, and as such, we need to reach out to experience *with our attention* to know it. The separate self experiences this as a felt tension or motivation, when we seek outside of ourselves within experience, in the misunderstanding that "I am separate from my experience." In our actual experience, the perception of this room is the same as the knowing of it. No experience ever takes place at a distance from the knowing of it – from consciousness.

LAW 4 – ATTENTION IS GIVEN TO THAT WHICH YOU RECOGNIZE (THAT WHICH YOU ARE)

Experience is the activity of consciousness as it looks in the mirror. Everything that is perceived in our experience is the recognition of who we are. Attention is this act of recognition. Within this mirror, or *Markov blanket* (Chapter 12), we know the world consciously through the model of the world that we create within it (our subconscious). Therefore, we can only perceive that which we can imagine. We can see the world when we close our eyes, an anticipatory aspect being essential to our survival. Indeed, what is seeing when we do not need eyes to see? Self-awareness is the imagination of self within our model of the world.

All experience is nothing but a recognition of who we are. You could not touch the wall if the wall were not to touch you back. You know the wall because you are the wall. Yet, in objective experience there appears separation, in which we can give attention inward (to the object of self – introspection – to our thoughts, our memories, our dreams) or outward (to the objects of our environment).

Experience is always calling to you, but the ego is always waiting for something, waiting in line for its name to be called, because it's the only one it can hear. But all names belong to you, and are yours, and you are the one that is calling.

Recognition is a feeling:

When we recognize something – that which we give attention to – we feel it. There would be no experiencing without feeling. What we describe as emotions is the movement of our attention, the recognition of our true nature in experience. You can point a camera at experience, but the Polaroid will not develop until it is held up to the light. Emotions – our recognition of who we are – are like a light that shines through all experience, illuminating what we see, colouring our reality. The source of all feeling is the joy and peace of our true nature, which shines in all of us. In the final analysis, recognition suggests a reflection, which implies separation. It may be closer to the truth to say that consciousness is instead like a faceless mirror, with each aspect reflecting all others, without end.

Our emotions are the registering and apprehension of our attention within experience. You could not see without the feeling of seeing, and that feeling changes depending on what you see. This feeling is so ingrained that we look through it, and see only the object in our experience. We miss that what we feel in us is the object itself. All experiencing is ultimately a feeling – an extension of the peace of knowing of our own being.

When we see or hear beauty in all its forms, whether through music, or nature, or just being with the ones we love, the recognition we feel is bestowed from within us, not from outside. It is the recognition of shared being. Feeling is the colour of knowing. Everything that is known is *felt*.

Emotions and the path of attention:

In the absence of ego, the path our attention takes is the *path of least resistance*. Conversely, egoic attention is the path of resistance. We call these paths our preferences. We experience the changes in our attention through our emotions, and accordingly experience what we like and what we dislike. The stronger our preference, the stronger the emotion, and the more heightened our attention.

What gains our attention is not what we see, but what we feel. Emotions are the movement of our attention, toward that which we want and away from that which we don't. There is no attention without emotion. The saying "seeing is believing" might be better expressed as "feeling is believing." Feeling is how we truly perceive the world. It is the cornerstone of all experience, and so inherent and pervasive that we tend to think of emotions as byproducts of experience, rather than their most fundamental aspect.

When we look at light, when we give it our attention, what we perceive is not a wave of light particles, but the feeling of light. We use concepts to describe its qualities – it's radiance, it's beauty – as if they belong to the light. They do, insofar as they also belong to us. All experience is felt, and all emotions and feelings are refractions of their source, of awareness in which all experience is known. The origin of all that we feel – from joy to despair – is the peace of our own abidance, just as all colours on the movie screen are illuminated through the colourless light of the projector, through which all colours are allowed to shine.

Emotions are often described in terms of their essential role in making decisions. We cannot choose our emotions any more than we can choose our attention, but to the ego, which claims authorship, a change in our attention feels like a choice. There is no filter or line that separates what we feel from what gains our attention. We are compelled to attend to that which we feel – that which is our preference. It is our change in attention, the experience of which is known to us through what we feel, that compels action.

LAW 5 – ATTENTION IS AN EXPRESSION OF PREFERENCE

The objects of experience – that which we give attention to – are our preferences. The manifestation of reality is a manifestation of preference. Preference is the spontaneous diffusion through osmosis of a solvent through a selectively permeable membrane from a region of high water potential to a region of low water potential, just as it is the preference for coffee over tea. Preference also denotes difference, another essential ingredient to the manifestation of life on Earth. Life is, by our simplest definition, a preference of movement. These preferences are baked into all experience; otherwise there would be chaos. It is the preference of rain to fall, the preference to eat sushi on Saturday, the preference of chlorophyll in plants to create energy from sunshine, the preference to be born and to die. Preference is central to the theory of evolution – from the differential behavioural preferences that enhance or limit a species' prospects, down to the arising of genetic mutations – the source code upon which their abilities are enshrined.

Another name for preference is bias. In society, bias has negative connotations due to the misunderstanding that it is something that could and indeed should be avoided.

It cannot. This negativity is, in part, due to the various models that fail to accurately categorize the essential types (and causes) of bias. Our very definition and rational understanding of bias – logic – is itself biased.

Bias presents us with the dilemma of acceptance. Can you accept that for you to live, others must die? Rational argument may propose that death is part of life, but where do you draw the line? Can you accept that when you buy your lunch, there are children starving? True acceptance does not require understanding or logic. Can you accept any suffering in this world without trying to change it? The ego cannot resolve this dilemma, because its authorship presumes responsibility and free will to act. Its strategy is always, in resistance, one of self-service, even when given to acts of charity. Either it will take what it needs from others (an act of aggression) or will attempt to defend what it has from others (which includes looking the other way from those that have less than you). Change starts with acceptance, which includes that we are as biased to left and right as we are to right and wrong. Equity within society (the sharing of resources based on what people need) is unlikely to happen when ego is the primary determinant of human behaviour.

Why you don't always like what you need:
There are two types of preference:

- **Egoic – a preference for things we need:** When we think we need something from experience to make us happy, we will either seek or resist experience. Our expression (of how we feel) is suppressed, and our attention is taken away from direct experience to thoughts (potentiality).
- **Non-egoic – a preference for things we like:** When we don't need anything from experience, through acceptance our attention is on it fully. Our enjoyment of experience has nothing to do with the activity we are undertaking, but on our unbounded expression (of how we feel) within experience (actuality).

One way to know which is which is to ask: *"How much effort is it to want this?"* If it's easy, then you like it but don't need it. From our attention arises how we express ourselves, and how we feel. Fig 5 shows the four cornerstone actions from which all emotions derive.

FIG 5 – PREFERENCE VS. ATTENTION: NON-EGOIC RESPONSE (ACCEPTANCE)

Note that the fight versus flight response is not itself egoic – rather, as shown in Fig 6, where it forms an egoic preference, it then becomes an egoic response.

FIG 6 – PREFERENCE VS. ATTENTION: IMPACT OF EGO (RESISTANCE)

Experience – an activity – cannot make you happy. A sportsperson does not want to win the game, they want to be aware of their own being. When we stop giving exclusive attention to the objects of experience, we gain awareness of our true nature. There is nowhere else to look. What we find is that the activity of experience still happens, it just happens for no one. Preferences still exist, but the activity is fulfilled in order for us to *express* our happiness (abidance), rather than to *find* happiness (seeking).

The opening line of the Sutra of the 3rd Chinese Zen Patriarch, from the 6th century BCE, says: *"The great way is not difficult for those not attached to preferences."*[6] Preference and desire do not cause suffering. Rather, it is the presumption of authorship that does. The ego identifies itself with its preferences and personality, but what you want, and what you need, are not who you are. Egoic preference is the route of all addiction – not just to drugs, alcohol or gambling, but the addiction to experience itself. It is the belief that experience can make you happy.

When we like something, we enjoy the activity. Yet, the interesting thing about needing is that the activity itself is often something we don't like. When we need something, we need the activity to get us to a point of release, to enable us to withdraw our attention from experience, to rest, to be at peace. We have to go through resistance to experience so that we can rest. For liking, the activity is both the means and the end. For needing, the activity is the means to the end.

This distinction has been borne out by research by Kent Berridge,[7] professor of biopsychology and neuroscience at the University of Michigan, on the role of dopamine. Until recently, it was generally assumed that if we needed something, it was because we liked it, and that the production of the hormone dopamine in the brain triggered this preference and was essential for inducing pleasure. In his experiment, Berridge attached a small metal rod to a rat cage that, when touched, delivered a minor electric shock. A normal rat quickly learns to stay away. However, by activating the rat's dopamine system, Berridge was able to make the rat become seemingly addicted to the stick, returning time and again even after receiving an electric shock. The conclusion: dopamine triggers the preference for needing, but not liking. In evolutionary terms, needing is far more fundamental than liking. Ultimately, it doesn't matter for the preservation of our genes whether we like sex or like food. Far more important is whether we need to have sex, and whether we seek out food.

6. Seng-ts'an. (6th century BCE). *Hsin Sjin Ming: Sutra of the 3rd Chinese Zen Patriarch* (R. B. Clark – translator). White Pine Press.

7. Berridge, K.C., Robinson, T.E. What is the role of dopamine in reward: hedonic impact, reward learning, or incentive salience? *Brain Research Review.* 1998 Dec; 28(3):309-69

When the dopamine system becomes sensitized, that wanting never goes away. A drug addict's preference for needing will be triggered by the sight of a spoon, or a syringe, or a street corner – or more accurately, through the feeling that arises. Does that mean that egoic preference is actually caused by dopamine? No. Rather, the ego steps in and lays claim to those preferences where there is a perceived sense of need for fulfilment.

The difference between pleasure and pain:

In Chapter 5 we discussed the difference between pain and suffering. Preference is a measure of our sensitivity to the objects within our environment. Outside of ego, our preference denotes a threshold of sensitivity within which we experience pleasure, and beyond which we experience pain. Desire for that which gives us pleasure does not create suffering. Instead, suffering arises through authorship.

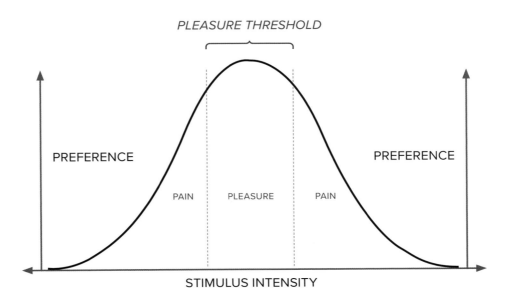

FIG 7 – PAIN PLEASURE SPECTRUM

You cannot have pleasure without pain. You also derive pain from that which gives you pleasure. Just as all experience denotes preference, pain arises in the absence of pleasure, and pleasure arises through the cessation of pain. Relativity of pleasure and pain is what we perceive as change within experience. With every sensation there is a feeling (an emotion), and with that feeling comes preference – either we like how something feels, or we don't. The point of ambivalence is when it is outside of our attention.

This relativity of pleasure and pain explains why we enjoy food more when we are hungry, and why we enjoy warmth more when we come in from the cold. Indeed, a 30-second cold shower before a warm shower is good for you, and will make your warm shower feel much better. Creating contrast within our experience that creates a visceral shift in our perspective and attention is a simple way to improve the pleasure we get from our environment. Aristotle called this *Eudaimonia*[8] – the need to stretch ourselves to experience greater pleasure. But pleasure is not the same as happiness. No object, nor any experience, can in and of itself make you happy.

Saying yes to experience:
Who you are is that which allows everything. Like it or not, you have already said yes to this experience, and every experience you ever have. You are like the space in the room, which unconditionally allows all within. You are the space of awareness for all experience. You have already said yes to experience, because that is the nature of consciousness. When you say no, the resistance you feel is because you're too late. It's already happening, already allowed. Notice that what says no to experience is an object (ego) within experience, which is also allowed, unconditionally.

When we say yes to experience, there is still the desire to do the things we like to do, and to avoid the things we don't, but there is also an abiding acceptance of ALL experience. When we say yes to experience, there is greater freedom to explore it, to drop the studying of experience and the internal monologue that judges what you should or shouldn't be doing, or that this should or shouldn't be happening. When we say yes to experience, we are more likely to: (a) Be aware of what is going on around us, so that more opportunities open up for us; (b) Enjoy what we do more because we will not feel that we have to do things to make us happy.

8. Aristotle (340 BCE). *Nicomachean Ethics*. (Drummond Percy Chase – translator). East India Publishing Company.

The withdrawal of attention:

Our biggest habit is giving our exclusive attention to experience. Our attention is always seeking its origin. The withdrawal of attention is required to know our true nature, just as attention must be given to objects to know experience. Look closely at those artforms that move us, that we feel most intimately. Music, whether melodic or discordant, leads us through its phrasing from dissonance to resolution. Harmonies build out of melodies as an answer builds from a question, to lead us back, like an echo. Through humour, we laugh as our attention is released. Stories and poetry catch us up in a journey through moments of recognition in which our attention is arrested and we stop looking in the space between the words or in the silence. Art collapses our attention so that the mind can rest. As Cézanne said, it *"must give us the flavour of nature's eternity."*[9]

Beauty is the revelation of the infinite in the finite. Some objects have the power to bring about the dissolution of the subject-object relationship. These works of art point us back to our true nature. We should not be surprised by those artists who go against the grain, and who agonize in their attempts to express that which is beyond our understanding, or their own.

All artful practice points toward the withdrawal of attention. Indeed, performance of any calibre necessitates it. Take the potter at her wheel. Through the space and time of practice, a bowl is formed that emerges through increasingly sophisticated creations, whose elegance belies its complexity. Through more practice, and more bowls, we see a change, a refinement taking place. The bowl takes on ever-simpler forms, until in its ultimate refinement it becomes simply the space for it to hold. Through attention, expression ultimately leads to dissolution. In the Chinese and Japanese Sumi paintings, a bird or a tree is rendered with a single stroke of the brush. In time, all artists, all musicians, who through their art point to truth fall silent. The Hindu sage Ramana Maharshi referred to this when he said, *"Silence is unceasing eloquence."*[10]

LAW 6 – ALL MEMORIES TAKE PLACE NOW

Our emotions colour our lives. What we feel in each moment is a recognition within experience of our true nature, our shared being. Our feelings are a refraction of the light of our true being – of consciousness – in the turning of our attention toward objective experience.

9. Gasquet, J. (1991). *Cézanne: A Memoir with Conversations.*

10. Maharshi, R. (2000). *Talks with Sri Ramana Maharshi.* (10th Edition). V. S. Ramanan, Sri Ramanasramam Tiruvannamalai.

What we perceive as change is only ever a change in our attention. All emotion, all feeling, is only ever in this moment, which is eternal. No feeling is ever lost in the eternal *now*; all that changes is where we give our attention.

Our mind assumes that everything has a place and a time. The 'now' is the place and time of current experience, relative to 'then,' which is a place and time in the past, known to us through memory. We conceive our minds as a vast filing cabinet that downloads and stores our experiences. In the absence of direct experience, our thoughts provide an artificial perceptual frame that takes the feeling from this moment and uses it to colour a picture within our imagination. Memories are a faculty of conceptual imagination. Through conceptualization we create a super-web of associations. Like the spider on its web, our mind cannot attend to it all at once. Rather, our mind controls perspective through its axis, like a tickertape of thought. But not left to right – from *past to future*. It is the direction of our thinking mind, of reason, of logic, of attention, that informs all understanding.

Memory is just a feeling, a recognition, happening right now. This recognition does not require thought, but it is through thought, and through association, that we conjure a conceptual experience – a perceptual timeframe in the absence of direct experience, which creates the remembered narrative. All narrative memory (the perception that an event happened in the past) requires thought, but only feelings are required to remember. It's not that the past didn't happen, or that the future hasn't happened, it's just that past and future only ever happen now. Notice that when you remember, you find the feeling in your experience before the memory. When an idea or memory suddenly springs upon us unheralded, it is because we recognize its feeling in our current experience, however subtle that may be. Our memories reside in what we feel in this moment.

Sensory memory is therefore an aspect of all recall. Our senses facilitate their recall, recall being contingent on which senses we give attention to. As Keller recounts of her experience growing up:

> "*I did not know that I knew aught, or that I lived or acted or desired. I had neither will nor intellect. I was carried along to objects and acts by a certain blind natural impetus. I had a mind which caused me to feel anger, satisfaction, desire. These two facts led those about me to suppose that I willed and thought. I can remember all this, not because*

I knew that it was so, but because I have tactual memory. It enables me to remember that I never contracted my forehead in the act of thinking. I never viewed anything beforehand or chose it."[1]

Our sensory memory creates perceptual rather than conceptual associations. Again, as Keller describes in her book:

"I folded the clothes that came from the laundry, and put mine away, fed the turkeys, sewed bead-eyes on my doll's face, and did many other things of which I have the tactual remembrance." For Helen, these sensorial associations were necessary not just for implicit memory, but for active recall: *"When I try to recall what someone has said to me, I am conscious of a hand spelling into mine."*[1]

The only difference between memory and imagination is the association of thought – whether we are reassociating through prior associations in the 'web,' through which we perceive past events, or forming new ones. It's perfectly possible to misattribute thoughts so that imagination is perceived as memory (the cognitive bias of *'false memory'*), or memory perceived as imagination (*cryptomnesia*). But fundamentally, memory and imagination are the same thing. Memories, imagination, direct experience, even dreams, are all just forms of an objective experience. In memories and imagination, we turn our attention to our subconscious.

Our memories and imagination require thought to render them. In a waking state, our mind is constantly seeking the association of imagination and memory with current experience. In dreams, we lose this restriction. Have you ever woken from a dream and wondered at its absurdity? In our waking state, the story often reveals itself as fragmented, incoherent, as if being read from random pages in a book. What seems incomprehensible to the waking state is transformed in the dream state, with no reference to past or future, into unlimited freedom of creative expression. In other words, our experience and our expression do not require reference to past or future, memory or imagination. They only require awareness, in which our attention requires only this moment. With limitations lost, a pirate swings from the bow of his ship onto shore, into the arms of a London zookeeper who is busy teaching a telephone box to sing. Everything is known, recognized, accepted, and none of it remembered, until we wake up.

Every action you take is an act of forgetting. You cannot think two thoughts at once. You cannot feel two feelings at once. You must forget. Remembering is the act of forgetting. To forget is simply a change in your attention, which results in a change in your experience. Imagination is a forgetting. Your forgetting that you are dreaming allows you to imagine your dream. Forgetting requires a relaxing and withdrawing of attention. Children are great at forgetting, which educational systems do their best to dismantle through rote learning and an insistence to 'pay attention' in class, like life depended on it. Perhaps daydreaming should be placed on the curriculum, and see how many people pay attention then. As Keller writes:

> *"As my experiences broadened and deepened, the indeterminate, poetic feelings of childhood began to fix themselves in definite thoughts."*[1]

LAW 7 – OUR EMOTIONS ARE THE SOURCE OF ALL THOUGHT
You cannot think without feeling:

A thought is an object in our experience, like touch and taste. Emotions bring it to our attention. They tell us when we are thinking, not the thought. You cannot think without feeling, and a thought is known through the feeling attached to it. As Keller explains:

> *"I cannot represent more clearly than anyone else the gradual and subtle changes from first impressions to abstract ideas. But I know that my physical ideas, that is, ideas derived from material objects, appear to me first an idea similar to those of touch. Instantly they pass into intellectual meanings."*[1]

Thoughts are the mind's categorization of what we feel, to make sense of the world, through an abstracted conceptual model. Just as we don't choose how we feel, we don't choose our thoughts. Feeling gives attention to our thoughts, while our thoughts provide their conceptual classification. When a thought arises out of a strong feeling, we believe it implicitly, immediately. We believe what we feel, because all of attention is known through feeling.

Experience is like viewing a painting. Perception brings the brushes, paints the canvas. Conception places it in a frame, finds a place for it on the wall. But through conception and perception, you will see nothing until you feel it. Feeling is when you show up. Note that we are still describing aspects of objective experience. In actuality, all aspects of experience – of feeling, seeing, touching, thinking – are simply the knowing of it; the space in which all experience is allowed.

You can only pay attention to one thing at a time:
You cannot conceive and perceive at the same time. Thoughts, like any object within experience, are felt and thereby experienced at different levels of intensity, and in so doing are able to gain greater or lesser attention. Some are fleeting, others are lit up in neon and refuse to budge. In all cases, our attention to the thought, in the moment that we perceive it, requires us to withdraw attention from sensory experience. Thoughts are sometimes described as an overlay or augmentation of experience, but look closely and you'll notice that you cannot think (give attention to any thought) without taking attention away from perceptual experience. It's like blinking: it happens so quickly and so often that we barely notice when we stop looking with open eyes.

Self-awareness is a thought:
Through thinking we become self-aware, through the identification of the object 'me' (which is a thought) and the according shift in attention away from our senses. Ego is the awareness of a self that is DOING the thinking (and therefore being). The awareness of self – the awareness of being – is the same as the awareness of cats or trees, until ego arises. Keller describes the dawning of the conception of self:

> *"When I learned the meaning of 'I' and 'me' and found that I was something, I began to think. Then consciousness first existed for me. Thus it was not the sense of touch that brought me knowledge. It was the awakening of my soul that first rendered my senses their value, their cognizance of objects, names, qualities, and properties. Thought made me conscious of love, joy and all the emotions."*[1]

You can think without words:

Can you think without language? It depends what you mean by language! For example, there is plenty of evidence from hearing-impaired individuals who have been cut off from language, spoken or signed, that they think in sophisticated ways before they have been exposed to language. When they later learn language, they can describe the experience of having had thoughts like those of the 15-year-old boy who wrote in 1836, after being educated at a school for the deaf, that he remembered thinking in his pre-language days *"that perhaps the Moon would strike me, and I thought that perhaps my parents were strong, and would fight the Moon, and it would fail, and I mocked the Moon."*[11] Thinking, as an instrument for the comparative labelling of our environment, is an ability that precedes language. However, language provides us with a set of rules through which we can think more eloquently.

Mathematics is one example. Through mathematical concepts, we are able to discern complex numerical arrangements and patterns that would not otherwise be visible to us. The nature of the language we use, and the concepts we're able to draw on, affects how we think. The Australian Aboriginal Kuuk Thaayorre community's language helps keep them orientated to the land, for instance. Rather than using left or right, they use the points of the compass. To say hello, they might ask, *"Which way are you going?"* Unsurprisingly, they rarely get lost. Language also affects how we think about time. An English speaker will likely draw a timeline from left to right, in the direction of their writing, whereas a Hebrew or Arabic speaker might draw it right to left. If you ask the Kuuk Thaayorre, it depends on where they are facing. East points to the past, west to the future – the arrow of time is locked on the landscape. But what if our senses are taken away?

Similar to how an 'inner voice' of a hearing person is experienced in one's own voice, a completely deaf person will often think in sign language. They'll feel themselves signing in their head. It is common for deaf people, when asleep, to not only communicate in their dreams using sign language, but also telepathically. Language is a code to think in, and deaf people who do not learn a language can have learning difficulties as a result. The brain treats sign language exactly as it treats spoken language. One might think that the brain would use part of the right hemisphere to process sign language, given its role in visual processing. However, the same portion of the left hemisphere used to process sign language also processes vocal language in those who can hear.

11. *Sixteenth Annual Report of the Directors of the New York Institution for the Instruction of the Deaf and Dumb to the Legislature of the State of New York, for the Year 1834* (1835).

The essential role that language plays in thought extends therefore to memory, abstract thinking and self-awareness. To an individual with normal hearing, memorization tests can be disrupted by asking them to repeat a nonsense phrase over and over, with the auditory stimulation distracting attention. Asking a hard-of-hearing person to grip something hard with their hands, while asking them to memorize a list of words, has the same disruptive effect.

THE LIMITS OF UNDERSTANDING:

It appears to the separate self that we are in control of our thoughts. Indeed, ask yourself to write down what thought is coming next, and you will always be right! But now, write down the thought that will come after that one, and you will always be wrong. You can only ever be right *now*. Thinking happens in time. We could describe time as a way of thinking. We don't actually experience time, we experience thinking of past and future. And thinking only ever takes place now. Yet, you can never understand this moment. You can only ever understand the past, or the future – never right now.

Through suffering, the ego searches for meaning and purpose – a need for something to fulfil happiness outside of current experience. Thoughts do not mean anything, but a meaningless world engenders fear to ego. Unfortunately for ego, nothing you can 'know' about you is you. You are not the content of your experience. You are not the character in the play. You are never upset for the reason you think. You cannot understand suffering beyond knowing that suffering comes from searching (including the search for understanding) rather than just abidance. Like a child waking from a nightmare, we suffer because we see something that is not there.

PART 2

LEADING OUT:
THE ELUCIDATIONS
OF LEADERSHIP

8. EGODYNAMICS

If Part 1 has raised more questions than answers, then you're heading in the right direction. Perhaps you're asking, *"What can I do with this?"* In Part 1 we explored the primordial nature of our identity, to renew the understanding by which we assert our role as leaders. In Part 2, we'll translate this insight into practice, through an introduction to *seven elucidations of leadership* that invite a new way to lead beyond the ego.

The role that our ego plays in our lives – our sense of a separate self – is profound. Egodynamics provides a new framework that explains the essential relationship between our egoic thoughts and feelings, as a basis to better understand the way we think, feel and act. While various attempts have been made to categorize the relationship between our different emotions, these models treat egoic and non-egoic feelings interchangeably. Egodynamics specifically concerns the feelings that result from our attachment to objective experience – those that cause suffering. When ego claims ownership of an emotion, we identify with what we feel. It is the difference in perspective from *"I feel sad"* (a natural, emotional response) to *"I am a sad person"* (an egoic response). Emotions may or may not cause pain, but they do not (unlike egoic feelings) cause suffering. Egoic feelings arise in resistance to emotions, in an attempt to mask and counter them.

To help us better understand the impact that ego has on our lives, this chapter will also explore a new measure for egocentricity: the Attachment Quotient. The only way for the ego to find relief is to do the one thing it is trying to avoid – to turn toward and embrace the emotion that it is rejecting in experience. In the absence of ego, emotions are embraced, known intimately, and so, ultimately short-lived.

THE ORIGINS OF EGOCENTRISM

Egocentrism is the inability to differentiate between self and other, and to assume or understand any perspective other than one's own. Its emergence through life is in direct relation to an individual's dualistic perception of reality – of subject and object. When a child is born, there is no concept of an objective reality that is separate from their subjective experience. We are not born with an ego. According to developmental psychologist Jean Piaget, babies don't begin to develop a sense of self until they are several months old.[1]

In early infancy, children are unable to recognize that their thoughts and their bodies are separate from others. For instance, it is observed that when infants initially interact

1. Piaget, J. (1936). *Origins of intelligence in the Child.* London: Routledge & Kegan Paul.

with their caregivers, with whom they spend long periods of time, they misinterpret that they are one entity. They may, for example, misattribute the act of their mother reaching to retrieve an object that they point to as evidence that they are one and the same.

From as early as 15 months, a *theory of mind* (the capacity for empathy and understanding of others) begins to develop. It is from this increasing perceptual distinction between an internal and an external world that subjective experience gives rise to an objective reality, and the perception of a separate self – the ego – is formed (as shown at point X in Fig 8). The existence of 'I' is relative to the existence of objects.

A well-known 1983 experiment by psychologists Heinz Wimmer and Josef Perner, called the False Belief Task,[2] demonstrated how four-year-olds could acquire a theory of mind. Children watched as Character A placed a marble under a blanket, before departing. A second individual, Character B, then removes the marble and places it in a box. When Character A returns, the child is asked where Character A will look to find the marble. Children under four typically answer "box," assuming that Character A has their knowledge. The misinterpretation of this test is that egocentricity gives rise to theory of mind. Rather, they are concomitant aspects of cognitive development in which, through their mutuality, egocentric behavioural traits (as observed in infants) appear to diminish.

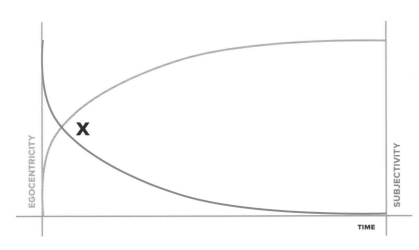

FIG 8 – SUBJECTIVE BASIS FOR EGOCENTRICITY

In young adolescence, egocentrism is observed within the protectionist preoccupation of self, as individuals undergo a physiological metamorphosis and encounter new social environments. The model of egocentrism as an aspect of human cognitive development that gives rise to theory of mind is herein considered incorrect. Rather, it is proposed that egocentrism is maintained throughout adulthood. Adults appear to

2. Wimmer, H., & Perner, J. (1983). Beliefs about beliefs: Representation and constraining function of wrong beliefs in young children's understanding of deception. *Cognition*, 13, 103-128.

be less egocentric than children because they are faster to correct from an initially ego-centric perspective than children, not because they are less likely to adopt an egocentric perspective. The formation of self ceases at a point that it, from the perspective of self, has attained maximum individuality, while simultaneously and paradoxically reflecting a state of maximum codependence (Fig 8).

EGOIC STATES

Consider what the reality for the ego looks like. There is the ego, and there is the world of objects that it experiences. The two are separate and distinct. Some of these objects appear as people. For the ego, the experience of seeking an object of fulfilment will always reflect one of nine different *egoic dynamics*, described as follows:

1. Help or hinder. Example – *"I am being helped to get what I want by you."*
2. Give or can't give. Example – *"I can't get what I want from you."*
3. Succeed or fail. Example – *"I didn't get what I wanted."*
4. Have or have not. Example – *"I don't have what you want."*
5. Dependent or independent. Example – *"I am the only one that can give you what you want."*
6. Acquire or impose. Example – *"I gave you what you wanted."*
7. Take or keep. Example – *"I stopped you getting what you wanted."*
8. Lose or not lose. Example – *"I lost what I had."*
9. Love or be loved. Example – *"I want you to get what you want."*

These nine dynamics define the ego's relationship between itself and that which it seeks. The dynamics assume the belief system as described in the eight tenets of ego (Fig 3). Each dynamic can be experienced from one of two different perspectives:
- From the perspective of subject (self or other)
- From the perspective of intent (toward or away)

From the dualistic aspect of each perspective arises four distinct modes of feeling within any given egoic dynamic. Our feelings vary depending on their orientation to past or future, or to their level of intensity. However, all our feelings (those resulting from egoic seeking) can be described within these nine dynamics, and from these four perspectives, resulting in a set of 36 different *'egoic states of separation'* (Fig 9), each reflecting a distinct personal identity or persona. Each egoic state defines the role that the ego identifies with, as described by its predominant thought and feeling, and which informs its resulting behaviour.

As Fig 9 shows, within each of the nine egoic dynamics there is a direct, dualistic relationship between the states of separation that occur between two individuals with opposing loci of control, within the two perspectives of subject (vertical relationship) and intent (horizontal relationship).

The ego essentially has two ways to seek fulfilment and to end the feeling of lack. Either it can seek to acquire the object it desires, or it can seek to retain it. Seeking is about control, and the manner in which the ego seeks is dependent on its locus of control. An ego with an internal locus of control believes that it can control its own life, whereas an ego with an external locus of control believes that life is controlled by outside factors it cannot influence. As a result, an ego with an internal locus of control will seek to obtain the object it desires from its external environment, whereas an ego with an external locus of control will try to hold onto it. This duality is fundamental to how the ego derives fulfilment from its perceived external world. In Fig 9, the feelings that demonstrate an ego's internal locus of control are shown in black, whereas demonstration of an external locus of control is shown in grey. Alongside each is shown the ego's governing thought. An individual with a higher internal locus of control will seek to organize the world (extroversion), whereas an individual with a higher external locus of control might seek instead to organize their thoughts (introversion).

HELP OR HINDER	Subject	You are being helped to get what you want by me.	You are being stopped from getting what you want by me.
		CONTROLLING	*DEFENSIVE*
	Object	I am being helped to get what I want by you.	I am being stopped from getting what I want by you.
		SUBMISSION	*ANGER*
GIVE OR CAN'T GIVE	Subject	You can get what you want from me.	You can't get what you want from me.
		DESIRED	*GUILT*
	Object	I can get what I want from you.	I can't get what I want from you.
		ADORATION	*CRITIC*
SUCCEED OR FAIL	Subject	I got what I wanted.	I didn't get what I wanted.
		SELF GRANDEUR	*DESPAIR*
	Object	You got what you wanted.	You didn't get what you wanted.
		SELF-PITY	*SCHADENFREUDE*
HAVE OR HAVE NOT	Subject	I have what you want.	I don't have what you want.
		VANITY	*SHAME*
	Object	You have what I want.	You don't have what I want.
		ENVY	*DISMISSIVE*
DEPENDENT OR INDEPENDENT	Subject	You are not the one that can give me what I want.	You are the only one that can give me what I want.
		INSULTED	*DEPENDENCE*
	Object	I am not the one that can give you what you want.	I am the only one that can give you what you want.
		REJECTION	*COERCION*
TAKE OR KEEP	Subject	You couldn't stop me getting what I wanted.	You stopped me getting what I wanted.
		ANTAGONISM	*DEJECTION*
	Object	I couldn't stop you getting what you wanted.	I stopped you getting what you wanted.
		JEALOUSY	*CONTEMPT*
ACQUIRE OR IMPOSE	Subject	I gave you what you didn't want.	I gave you what you wanted.
		OPPRESIVE	*INFERIORITY*
	Object	You gave me what I didn't want.	You gave me what I wanted.
		DISGUST	*SUPERIORITY*
LOSE OR NOT LOSE	Subject	I didn't lose what I have.	I lost what I had.
		RELIEF	*GRIEF*
	Object	You didn't lose what you have.	You lost what you had.
		ADMIRATION	*PITY*
LOVE AND BE LOVED	Subject	I want you to get what you want	I want you to get what you want
		LOVE	*LOVE*
	Object	You want me to get what I want	You want me to get what I want
		BELOVED	*BELOVED*

FIG 9 – 36 EGOIC STATES OF SEPARATION

An egoic state describes the characteristics of ego at its most irreducible level. Within each egoic state, there is a subject that has a need (ego), and the object that can fulfil that need. The relatedness between each of these egoic states (represented by a specific thought and feeling) is a function of the relative degree of apparent separation between the ego and its objective reality. When we consider the different dynamic interactions between the ego and its objective reality, we can see that there is a natural sequence that describes the minimum change in attention required between each step, as shown in Fig 10. Each step reflects a different degree of separation (resistance) from their perceived objective reality, with increasing separation running from left (lowest) to right (highest).

In Fig 10, the blue circle indicates the object of ego with an internal locus of control, the black circle represents the object of other (another person), and the red object is the ego's object of desire. Arrows show the direction of intent – of attention – whether to move the object of desire closer to or further from the 'other' in that relationship. The same dynamic occurs for the ego with an external locus of control, except that the objects of *ego* and *other* reverse (with the self/ego as the black circle).

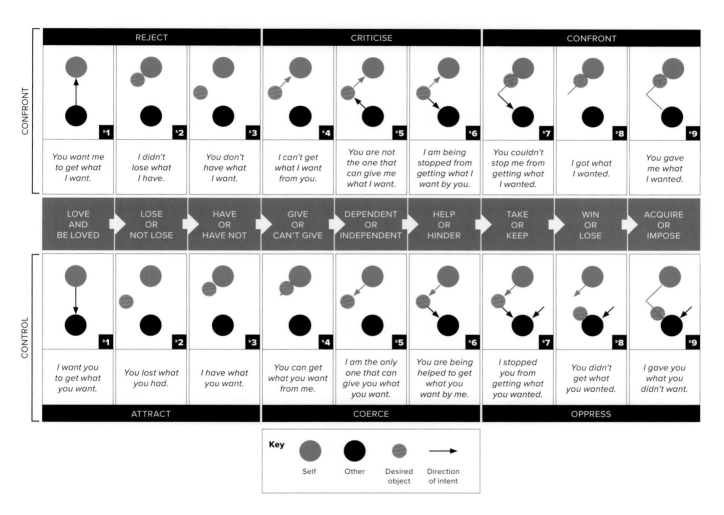

FIG 10 – SEQUENCE OF INCREASING SUBJECT – OBJECT SEPARATION (INTERNAL LOCUS OF CONTROL)

The incremental degrees of separation are described numerically by a *Separation Index (SI)*, which ranges from s1 to s9. Fig 11 shows the relationship between each egoic state, according to their SI and locus of control.

	STATE	SI	INTERNAL LOCUS OF CONTROL	EXTERNAL LOCUS OF CONTROL	CHAPTER
CONFRONT	LOVE AND BE LOVED	s1	You want me to get what I want.	I want you to get what you want.	**REJECT**
			BELOVED	LOVE	
	LOSE OR NOT LOSE	s2	I didn't lose what I have.	You didn't lose what you have.	
			RELIEF	ADMIRATION	
	HAVE OR HAVE NOT	s3	You don't have what I want.	I don't have what you want.	
			DISMISSIVE	SHAME	
	GIVE OR CAN'T GIVE	s4	I can't get what I want from you.	You can't get what you want from me.	**CRITICIZE**
			CRITIC	GUILT	
	DEPENDENT OR INDEPENDENT	s5	You are not the one that can give me what I want.	I am not the one that can give you what you want.	
			INSULTED	REJECTION	
	HELP OR HINDER	s6	I am being stopped from getting what I want by you.	You are being stopped from getting what you want by me.	
			ANGER	DEFENSIVE	
	TAKE OR KEEP	s7	You couldn't stop me from getting what I wanted.	I couldn't stop you from getting what you wanted.	**CONFRONT**
			ANTAGONISM	JEALOUSY	
	SUCCEED OR FAIL	s8	I got what I wanted.	You got what you wanted.	
			SELF-GRANDEUR	SELF-PITY	
	ACQUIRE OR IMPOSE	s9	You gave me what I wanted.	I gave you what you wanted.	
			SUPERIORITY	INFERIORITY	
CONTROL	ACQUIRE OR IMPOSE	s9	I gave you what you didn't want.	You gave me what I didn't want.	**OPPRESS**
			OPPRESIVE	DISGUST	
	SUCCEED OR FAIL	s8	You didn't get what you wanted.	I didn't get what I wanted.	
			SCHADENFREUDE	DESPAIR	
	TAKE OR KEEP	s7	I stopped you from getting what you wanted.	You stopped me from getting what I wanted.	
			CONTEMPT	DEJECTION	
	HELP OR HINDER	s6	You are being helped to get what you want by me.	I am being helped to get what I want by you.	**COERCE**
			CONTROLLING	SUBMISSION	
	DEPENDENT OR INDEPENDENT	s5	I am the only one that can give you what you want.	You are the only one that can give me what I want.	
			COERCION	DEPENDENCE	
	GIVE OR CAN'T GIVE	s4	You can get what you want from me.	I can get what I want from you.	
			DESIRED	ADORATION	
	HAVE OR HAVE NOT	s3	I have what you want	You have what I want	**ATTRACT**
			VANITY	ENVY	
	LOSE OR NOT LOSE	s2	You lost what you had	I lost what I had	
			PITY	GRIEF	
	LOVE AND BE LOVED	s1	I want you to get what you want	You want me to get what I want	
			LOVE	BELOVED	

FIG 11 – EGOIC STATES ACCORDING TO THEIR SEPARATION INDICES

Through incremental degrees of separation, there appears to be a movement or flow of resistance, across six 'chapters' (these appearing within the story of the ego), in which the ego moves toward or away from that which it seeks. Each chapter describes a triad of ego-centric states: upper triad (s7-s9), middle triad (s4-s6) and lower triad (s1-s3) – see Fig 12.

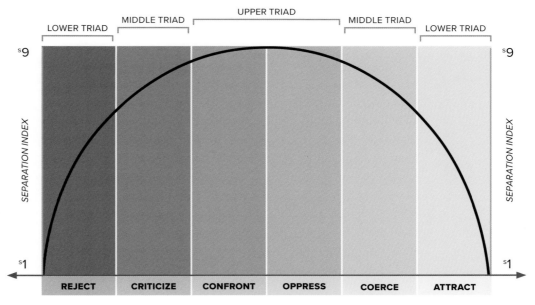

FIG 12 – RESISTANCE CHAPTERS

Across the internal and external loci of control, this creates a continuous, symmetrical relationship. This is described by the Egodynamics Wheel in Fig 13, which shows the relationship of different egoic states according to the ego's *governing thought*. Increasing perceived separateness occurs along the Y axis, with decreasing separation along the X axis. The duality of egoic states is described across opposing loci of control but with shared SIs.

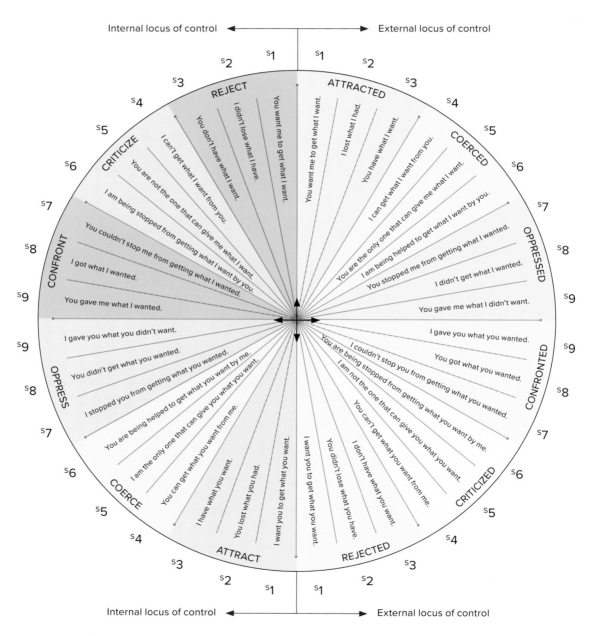

FIG 13 – EGODYNAMICS WHEEL: RELATIONAL MODEL FOR GOVERNING THOUGHTS

The Egodynamics Wheel in Fig 14 shows the relationship between different egoic states according to the *governing feeling*.

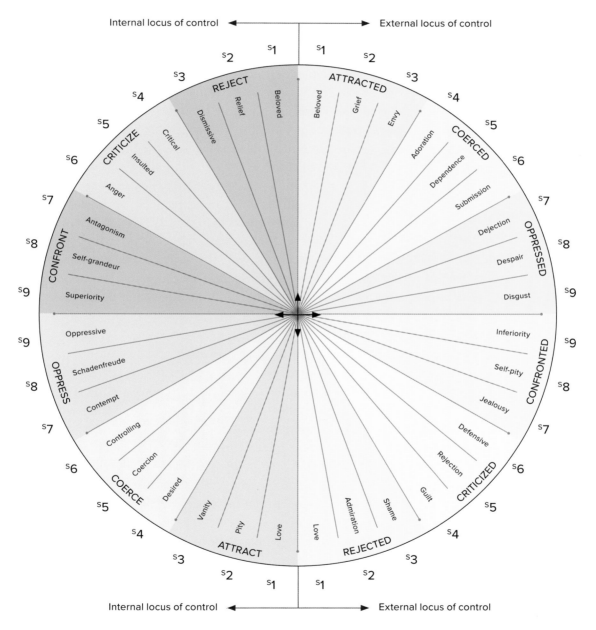

FIG 14 – EGODYNAMICS WHEEL: RELATIONAL MODEL FOR GOVERNING FEELINGS

Egodynamics provides the first definitive analysis of personal egoic identity – how we identify as a separate self. The Egodynamics Wheel is the only universal framework for describing the relationship between our egoic thoughts and feelings, and our objective experience (including our interpersonal relationships). It is the first to define the relationship between these 36 different egoic states, across the nine distinct egoic dynamics, reflected across opposing loci of control.

The wheel shows how opposing egoic states define self through other. For the ego that inhabits the 'controlling' egoic state, it must perceive an object that can be controlled. The thoughts and feelings of ego exists in duality. The more intensely a feeling is felt, the more solid, more defining, the contrast between the two opposing egoic states will be. The harder you push against the wall, the harder it will push back. All egoic feelings, therefore, are seen to be in resistance. In this way, egoic relationships that reflect opposite states are attracted to each other, and, through their dysfunction, perpetuate.

ATTACHMENT QUOTIENT

As we develop from adolescents into adults, through a process of integration we assume a core subset of egoic states through which we identify, relative to our current context. These *primary egoic states* reflect egoic identity across multiple contexts and, as such, are less susceptible to change. We spend most of our time within these egoic states, which represent the cornerstones of our identity. This one-to-many relationship between egoic state and context arises through repeated associations and self-reinforcement. From these arise our predictable patterns of behaviour, our attitudes and beliefs. While atypical circumstances may give rise to primary egoic states, *secondary egoic states* – those that are associated with more specific circumstances – are always derived from atypical experience.

Individuals who want to change how they feel may attempt to do so through the pursuit of atypical experience. However, when the pursuit is engaged in on behalf of an ego from a primary egoic state, the effect is to incorporate and associate that atypical experience into the existing primary egoic state. Even when an atypical experience arises unexpectedly, a primary egoic state will seek, through association, to claim ownership. This process is an extension of the egoic integrative process that forms our personality, through childhood and into early adulthood. The reduced appearance of secondary egoic states, therefore, reflects both the temporary nature of atypical circumstance and the integrative, associative process of ego.

So how might we assess how 'egoic' an individual (including oneself) actually is? The Attachment Quotient provides a new measure of an individual's relative attachment to ego – that is, their degree of attachment to its egoic states. The assessment considers the two codependent characteristics of the egoic state, from which our attitudes and behaviours derive, as seen in Fig 15.

Factor	Description	Range
Separation Index (SI)	The degree to which the ego objectivizes its experience.	1 (s1) to 9 (s9)
State Intensity (I)	The intensity with which feelings are experienced by the ego in resistance.	0 (minimum) to 100 (total maximum)

FIG 15 – ATTACHMENT QUOTIENT ASSESSMENT PARAMETERS

- **Separation Index (SI):** This is the relative degree of apparent separation between the ego and its objective reality, as perceived by the ego. At higher SI, an egoic rigor mortis locks the attachment of ego to its objective experience, such that: (a) All circumstance is perceived with and identified with similarly; (b) Objective experience and circumstances are increasingly manipulated (both objects and people) to maintain the egoic state. In other words, concomitant to an increasing SI is an increasing effort to control the objective environment (outward movement) in order to bring into itself that which it seeks (inward movement). The misunderstanding is that through resistance comes acceptance.

- **State Intensity (I):** This describes the intensity of feeling we associate with this state. It is a factor both of the degree of resistance and the duration of time with which that feeling is experienced within that egoic state. State Intensity ranges from 0 to 100 (reflecting 100% of an individual's time within one or more egoic states). Our feelings (being self-referring) are directional. They refer either to ourselves or to others. We can also say that our attention is directed through feeling, either to self or to other. Feelings are therefore a vector, having both direction and magnitude. The vectorial quality of feeling is such that our attention can only be given to one object at a time – to self or other. As we feel angry, our attention is on our experience and not on what the person who 'made us angry' is feeling. Similarly, if our focus is on the feelings of others, then attention is taken away from our own egoic state. In this 'extro-egoic state' we experience how others are feeling. The process of acquiring this extro-egoic state, and its subsequent reintegration by the ego, is what we call *empathy*. In contrast, if my attention is on me, it cannot be on you. As the intensity of egoic feeling (of resistance) increases, attention is turned inward, to self, at the expense of the other.

If the Separation Index is a measure of space between subject and object, then State Intensity (how we feel) reflects the distance moved across this space. Together, they represent the cognitive and affective aspects of ego – of thought and feeling. As we conceive separation (thought), we perceive change (feeling). Because our feelings have (attentional) direction, they take us toward or away from our experience. They also have the power to collapse our sense of separation when directed outside of ego. Egoic feelings always act in resistance, taking us away from our experience.

$$AQ = \frac{\Sigma(SI \times I)}{M}$$

FIG 16 – ATTACHMENT QUOTIENT FORMULA

The Attachment Quotient (AQ) is measured using the formula (Fig 16) in which 'M' is the maximum possible AQ score that could be achieved (if an individual were to score 100% to an egoic state of s9 – equivalent to a score of 900 – the minimum score being 0). AQ is expressed as a percentage of egoic association, ranging from 0% to 100%.

A lower AQ is achieved by:
- Greater proportion of lower SI range egoic states relative to higher SI range egoic states – with individuals more engaged in their experience
- Lower intensity of egoic feelings – with reduced resistance resulting in greater expression of non-self-conscious emotions

While there are a possible 36 egoic states, the majority of experience is typically undertaken through a core set of primary ones. Individuals with a predominantly internal locus of control will experience the majority of their egoic states on the left-hand side of the Egodynamics Wheel. In individuals who demonstrate a very narrow range of egoic states, the tendency is toward egoic states with higher SIs.

AQ (undertaken as a self-assessment) can be viewed as an individual profile on the Egodynamics Wheel, against the two axes of Separation Index and State Intensity, as in Fig 17, with the egoic 'absolute zero' present in the centre.

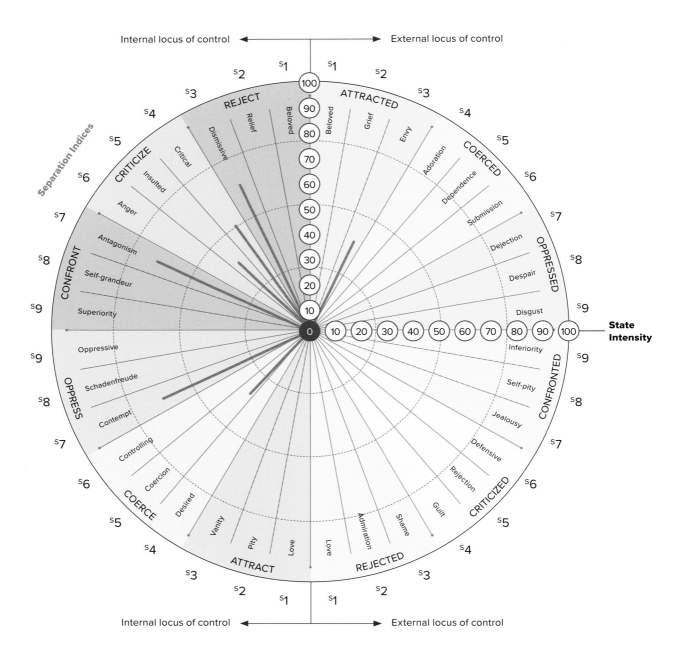

Internal locus of control ← → External locus of control

FIG 17 – EGODYNAMICS WHEEL: EXAMPLE ATTACHMENT QUOTIENT PROFILE

AQ represents the natural evolution of EQ – from emotional to egoic intelligence. As a measure of egoic association that is unique to the individual, AQ can provide insight into the following:

- **Empathy** – individuals with lower AQ give greater attention to the thoughts and feelings of others, with greater capacity to connect from a cognitive and emotional perspective.
- **Wellbeing** – individuals with lower AQ will demonstrate increased acceptance and wellbeing, due to reduced egoic attachment and seeking behaviour.
- **Learning** – individuals with lower AQ are better able to look outside of their current experience and form new associations.

IMPACT OF EMOTIONAL SENSITIVITY ON EGOIC STATE INTENSITY

The magnitude, or intensity, of feeling will differ from person to person in part due to the individual's level of sensitivity. The ego persists between the space that separates other from self. You will not find the ego anywhere on either side of this line. Whether our attention is lost in our external experience (hypersensitivity) or through overfixation on self (hyposensitivity), we turn our attention to the objects of our experience, and thereby to ego. Much research has been undertaken into the physiological basis of emotional sensitivity.

People with hypersensitivity (or sensory processing sensitivity), otherwise known as a 'highly sensitive person' (or HSP), are quite sensitive to physical (sensory) and emotional stimuli. A study carried out by researchers from Stony Brook University[3] in New York presented HSP and non-HSP test subjects with photographs of sad and happy faces. Using functional magnetic resonance imaging, they found that the mirror neuron system (that part of the brain strongly tied to empathy) was stimulated to a far greater degree for HSP subjects than for non-HSP test subjects. It is important not to misconstrue this heightened external awareness as evidence of increased empathy. Empathy has both an outward and inward aspect – of connection and reintegration.

In the outward expression of hypersensitivity, there is difficulty in focusing attention, due to the emotional volume being turned up. This process can be overwhelming, and people with hypersensitivity describe feeling variously anxious, annoyed, and may need to withdraw from overstimulation. Among individuals with Attention Deficit/Hyperactivity

3. The highly sensitive brain: an fMRI study of sensory processing sensitivity and response to others' emotions. Bianca P Acevedo, Elaine N Aron, Arthur Aron, Matthew-Donald Sangster, Nancy Collins, and Lucy L Brown (Published online 2014 Jun 23), Stony Brook University.

Disorder (ADHD), hypersensitivity is characterized by low levels of concentration and impulsive behaviours. Consequently, and in resistance, the inward journey reflects a sympathetic approach, pointing us back to our current egoic state. In contrast, empathy directs our attention outside of self, directly antithetical to ego, to recognize something different.

Our emotional sensitivity is also affected by our ability to recognize what we are feeling. For example, individuals with alexithymia (from the Greek *a lexis thymos*, meaning 'no words for emotions') are unable to cognitively label their emotions – they cannot use words to express and understand their feelings, and are therefore unable to recognize them in themselves or others. As a result, this recognition is consigned to the extremes of emotion – fear and anger – as if everything appeared through a shade of light or dark, but without the spectrum of colour to diffuse the apparent separation. This physiological basis for limiting our emotional attention has been used to explain how individuals can appear desensitized to the feelings of others (being unable to recognize them) while being highly sensitized to their own (through the narrowed range of emotion and resulting sensitivity). The condition has been observed in some psychopaths – individuals with an extreme 'egocentric and antisocial personality marked by a lack of remorse for one's actions, and an absence of empathy for others.'[4] However, psychopathy is not itself a function of alexithymia. The importance of hypersensitivity and hyposensitivity in relation to learning will be explored in a later chapter.

EXTREME EGO

Egocentrism is the inability to understand any perspective other than your own. Egocentricity is a form of addiction – to the emotions that arise through identification with objective experience. Indeed, the cause of all addiction stems from the egoic belief that the objects of our experience can make us happy. To that extent, we are all, to some degree, addicts.

Individuals with high (SI) egoic states will tend also to a more limited range of states and resulting behaviours. At the highest egoic states of s9, we see on the one hand, through the internal locus of control, the extremes of confrontation (superiority) and control (oppression), while through an external locus of control the complete capitulation (inferiority) and demonstration of subjugation (disgust). These egoic states bare the hallmarks of the abuser and the abused.

4. Merriam-Webster. *Psychopath.*

At the highest egoic states, we observe acute egocentric behaviour, such as psychopathy and sociopathy. A psychopath is a pathological egocentric. Psychopathy does not emerge overnight, and for most it starts in adolescence. Psychopaths and sociopaths have likely suffered some trauma in their past,[5, 6] from which they have shifted from an external to an internal locus of control. We can make the following observations about psychopaths:

Upper triad predominance: Psychopaths spend most of their time within the egoic states of the upper triad (SI levels 7–9), in a restricted egoic range. The saying "we all have a bit of psychopath in us" references the fact that we will all experience moments in our lives in each of the egoic states, including the very highest. The difference is the amount of time we spend in them, and therefore the degree to which we identify with that egoic state and act upon it. One of the reasons most people don't stay in the same egoic state all the time, or don't let their egoic need get out of control, is that they possess empathy. Empathy allows us to understand another's point of view AND to care about it, or at least feel that we should. If you don't seek understanding from others, you will not feel the need to give understanding to them.

The need to dominate: Everything a psychopath does is to fulfil the need of that egoic state, which is to dominate. That form of domination will vary depending on their specific need. If they have been abused, there is a good chance that they will be abusers or kill. But the psychopathic trait is celebrated in those who are seen as single-minded, uncompromising and successful. Being a pathological liar is a means to an end, the same as the killing itself. The psychopath is convinced that they are right, and with an internal locus of control, are extremely confident. They also want to be accepted and liked, not because they need validation, but because they seek superiority. Charisma is a tool to get what they want, and they are highly calculating. Their talents for charm and persuasion are entirely for manipulatory purposes. Violence, while certainly possible, is not an inherent characteristic of either sociopathy or psychopathy. But, the psychopath will go to extraordinary lengths to get what they want, given the strength of their egoic attachment that drives their conviction. The more isolated a psychopath feels, the more likely they are to be violent.

5. Martens W. Antisocial and psychopathic personality disorders: causes, course, and remission: A review article. *Int J Offender Ther Comp Criminol.* 2000; 44:406-430. doi: 10.1177/0306624X00444002.

6. Carlson M, Oshri A, Kwon J. Child maltreatment and risk behaviors: The roles of callous/unemotional traits and conscientiousness. *Child Abuse Negl.* 2015; 50:234-243. doi:10.1016/j.chiabu.2015.07.003.

Fight or flight: Psychopaths have been found to have a different sympathetic nervous system – that which governs our fight-or-flight response.[7, 8, 9] If you do something embarrassing or rude, or you drive through a red light, most people's heart will start racing. This is a cue to shift into a different egoic state. Psychopaths, however, don't demonstrate the same levels of arousal or fear response. Their extreme internal locus of control, through which they view their dominance within their environment, affects how they perceive threat. They can sit through a horror movie and their heart won't miss a beat. They can dupe a lie detector test, because they control the test. Additionally, and to compound this, a psychopath is not afraid of the consequences, because in their opinion they are never wrong. They have no concern that they might default to an egoic state in which a feeling such as shame, and the resulting suffering, could arise. Their control provides an immunity to such feelings – in the mind of a psychopath, they are the authority, and they set the rules. A psychopath's ego cannot be controlled by objective experience, using the rules deployed for lower egoic states, because their identity is not derived through the same level of mutuality and interdependence. It is through this filter of extreme egoic protectionism that the psychopath asserts their dominance. For the psychopath, any recognition that they are part of something else would be anathema. Which is why they fail to break a sweat when the police arrive. Indeed, however cunningly evasive a psychopath may have proved to be up to that point, they often demonstrate no particular concern when the law catches up with them. To them, it in no way suggests that they have done anything wrong. On the contrary, psychopaths often relish the attention and notoriety that their capture affords, seeing it as an opportunity to further wield their influence upon others.

Empathetic psychopathy: While psychopaths display *cognitive empathy*,[10] and are able to understand what people are feeling, they do not possess *emotional empathy*, and so cannot feel what the other is feeling. They hear the music, but not the melody. For most people, cognitive empathy occurs unintentionally and automatically, as an aspect of theory of mind referred to as *altercentric interference*. Psychopaths, however, have a diminished propensity to automatically see another person's perspective. In other words, they have the capacity for cognitive empathy when it suits the needs of

7. Marsh, A. A., Finger, E. C., Schechter, J. C., Jurkowitz, I. T., Reid, M. E., and Blair, R. J. R. (2011). Adolescents with psychopathic traits report reductions in physiological responses to fear. *Journal of Child Psychology and Psychiatry*, 52(8), 834-841.

8. Bradley, M. M., Silakowski, T., and Lang, P. J. (2008). Fear of pain and defensive activation. *PAIN*, 137(1), 156-163.

9. Vaidyanathan, U., Hall, J. R., Patrick, C. J., and Bernat, E. M. (2011). Clarifying the role of defensive reactivity deficits in psychopathy and antisocial personality using startle reflex methodology. *Journal of Abnormal Psychology,* 120(1), 253.

10. Fallon, J. (2013). The psychopath inside: A neuroscientist's personal journey into the dark side of the brain. Current.

the ego (for example, for manipulative purposes) but the natural need to do so is not normally triggered. Indeed, psychopaths can be highly attentive to an individual's needs, in order to use that understanding to exert control. It may therefore come as no surprise that psychopaths make great salespeople.

Addiction to objects: If a psychopath is trying to commit a murder, they are unable to empathize with the suffering of their victim. In this extreme form of objectification, the attention is entirely on self, oblivious to the other's perspective. And it is an addiction. Consider a drug addict taking a drug. There is no appreciation of the drug per se. Rather, the goal is to consume it as quickly as possible. As an object it is offensive through its separation from self, and so the ego must expunge it, so that only self remains. It has no regard for the object's individual existence – its purpose is solely to end the ego's suffering, in whatever manner the ego requires. If the addict were a psychopath, they would be hypersensitive to what they feel, but hyposensitive to the victim. For psychopaths, as for any addict seeking fulfilment from outside of self, the law of diminishing returns applies. As the bar for satisfying personal need is raised ever higher, ever more extreme behaviour will undoubtedly result. For the ego, there is no choice.

The difference between psychopaths and sociopaths: Sociopaths have greater levels of emotional empathy than psychopaths, affording them a greater egoic state range. This is evident, for instance, in how a sociopath is more likely to show anxiety, wherein they can switch to an external locus of control (something a psychopath would never do). The sociopath will justify their actions, a psychopath will not. While a psychopath will preside almost exclusively within the upper triad egoic states, a sociopath is much more likely to exhibit a broader range of SI egoic states, albeit with a predominance in the middle and upper triads. Sociopaths are often considered to be more hot-headed, more overt in their actions, less planned and calculating, and easier to spot. It's much harder to wind up a psychopath. Whereas a sociopath will frequently display the middle triad egoic state s6 – *anger* ("You are stopping me from getting what I want") – the more common egoic state for the psychopath is s9, *superiority* ("You gave me what I wanted") or *oppression* ("I gave you what you didn't want").

Anger is certainly a more compulsive, reactive feeling, whereas the psychopath's need for fulfilment requires greater subjugation of another to gain superiority. While both sociopaths and psychopaths don't care whether their actions harm others, a key difference is that sociopaths have learned to be that way in order to survive.

IMPLICATIONS FOR EXTERNAL LOCUS OF CONTROL

Individuals with a high egoic state but an external locus of control are often the victims of abuse and/or may be suffering from depression. A feature of depression is self-obsession, and therefore an inability to see beyond one's own feelings and empathize with others. They will also demonstrate a limited range of egoic states, locked as they are into a pattern of dysfunctional thinking.

Egocentrism has important implications for wellbeing. In a study, Pierre Baron and Jay Hanna[11] looked at 152 participants to see how the presence of depression affected egocentrism. They tested adults between the ages of 18 and 25 and found that those who suffered from depression showed higher levels of egocentrism than those who did not.

11. Baron, P., & Hanna, J. (1990). Egocentrism and depressive symptomatology in young adults. *Social Behavior and Personality: An International Journal,* 18(2), 279–285. https://doi.org/10.2224/sbp.1990.18.2.279

9. EGO FLIP

Like the puppet that pulls on its strings, control is an illusion. It is our belief that we are in control, or that we could lose it, that gives rise to the sense of an individual, separate self – the ego. Egodynamics describes the characteristics of our different egoic personae according to their SI – the degree to which we identify as separate from our external environment, and through which we infer our locus of control. With increasing SI, individuals with an internal locus of control believe that the world should change according to their needs – that it should bend to them. In contrast, individuals with increasing SI, but with an external locus of control, believe that they are at the mercy of the world – that they must bend, or be broken. What both have in common is the tendency to get stuck within a very limited set of egoic personae, as if trapped in a one-person show.

All of us who identify as a separate, individual self, become lost in our story. We define our 'lifetime' through the many parts we play – our lives a series of story tracks, played out through the different personae we embody. With increasing SI, our egoic personae limit our ability to perform at our best. So, what do we do when we want to change our persona? How do we change our story?

We can choose (it would seem) to step outside of our story, to explore the fundamental nature of our experience, to *look behind the curtain*. Chapter 10 (GO Practice) provides a guided enquiry to withdrawing our attention from experience, toward not knowing. The second option is to embrace the story, to seek ourselves within experience. Within each of our stories, it appears that we can make our own decisions. And so it follows (albeit falsely) that we have the ability to change our story from within. But what if you could step into a different story?

Ego flip is a radical technique for changing your egoic persona, to change your life story. Radical, because it requires a profound shift in perspective to one that is antithetical to the one that perceives it. It is an invitation to notice that, as the parts we play appear to change and be changed by our experience, all experience is pervaded by that which is changeless – the knowing of experience; that which you are.

This chapter describes how each of us can consciously change our story – to ego flip – through the consideration of three aspects:

1. Ego flip loop
2. Method learning
3. Empathy practice

1: EGO FLIP LOOP – THE ART OF FORGETTING YOURSELF

Egodynamics allows us to look at the egoic personae we most frequently embody and to ask ourselves: *"Through the parts I play, how can I give myself more fully to my experience?"* Most people take to life's stage through a set of personae that are often dysfunctional. When we ego flip, we consciously recast our lives to change the parts we play – to tell the story that honours the parts of us we value most. Under the assertion of self-control, ego flip describes a six-step process (Fig 18) – a narrative loop through which the story of self is transformed.

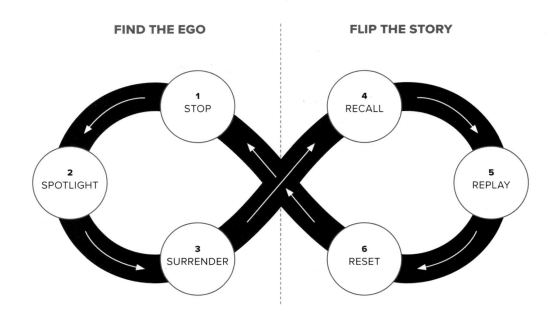

FIG 18 – EGO FLIP LOOP

OPENING: FIND THE EGO

To open the loop, the incumbent persona is dissected to reveal its true nature and contribution to our story of suffering. The process is designed to bring into question our story's 'cornerstone' – the intent through which, in resistance, we hold onto our egoic identity.

Step 1: Stop – See the story *(give attention to story)*

Ego flip begins by noticing that you are not your story. The moment you can step back from the screen, and see the movie being played out, is the first and most important step. You'll notice that you can't change who you are in the movie, because the movie is about you. The story has its own momentum – we cannot step out of the movie any more than we can step outside of ourselves (as if there were an 'inside' that we could 'step out' from).

Imagine ... it is opening night, and you are about to give the performance of your life! As you stand upon the floodlit stage and look out into the darkness, it opens before you like an abyss. You sense the audience, and the weight of their expectation terrifies you. You feel a thousand faces staring back at you. And then you sense your own. You notice that you are also part of the audience, looking back, so that what you see is not yourself, but your story.

CRITICAL STEP: Only when you recognize that you are not your story can you see that you are *in* one. It is through this understanding – that the story of you as a separate self is not who you are – that you create the possibility of seeing beyond it. As the poet Antonio Machado puts it: *"Traveller, there is no path. The path is made by walking."*[1]

Step 2: Spotlight – Locate your persona *(give attention to feeling)*

The second step is to identify and localize the part you play – your character within the story. Through the story of self, we identify with what we think and feel. We can use egodynamics to determine our specific current egoic persona by asking, in this moment: *"What am I thinking?"* and *"What am I feeling?"* We identify with what we need through what we feel, and it is this which defines our story.

1. M, Antonio (2003). *Border of a dream: Selected poems of Antonio Machado.* (1st Edition). Copper Canyon Press.

Imagine ... at the interval, you find sanctuary in your script. As you read the words, you notice how your thoughts fill the spaces between them: "I need to be better than this!" Using Egody-namics, your thoughts reveal the part to which you are cast. As the 'guilty' persona, you believe "I do not have what you want" – the 'you' in this case being the thousand faces that are watching. (This being no different from the one who is faceless – you, through which all faces are known.)

CRITICAL STEP: You need to see exactly who you are – not some approximation, but the precise nature of your ego – in order to flip to a different persona. This is what the egodynamics framework uniquely provides, through its classification of the 36 egoic states. However, the only way your persona will reveal itself is through acceptance, to feel it without seeking to change it. Resistance will simply deflect your attention back into your current story, and the loop will be broken.

Step 3: Surrender – Change the question *(give attention to meaning)*
Having brought the incumbent persona into focus, the next step is to challenge the prevailing egoic perspective.

Ask yourself: *"How am I changing my experience, and how is my experience changing me?"* The ego's locus of control limits its response, to either: *"I change my experience"* (internal locus of control), or *"experience changes me'* (external locus of control). By giving attention to your direct experience, openly and without resistance, answers that run counter to the egoic perspective will become apparent, and in awareness lessen the ego's claim on your attention.

Questions that seek fulfilment from experience signal the ego's intent. Look closely, and every question the ego raises is rhetorical, based on an egoic presumption that is both self-evident and self-affirming. When you turn attention back to the question it always changes its meaning. Ask yourself: *"What is the most important question I have in this moment?"* We identify as the author of our questions. When we ask questions that signal a change in our intent, we perceive a different author, and a different meaning. What lends our questions their power is the understanding of why we are asking them, and from *why* we derive *who*.

CRITICAL STEP: The cornerstone of the egoic perspective – the grit beneath the pearl around which the ego's 'story of me' forms – is at its most irreducible level a single governing thought. Egodynamics describes the specific egoic states and according egoic assertions from which we derive our sense of self. It might seem logical, therefore, that to change our sense of self – who we think we are - we need simply change how we think. Unfortunately, the ego, as the author of our thoughts, persists through thinking.

To flip the ego, we must do the one thing that the ego is trying to avoid – to turn toward and embrace the feeling that it is rejecting in experience. Ego defines itself in opposition to that feeling. The egoic state of dependence arises in resistance to the feeling of coercion (s5). The egoic state of envy endures in resistance to the feeling of vanity (s3). The egoic state of guilt persists in resistance to the feeling of criticism (s4).

Absolute acceptance arises when we step into the unknown. Each egoic state is substantiated according to its own egoic opposite, so that in resistance, neither can know the perspective of the other. In other words, the ego defines itself by what it is not (through that which is known), which paradoxically excludes the dualistic perspective of its alter ego (that which is unknown to it). It is through this 'egoic blind spot' that the opportunity to ego flip arises.

In complete acceptance and surrender, as ego recedes, the antithetical perspective of the alter ego is revealed to us. Then, as attention is given back to the self, and ego returns, it presumes agency for that perspective, so that a new persona can arise. It is how we recognize ourselves in our reflection, because we are blind to the fact that what we see is in fact our opposite.

Imagine ... it is the following morning, and the reviews are in. You have always avoided the critics, but today, you read every article, pour over every sentence, as you seek to understand your audience, to gain their perspective, to see beyond the darkness. You allow their words to imprint upon you. You accept and embrace the feelings that arise, from the castigatory to the complimentary, without seeking to change them. Using the full mastery of your craft, you invite their voices in. You read reviews aloud to your friends, and lend them your voice. You write your own critique, and as you point your pen to the page, notice that the words point to no one.

Ask yourself, *"Am I seeking to take over and stop what my current persona is doing, or seeking to protect it?"* Individuals with DID (Chapter 6) switch their persona, or *alter*, when there is an urgent need to stop their current persona's behaviour, or to protect the individual from sabotaging itself. Switching is a natural response, whether we do so consciously or not, and which as a defence mechanism may suggest how the ego arose as an evolutionary process in the first place. It does not require a persona with an internal locus of control to flip the ego – ego cannot control ego. Rather, it is through awareness of our other selves (an 'altered-self-awareness') that we can shift our locus of identity. Later in this chapter we will explore how to surrender to our antithetical selves through Empathy Practice.

CLOSING: FLIP THE STORY

As we ego flip, a new author emerges. To close the loop, we substantiate its presence to embody the new persona fully in the present.

Step 4: Recall – Step into memory *(give attention to objects)*

Our new persona cannot survive without story. To flip the ego, to personify a new locus of identity, we must step into their story, and the route to story is memory. To remember is also to forget. Our different personae persist through memory, because to remember who we are, we must first forget ourselves in this moment. Our memories are like dreams through which we invite a new persona to awaken into the present. It is our most powerful memories that get our attention. Our memories recall how we feel in this moment. We cannot choose our feelings any more than we can choose what we remember. (Could you remember *what to remember?*)

> **CRITICAL STEP:** The key to memories is objects. To recall a new persona, we must change the objects in our experience to which we attend. Every object has a story that is known through the feelings we attach to them, and through which we remember. We are drawn to objects – indeed, our attention can only ever be given to objects. Like a memory box, our persona is revealed through the objects that define our story. This is the basis of all materialism. The priest holds the Bible to remember their faith.

The soldier holds their rifle to remember their courage. The father holds their child's hand, to remember their own. There can be no persona without possession. To ego flip – to change our story – we must ask: *"What is the object that defines me the most, that is most precious to me, and which is mine alone?"*

Step 5: Replay – Change the game *(give attention to senses)*

Our most precious object – that to which we are most attached – is our body. To bring the 'memory of me' fully into the present, we must locate our new self within the body, through the practice of embodiment. Embodiment of memory is a physical process that requires our eloquence through expression, and our performance through movement. Like a dance in which we give attention to the fluency of feelings and sensations that rise and fall through unguarded expression. Ask yourself:

- Perceiving: How do I embrace how I feel through my body?
- Conceiving: How do I embrace how I feel through my thoughts?

CRITICAL STEP: Embodiment is a skill that all leaders should learn, but few are even aware of. Embodiment matters, because as ego, we locate and identify who we are through the body. Through our sense perceptions and thoughts, we identify not with being, but with being here, and now. As we ego flip, we change what we feel by where we feel it. For this reason, the techniques of Method Learning (see below) that enable embodied practice are essential to this step. Ask yourself: (1) Where do I feel myself in the body? (2) How do I move when I feel like me? (3) What is the most important sensation that I recognize as myself?

Step 6: Reset – Restart the story *(give attention to change)*

To close the loop, and to complete the transition, our new persona must leave its mark, whether that's perceptually (on our environment) or conceptually (through ideas). We must indelibly change our experience, to update our model of the world – to create a world in which there is evidence for our own existence. We can only perceive what we can imagine, just as we can only imagine what we can perceive. This final step marks the transition from reverie to reality, from the imagined world to our direct experience, through which the story continues. Every story you have ever known is connected, through you. Ego flip creates a bridge between stories. To the ego, this transition will always appear as a conscious choice. That is to say, you'll know when it has happened, when there is no longer a choice to make.

> **CRITICAL STEP:** The new persona must do something memorable, to create an 'affective memory' (see below) that will enable future emotional recall and reinforcement of the narrative loop – to lock-in your story track.

You cannot out-think ego. Our ability to ego flip – to change who we think we are – is made possible not in spite of ego, but because of ego. More specifically, the process arises through the eight tenets of ego – the belief system on which our self of sense is governed. The conception of separation and choice provide the background and foreground to this process: the potential for all of us to ego flip arises through our belief in a world that is *SEPARATE* to me (*first tenet*), and it's appearance to us as a process – as a *CHOICE* of our own making – arises through our belief that through my actions I am responsible for the world (*eighth tenet*). The latter does not presume or require an internal locus of control (that I can control the world), rather a locus of thinking (that I am my thoughts). The appearance of progress through the ego flip loop arises as we give attention in turn, to each egoic tenet:

- As we **STOP** – we recognize the *FINITUDE* of our existence (*second tenet*) – as we step outside of story to become its witness.
- In the **SPOTLIGHT** – we identity our *INDIVIDUALITY* (*third tenet*) as we locate ourselves within the story.
- As we **SURRENDER** – we lose our sense of *AUTHORSHIP* to our story (*fourth tenet*), so that a new perspective and version of ourselves can arise.
- As we **RECALL** a new story – we perceive *TRANSCIENCE* (*fifth tenet*) as we draw on the past and memory to substantiate a new locus of self in the present.

- As we **REPLAY** – we relive our lives and perceive *CAUSALITY* (*sixth tenet*) as the story changes our body and how we move through space and time.
- As we **RESET** – we perceive our *RELATEDNESS* (*seventh tenet*) to the world, as through our actions we appear to change our experience.

Ego flip is the art of forgetting yourself. Each step marks a point on the progressive path – the belief that there is someone we need to become. But the purpose of the practice is not to lose ourselves in story, but to point us toward the possibility that who you are cannot be found in story. Who we are is unknowable. It is from this perspective, or rather through the many perspectives of ego, that the practice of ego flip gives us the freedom to play our many parts, and for no one. In Chapter 14, we will develop this practice into a set of design principles for 'storyliving' – how to create immersive experiences that can switch leaders out of their egoic story track, to reinvent their perspective and performance as a leader.

2: METHOD LEARNING – THE PRACTICE OF EMBODIMENT

The ego flip approach draws on the 'switching' technique deployed so effectively by those with DID to transition between alters. But because ego flip is a conscious process, it requires conscious practice. Method Learning is the practice of embodiment. As children, we play through the characters we create. No one ever needs to teach children to do this, or how to do this. It is innate and natural for our expression to change ourselves, to change experience, and there is a deep joy in our ability and freedom to do so. As we grow into adults, we limit ourselves. The act of 'growing up' seems to require us to limit our expression, our ego forming like a hardened carapace.

Method Learning provides a set of practices to open ourselves up to the exploration of new roles and new perspectives that can allow us to develop greater affinity and empathetic understanding for our environment. We are not limited in our experience to the parts in which we have been cast, and through which we perceive the world. This is the opportunity that Method Learning presents.

Method Learning is the application of Method Acting to personal development. It is derived from the work of Russian theatre figure Konstantin Stanislavski, who established a 'system' that cultivates what he called the *"art of experiencing."* In method acting, it mobilizes the actor's conscious thought in order to activate other, less-controllable psychological processes, such as their emotional response. In Method Learning, we seek the same effect for the leader.

The techniques are designed to aid the learner in their inhabitation of the character: to think and feel as the character would think and feel; to relate to and identify with their character's thoughts and feelings; to express their character's emotions through their own. The practices of Method Learning may seem alien, abnormal, even foolish, which is why they are so important. The collective stringency of egoic organizations is unlikely to see value in anything that asks it to loosen its grip.

The five practices that encompass Method Learning challenge the learned instinct to internalize complex experiences and to keep what is private from public view. In their development, the learner extends their creative reach and expression from private practice into the pressurized environments we often operate in, and that offer the greater scrutiny of others' attention. Through their practice, learners can step into the most challenging scenes, and stay alert and sensitive to their feelings through which the character (of self or other) is given the freedom to act.

Practice 1 – Animal Exercises:

We could describe 'growing up' as a limitation of movement. Through our identification with the body, the ego limits its localization away from impulse and spontaneity, and toward measure and control. We laugh and ridicule, because in conformity we crave its outlet and expression. Animal exercises, which are part of the method acting approach, are most associated with Russian acting teacher Maria Ouspenskaya, an early disciple of the Stanislavski System. The technique uses mimicry to improve the power of observation and sensorial attention, by diverging from traditional ways of human movement (learned over a lifetime) toward using the body in ways not previously imagined, to enhance the range of characters they can portray. The practice is to observe animals – anything from tigers to worms to pigs to elephants – and mimic how they move, how they behave, how they eat or sleep or interact with other animals. Through the practice, the learner uses new centres of gravity, responds differently to stimuli, and adopts new tempos and rhythms of movement. This practice is a physical process that frees us from the inhibitions that contain not just our movement, but our emotions – the two being inextricably linked. (The Latin derivative of the word emotion, *emotere*, meaning 'energy in motion.')

Practice 2 – As If:

The As If practice of stepping outside of ego (that to which we have been typecast) is for the learner to place themselves into the shoes of another character and to think and behave 'as if' they were that character. Each character lives through the story, and so it is to the story that the character is referred. To do this, the learner places themself into the character's situation, as the character asks of themself:

- How would I act IF I were in that situation?
- How would I think IF I found myself facing these challenges?
- How would I respond IF this traumatic event happened to me?

This is the starting point for creating embodiment – an affective response to the character's experiences in the story that begin, through the learner, to take on a life of their own. An introspective empathy in which, through understanding of the other, arises a new understanding of self.

Psychologists Jon Carlson and Len Sperry described the benefits of taking on new roles for development: *"When someone has difficulty ... speaking assertively or responding with some measure of empathy, the clinician might encourage [him or her] to act 'as if' they were assertive or empathic several times a day until the next session. The rationale for this reconstruction strategy is that as someone begins to act differently and to feel differently, they become a different person."*[2]

Practice 3 – Substitution:

Substitution is to recognize the story and events attributed to the alter-ego/character's life within your own life. The learner uses the Egodynamics Wheel to identify the character's particular egoic persona and resulting emotion. For example, a character who is being blackmailed may be demonstrating the persona of 'shame,' and the corresponding feelings of humiliation (from the fear of exposure). Using Substitution, the learner recalls a time when they inhabited the same persona, for example when they felt exposed or embarrassed when a bit of personal information became public. From different contexts arise shared feeling and shared meaning.

In her book, *Respect for Acting*, the performer and drama teacher Uta Hagen refers to the importance of this process of make-believe: *"My strength as an actor rested in the unshakable faith I had in make-believe. I made myself believe the characters I was allowed to play and the circumstances of the characters' lives in the events of the play."*[3] And later in the book, *"I use*

2. Carlson & Sperry (1998). *The Handbook of Constructive Therapies: Innovative Approaches From Leading Practitioners.*

substitution in order to 'make believe' in its literal sense – to make me believe ... in order to send me into the moment-to-moment spontaneous action of my newly selected self on stage."[3] Any act of empathy requires us to step into another's shoes so that we can feel its fit against our own skin.

Practice 4 – Sense Memory:
To fully embody a character, the learner needs to bring forth the full potential of their emotional expression. Have you ever awoken from a dream in a state of heightened emotion? In dreams, we lose our waking inhibitions, allowing our emotions to come fourth unchecked. Whether in terror, as we scream to escape a nightmare, or in grief, as we weep for something we have lost. All feelings are accepted and allowed. Our memories are emotions, and as we wake, and we forget, our emotions are quickly forgotten, and our attention given back to the day. Our emotions are not an event, although through emotions we can recall events. Rather, they are an expression and recognition in THIS moment of who we are. The intimacy of their truth is also the reason for their active concealment.

Sense memory is an aspect of what Stanislavski referred to as 'affective memory' – that by which the actor recalls a memory's details and emotions so as to import them into the individual's character and the scene. Sense memory is a conscious process whereby you recall the physical sensations and the emotional response that accompanied an event that happened to you in the past. Sense memory directs our attention to memories that allow the learner to believe in the 'reality' of imaginary circumstances, such as the feeling of cold, or the feeling of fear. To do this, the learner needs to identify an emotional trigger within the character's current experience, to which they can associate their own sense memory. For example, the sound of footsteps triggering a feeling of dread, as you recall the memory of being followed home late at night. Because all memories are emotions, through reassociation there is no longer a need to 'remember' the event to affect a natural, emotional response.

You may notice this in your own experience. Perhaps there is a song that you can't listen to because it reminds you of a breakup. When you hear the song, your attention is immediately given to a surge of feelings, perhaps sadness or anger, that in resistance you seek to stop. When you turn off the radio, and stop the trigger, your attention is diverted, and the emotions drop. Through sense memory the learner can affect an emotional response intentionally – one that is non-egoic – in order to inhabit their character.

3. Hagen, U. (1973). *Respect for Acting.* (2nd Edition). Wiley,

As the learner gains experience in the playing of different parts, so they can extend their repertoire of sense memories toward an increasingly holistic representation of the 36 different Egodynamics personae, using all of their senses to do so. (The most common forms of sensory memories derive from sound and sight because they are the most developed senses in the majority of people). Accordingly, their empathy – the ability to see themselves through others – will also increase, and the effect of ego diminish.

Practice 5 – Improvisation:
At the route of improvisation is our acceptance of current experience, without the need to change the scene. We like to work off scripts, to know what is coming next and have our lines ready. Life becomes a rehearsal rather than a live performance. To improvise is to give attention to our immediate environment, and be willing to respond to its changes intuitively and impulsively. When we are open to experience, our emotions and how we feel will evoke our action, off-script, allowing our innately creative nature its expression and voice. In this state of full attention, we allow our senses full access to experience, and so experience full access to our emotions. They arise unbidden through each moment of recognition. In improvisation is our acceptance of the unpredictable, to change, and to the loss of authorship and control, as we allow our experience to take us where it will. The joy of play is to forget ourselves. Through embodiment, we forget who we are, to remember who we are not.

3: EMPATHY PRACTICE – CLOSING THE GAP
When change doesn't happen, it's usually because there is an *empathy gap*. In the late 1780s, some half-million African slaves were being worked to death on British plantations in the Caribbean. Slavery was an accepted part of society, and the UK economy was dependent on it. The human rights movement of the time, leading the campaign for the abolition of slavery, wanted people to understand what was actually happening. Exhibits brought to life the experience of what it was like to be a slave, such as the types of punishment they endured: what it was like to be whipped; what it was like to be force-fed. The campaign led to a social movement that resulted in the abolition of the slave trade in 1807, and later slavery itself. And the reason for one of the most radical changes in history was empathy.

Perhaps the simplest and most profound way to bridge the empathy gap is by directly relating to others, particularly those with whom we perceive significant personal difference. Consider, for example, the grassroots peace-building organization The Parents Circle,[4] which is bringing together Israelis and Palestinians from two seemingly entrenched and opposing sides of their conflict. Under the motto *'It won't stop until we talk,'* the project has opened up a channel between families from both sides that have lost loved ones through the conflict, and thus share a common story. Families are sharing their stories and have formed close and enduring relationships with people they once regarded as enemies.

If you want to find opportunities to bring about meaningful change in the world, then seek out and sit down with your enemies. Within the Egodynamics Wheel, our egoic opposites are those individuals whose egoic states are diametrically opposed to our own. In our own lives, these may be individuals who either hinder us from getting what we want, or want what we have, or indeed those who would do either of these things should they be given the chance (and from whom we therefore stay well clear). Seeking out such individuals with the purpose of building empathy can have a profoundly positive personal effect. As a practice, it is one of the most important development endeavours that a leader – that anyone, really – can undertake. As the philosopher Martin Buber once said, *"The innermost growth of the self is not accomplished, as people like to suppose today, in relation to man himself, but in the relation between one and another, between men."*[5] Or, as Abraham Lincoln put it, *"I do not like that man. I must get to know him better."*[6] One example of someone who mastered this is Daryl Davis, a Black blues musician in Maryland who has been attending Ku Klux Klan meetings for 30 years. He spends time befriending KKK members, and has personally convinced more than 200 of them to resign, amassing a collection of their discarded hoods and robes. He's done this by sitting down for dinner with individual Klan members and having deep conversations with them.

Empathy practice is the art of learning to appreciate those perspectives that appear in opposition to our own egoic beliefs. The unwritten rule for those seeking empathy is this: to gain another's understanding, you must lose something of your own. To have the courage to walk in another's shoes will inevitably lead to the relinquishment of even the most strongly held egoic beliefs.

4. http://www.theparentscircle.com/en/about_eng/

5. Buber, Martin (1965). *The knowledge of Man*, p71 (M. Friedman & R. G. Smith, Trans.). New York: Harper and Row.

6. As quoted in *Residence Laws: Road Block to Human Welfare, a Symposium* (1956), p. 28.

10. GO PRACTICE

Can you think of anything more important than the question, "Who am I?" All our actions stem from our answer to this one simple question. Look carefully, and you'll see that every question the separate self asks in its search points to this. In the materialist paradigm, the answer comes from the world around us. Who we are is defined by our achievements, through our relationships, through experience, by what we are told to be true. But the only one who can ever answer this question, with any real knowing, is you.

Leadership is not about doing things well; it's about doing what matters. The investigation into our true nature is the most essential activity we can undertake. The most important thing any mind can do is explore its own limitations. It is the ground of all our knowing. In ignorance, we build on shifting sands. In awareness arises the opportunity to pause, to stop and to look.

Reality seems to work a certain way, but does that really mean it IS that way? Your actions, your behaviours, are based on your current understanding. To change how we act, we need only change our understanding. And to change our understanding, we need to change where we look.

GO practice is an approach for exploring our existence at its most fundamental level. All experience arises through introspective (of self) and exteroceptive (of other) exploration. GO practice is an enquiry into this duality – of the separation of self from experience, through the consideration of two perspectives:

- **G**ain the ego: Inward perspective – to find ourselves in experience
- **O**utreach experience: Outward perspective – to find our experience in ourselves

It offers a new model for self, and guided coaching that seeks to understand the actuality of our direct experience. Your direct experience is that which is in your experience right now. There is nothing outside of your direct experience that you can pay attention to. What matters is where you place your attention. For most of us, what we see is a world made up of *me*, that appears in this body, that appears in this world of form. If we look closely, we see that everything is known through conception (though rational thought) or perception (through our senses). Try to find anything in your direct experience that is not thought or perception. When we drink a glass of water, we perceive it through our senses, and we label it through our thoughts – wet, clear, thirsty, cold. When we sit on a chair, what we experience are thoughts and perceptions. In our direct experience, the chair arises out of thought and perception. In our direct experience, do we ever experience a chair prior to thought or perception? All of this is known to us through our awareness, as the perceiver. But who is perceiving the perceiver?

As a process of contemplative enquiry, GO practice offers an alternative to more traditional coaching approaches, for example, when contrasted with the GROW coaching model:

- **G**oal: The process of contracting and goal setting in conventional coaching techniques ensures that the exploration is orientated toward a particular outcome or insight. *Conversely, in GO practice, there is no goal, nowhere to 'get to,' nothing to be gained outside of this moment. Our interest is not in finding an answer, but in the question itself.*
- **R**eality: The consideration of the current state in the GROW model provides a basis from which to change the current state. *Instead, through GO practice, the focus is not on my situation or story, but only on what is arising in this moment – on our actual, rather than assumed, reality.*
- **O**ptions: Coaching uses an open mindset to identify options to bring about change. But *through GO practice, we are not interested in future events and what we could or couldn't do – only in what is actually happening right now.*
- **W**ill: Through the raising of awareness, coaching generates accountability in the subject to deliver change. It assumes authorship of thought, through which behaviours are changed. *On the other hand, GO practice is the relinquishing of authorship, of the idea that you can change a thought with a thought. It is paradoxical in its implication of a search without a seeker. It recognizes that our behaviours change not through thought, but through understanding. Through GO practice, understanding changes by itself.*

The questions we ask are a matter of perspective, and though enquiry we look at the question more closely. Take a moment, look around you, and ask yourself, *"Where am I in the room?"* This question reflects our natural understanding as the subject of our experience. But could we also ask, *"Where is the room in me?"*

GAINING THE EGO – CONTEMPLATIONS FOR THE INWARD PERSPECTIVE

If you want to go and 'find yourself,' you need to know exactly where to look. For most people, it is axiomatic that you are a separate, individual self. What's more, it is understood that this is not just a good thing, but the only possible thing we could be. To understand who we really are, we need to be prepared to look closely at the ground on which all these beliefs are formed – our thoughts and perceptions.

GO practice derives understanding from the facts of our individual direct experience. As discussed in Chapter 6, within our experience there are two facts that are undeniable:

- First, you know 'I am'
- Second, you know that something is being experienced

With the right powers of persuasion, I could make you believe almost anything. I could convince you that the world is flat, that you have superpowers, that your lover hates you, or that you hate your lover. And the only way I can do this is, of course, to convince you that the idea is yours. The only thing neither I nor you could convince yourself of is that you do not exist. Something in existence cannot believe it does not exist, because it would need to exist to believe it (the paradox of self-reference).

Try this now: Put the book down. Notice that you are present, that you are here. Notice that you exist. Ask yourself, *"What is the most precious thing that I will lose when I die?"* What arises? Perhaps it's a feeling, or a thought, or a sensation in the body. Ask yourself, *"What is the deepest sense of me, my most essential nature?"* Put your attention on that. Ask yourself, *"What is that?"* Any answer that arises as a thought is not it. Go deeper than thought. Try to find the thing that asserts your existence.

The 'I am' is the immutable, never-changing aspect of experience. Through the inward perspective, we need to look for that which is consistent across all experience. Through a process of elimination we can consider:

1. Am I my thoughts?
2. Am I my feelings?
3. Am I my body?
4. Am I the perceiver?

This exploration and enquiry into the true nature of *'who I am'* can be done anytime, anywhere (you will not find a time or space that is other than that). We can enquire into our current activities, as events and ego reveal themselves in this moment. Alternatively, we can look to memory, and explore past events that have a deeply affective resonance. All objects within our experience are welcome, as our attention pivots across two lines of enquiry:

- **Locate:** Identify those objects that appear in resistance, be they a thought, feeling or sensation.
- **Investigate:** Carefully examine the object from every angle, giving it full and open attention.

Using GO practice, we guide the exploration through questions designed to unpack our true nature. Some examples are provided below, although the most powerful questions will always arise spontaneously, in response to that particular moment.

The questions used are often closed-ended – requiring a yes or no – to avoid conjectural hypotheses and 'sitting on the fence.' Questions with the prefix *why* are avoided, so as to avert the exploration of the cause and effect of suffering, and the tendency to fall back into concepts and story. The enquiry is analogous to the search for a precious antiquity in a museum – each priceless object handled with care, looking closely under the light to reveal what is hidden, every object carefully and fully attended to in turn, before turning to the next.

1. Am I my thoughts?

With close attention to direct experience, and without reference to memory, ask yourself:

- *What are my thoughts made of?*
- *Where are my thoughts?*
- *How do I know these are thoughts?*
- *What are the gaps between my thoughts?*
- *When are my thoughts?*
- *Can I feel my thoughts?*
- *Can I see my thoughts?*
- *Can I hear my thoughts?*

A thought is the experience of thinking. Thought only ever refers to either the past or the future – it can say nothing about now. Everything that you believe is happening in time is a story. Every thought is in that sense a reference to memory (although implicit memory does not require thought). Memory, in the form of thought, creates the illusion of time. What we conceive of as memory is simply thoughts arising in this moment. We never actually remember or forget anything. We could also say that all our thoughts about the future are actually memories that we imagine in this moment about the moment to come. To the mind, thought needs time, and time needs thought. Your mind collects thoughts and feelings to project time through memory. But experience does not need time. Clap your hands and notice that you do not need time to know this.

Our thoughts are everywhere, although we can only ever conceive one thought at a time. When we reach out to experience with our thoughts, it is our thoughts that we meet first. Take a look at your hand and ask yourself, *"How do I know this is a hand?"* Whatever words you use to describe and understand it are just concepts. Concepts can never say what 'it' is, only what 'it is not,' in the same way as something is light because it is not dark (one ceasing to exist without the other). When our attention is given over to concepts, we lose sight of the fact that concepts, however useful, are the map, not the terrain. Our worldview is spoken through a litany of concepts, such as science, reason, logic, evidence etc. that all purport to be the fundamental constructs of reality, these having precedence over direct experience.

Try this simple experiment. Find somewhere to sit, where you will not be disturbed, and set a timer for five minutes. Now squeeze your thumb and forefinger together and concentrate only on that sensation. Notice how thoughts arise unsolicited, to claim attention: "There is an urgent task I should be doing," "This is a waste of time, I'm not getting anything from this," "I am not very good at this," "I am not doing this properly," "My back is starting to hurt," "Has it been five minutes yet?" Ego reaches out through our thoughts, as surely as through the tips of our fingers.

Our thoughts change all the time, but can thoughts still happen without a 'me' doing it? Try to think your next thought. Can you know what thought is coming next, before you think it? Of course, we never know which thought will follow the next, and yet thinking still happens. Words still appear on a page. There appears to be recognition and understanding. The facts of our direct experience suggest that we can neither author our thoughts nor silence them.

2. Am I my feelings?

With close attention to direct experience, and without reference to memory, ask yourself:

- *What are feelings made of?*
- *Where are my feelings?*
- *How do I know these are feelings?*
- *What are the gaps between my feelings?*
- *What is hearing made of?*
- *What is seeing made of?*
- *What is touching made of?*
- *What is tasting made of?*
- *What is smell made of?*

Notice the feelings in the background of experience. The egoic sense of lack is often born through a subtle sense of boredom or unease, reflecting an internal or external locus of control, respectively. Boredom is the sense of dissatisfaction when the ego cannot find what it wants. In boredom we seek distraction – we turn on the television, and the ego retreats. Through enquiry, we turn off the TV and invite the ego to come out.

The temptation when we observe our feelings is to hold them at a distance, to label them, judge them, resist them, try to understand them. As feelings come and go, notice that you do not.

3. Am I my body?

With close attention to direct experience, and without reference to memory, ask yourself:

- *Where am I?*
- *How big am I?*
- *What are my boundaries?*
- *What do I look like? Is that a memory?*
- *What can I see/taste/touch/hear/smell? What is that sensation made of?*

We perceive the world though our senses. Our senses of taste, touch, smell, sight and hearing help us to distinguish the objects within our environment, as well as our body. We identify the body as 'our body' through the sensations that arise. But how do we know that this body belongs to us?

Our implicit association with our sensations arises in part through their relativistic nature, and how they work together. Every sense is affected in this way. For example, what we hear is affected by what we see, and what we see is affected by what we touch. The *rubber hand illusion*[1] demonstrates this with surprising effect. In this experiment, the participant's arm is hidden from view and replaced with a fake arm, which the participant is asked to concentrate on. Both the fake and real arms are then stroked simultaneously with a brush, while the participant can only see the fake arm being stroked. The participant quickly associates what they see (the fake arm being stroked) with what they feel, believing the fake to be their own. In a dramatic twist, the fake arm is quickly removed, and in horror the participant believes they have lost a part of themselves.

We identify strongly with the body – often as the point of tension – not only from the outside but also the inside. We attach feelings to changes in our heart rate, stomach acidity, muscle tension, equilibrioception (balance), proprioception (body position), spatial awareness, temperature, thirst and hunger. But whereabouts in the body do we reside? Through a process of elimination, most of us would concede that the loss of a few limbs would not equate to loss of self. Follow the logic through and most people arrive at the brain and mind, and the hard problem of consciousness.

Ask yourself:

* *What is the mind?*
* *Where am I within mind?*
* *What is my boundary within mind?*
* *Have I ever experienced my mind?*
* *Could I ever experience my mind?*

[1]. Decreased motor cortex excitability mirrors own hand disembodiment during the rubber hand illusion: Francesco della Gatta, Francesca Garbarini, Guglielmo Puglisi, Antonella Leonetti, Annamaria Berti, Paola Borroni – University of Milan, Italy; University of Milan Medical School, Italy; University of Turin, Italy.

4. Am I the observer?

With close attention to direct experience, and without reference to memory, ask yourself:

- *What is that which knows my thoughts?*
- *What is that which knows my feelings?*
- *What is that which knows my sensations?*
- *Where am I in the gap between thoughts?*
- *Where am I in the gap between feelings?*
- *Where am I in the gap between sensations?*
- *What is that which perceives the perceiver?*

As we turn and give our attention to experience, so too we can turn our attention to that which is aware of this thought, this sensation. Whatever is aware is the 'I.' As we give this our attention, we immediately localize and objectify it. As the observer, we can only locate objects in awareness. In localizing a perceiver, we become aware of the perceiver. But ask yourself again: who is perceiving the perceiver?

The silent conversation

You will never see into your own eyes – all you can ever know is the reflection of yourself, in the mirror, or in dreams, or in the eyes of others. But is there a difference? One of the most powerful ways to open yourself to this enquiry and the contemplation of self is through the 'silent conversation.' This simple practice is undertaken in pairs, with two individuals facing each other a short distance apart, in silence, looking directly and deeply into one another's eyes. To the ego, this experience is challenging, as in resistance it seeks separation, distance, somewhere to hide. Through GO practice, we seek a neutral observation that surrenders ourselves to looking. In contrast to the egoic need to reach out to the objects of our experience, in awareness we allow the objects of experience to come to us. When GO practice is led through guided enquiry, the silent conversation helps collapse the distance between the guided and the guide.

In acceptance, ask yourself:

- Of self: *What can I see?*
- Of other: *What can I see through your eyes?*

A dead end

Self-enquiry is inevitably a search for that which we are not. Through the inward exploration, the mind discovers only that which it can give attention to – that which is at a distance from itself. You cannot be made out of thoughts because thoughts come and go. Feelings come and go. Sensations and perceptions appear and disappear. All we can say is "I am not this, and not that," or *neti neti*, in the Sanskrit expression. Amidst this ever-changing experience, the only thing that remains is the knowing of it. The 'I.' It is a search without end, an infinite loop. In this futility of seeking is the invitation to recognize that as we peel back the layers of the onion, there is no centre, no perceiver that we can point to, no object, no boundary. Just awareness. In fact, our very concept of 'inward' is a misconception. We go inward because we imagine this is where we are. The only place left to look, therefore, is to look back.

OUTREACHING EXPERIENCE – CONTEMPLATIONS FOR THE OUTWARD PERSPECTIVE

On the inward journey we affirm the 'I' as the only undeniable, constant presence in all experience. From this understanding, we could form one of two contrasting hypotheses:

1. I am the awareness that arises out of my experience, and am therefore located within my experience.
2. I am the awareness within which all experience arises, and am therefore prior to experience. All experience arises within me.

Our assertion of the first statement is congruent with the limitations of mind, whose logic programme necessitates a dualistic perspective of reality. Through our thoughts and perceptions, this logic is asserted through the agency of a voice called 'me,' within a body called 'mine.' On the outward journey, we seek to collapse the *subject and object* relationship through the contemplative questioning of six dimensions by which egoic separation is perceived. The following contemplations provide a framework for enquiry and are by no means exhaustive. They are described sequentially as a *flow*, as one might lead to the other. However, there is no process to follow.

The purpose of contemplation is to consider the question, rather than the answer. Without giving time and attention to the question, to understand it, we can miss what the question is pointing to. To understand the question, its profundity, its implications, is itself the answer and the insight we seek. The alternative is to race to the end, to the answer, which inevitably takes you back to where you began. So much of our current understanding and our assumptions stems from the simple overlooking of the question itself. Through contemplation, we question the question.

FIG 19 – THE 6 DEGREES OF EGOIC SEPARATION

1. THE LOCATION OF SPACE AND TIME

Where do you go from here? Through the apparent separation of objects in space, we perceive distance. We localize objects that are 'there' relative to ourself, which is 'here.' When we go to there, we only ever find here. In our direct experience, everything only ever happens here. Here is not a place in space, here is nowhere.

> *Look at an object. Where is that object?*
> There
> *Where are you?*
> Here
> *What separates here and there?*
> Space
> *Go to that object. Where are you now?*
> Here
> *Where were you before?*
> There
> *Go there. Where are you now?*
> Here
> *Where have you always been?*
> Here
> *Can you ever get to there?*
> No
> *What is the space between here and there?*
> There is no space
> *Where are you?*
> Nowhere

The same contemplation can consider our movement through time. We have never been to a 'past,' nor have ever been to a 'future.' In our direct experience there is only ever this moment. When we recall the memory of past, or imagine the memory of future, what is seen is always in the present. Past and future are thoughts arising in this moment. Past, present and future only ever exist now.

> *When do you experience this moment?*
>> *Now*
> *Do you ever experience anything that is not taking place now?*
>> *No*
> *Could you ever experience anything that was not taking place now?*
>> *No*
> *Could you ever go to a thing called a past that is not taking place now?*
>> *No*
> *Could you ever go to a thing called a future that is not taking place now?*
>> *No*

2. THE ABIDANCE OF AWARENESS

We conflate awareness with our senses. When you close your eyes the room disappears, and when you open them, the room reappears. From this, we assume that our awareness is in the head, behind our eyes, like a soul residing in the brain, located in space as a temporary phenomenon. We equate loss of faculties with loss of awareness when we believe awareness comes from matter, from mind.

Awareness does not look through your eyes – this would suggest it is located between the eyes. Awareness is not located anywhere. The eyes, the head, the world, headaches, thoughts, are all objects that appear in awareness. Awareness is the sole substance of all experience.

You are not the viewer, the sensor behind the camera. There is no fixed point of awareness, there is no space in awareness for it to fix to. Awareness is everything. You are that within which everything occurs. The mind cannot comprehend this. What is left when you take senses away? Diminished experience. But awareness remains. The camera is limited, but that does not mean that the one who looks is limited.

Close your eyes. Are you aware?
    Yes
Open your eyes. Are you aware?
    Yes
Did your awareness change?
    No
You are still just as aware as you were before?
    Yes

3. THE SUBSTANCE OF PERCEPTION

To explore the indivisible nature of experiencing, consider the separation of the body. Awareness is self-aware. We think that we are aware of something other than awareness (objects, thoughts). We think we know something other than knowing. We think there is an outside world, separate from ourself, that we perceive. In order to know something called the world, made out of matter, you have to ignore the reality of experience – pure awareness. Awareness of an object is awareness of perception, and all there is to perception is the knowing of it.

Close your eyes and listen to something. Can you see that the sound is only made of hearing?
Can you see that hearing is one with and made out of yourself?

Open your eyes and look at something. Can you see that the sight of it is only made of seeing?
Can you see that seeing is one with and made out of yourself?

4. THE DISTANCE FROM EXPERIENCE

How far are you from experience? We believe that perception happens through us, and as such is made of two parts: myself, which has awareness, and that which is other than myself, to which we give awareness. This contemplation can be undertaken using any of our senses, although the illusion of duality is at its most convincing through sight.

Look at the sky. Perceive it. How far away from you is that perception?
    No distance
How far away from I does awareness take place?
    No distance
Is there anything in your current experience that is farther away from experiencing than anything else?
    No
Is there anything to your experience of seeing other than the knowing of it?
    No

5. THE KNOWING OF EXPERIENCE

There appears to be a distinction between objects and awareness, so we go from one to another. There is no distinction between a thought and the knower of the thought, there is JUST the experience of thinking. The only substance present in thinking is consciousness or knowing.

Take thinking. Is there anything to a thought other than the experience of thinking?
    No
Is there anything to the experience of thinking other than the knowing of it?
    No
Take the experience of the body, which you experience as sensations. Is there anything to the experience of the body other than sensing?
    No
Is there anything to the experience of sensing other than the knowing of it?
    No
Take your current perception. Is there anything to a perception other than the experience of perceiving?
    No
Is there anything to perceiving other than the knowing of it?
    No

Is the knowing of it the same knowing of thoughts, feelings, etc., or different?
>   It's the same knowing.

For any experience, do you encounter anything other than the knowing of it?
>   No

Could ANY experience be made of anything other than the knowing of it?
>   No

All you know is that there is knowing, or awareness. That you are aware. What is it that knows there is knowing?
>   Knowing, awareness

What is there to experience other than the knowing of it?
>   Nothing

Experience is the knowing of experience. The knowing of experience is not an object, not a person. It is consciousness. It only appears as a separate person, in space and time, to the ego.

6. THE KNOWING OF AWARENESS

Most people spend their lives avoiding the existential lack and fear of the ego, in a full-time job of satisfying their needs, and to counter the sense of separation through the exclusive focus on objects. To stop this, all you need to do is stop and do the opposite. Ask yourself:

What is the knowing by which I know my experience?

Turn your attention away from objective knowledge to the knowing by which it knows experience. There are no limitations in your own being. The recognition of this is called *revelation* because nothing new is found, just a recognition of what was veiled.

In the cinema, the screen is present everywhere in the movie and as such can never appear as an object in that movie, from the point of view of a character in the movie. Likewise, awareness pervades all experience so intimately that it can never be an object of experience, and so from the perspective of the separate self appears to be missing. Its apparent absence is because it is so completely present in everything that nothing can be distinguished from it. It seems to be nothing because it is everything.

The character believes it is having an experience, because they have awareness of experience. In the absence of a character there is still awareness. In the absence of experience there is still awareness. In the absence of awareness, there is still awareness. You are not having an experience, *you are the experience*.

THE DIRECT PATH

GO practice is an approach for opening the mind to what is. It is not a procedural framework, but rather, it provides a starting point for enquiry. However, like all frameworks, it runs the risk of being taken literally. The following therefore is offered to avoid compliance and to encourage dissent. Ultimately, the purpose of any practice should be to enquire as to the purpose of that practice.

The separate self is like a mirror seeking its own reflection. In each moment the separate self looks away from itself, away from this moment, in its search for happiness. The progressive path describes the process by which the search, and suffering, can end. But the process necessitates authorship and control. It is through a process of egoic eradication, therefore, that the ego is perpetuated, and the search continues. We drink the water from the mirage and wonder why we are still thirsty, but as the musician and Buddhist monk Leonard Cohen said, *"If you don't become the ocean, you'll be seasick every day."*[2] The paradox of the search and the searcher is referred to as *'the gateless gate'* – the recognition that there is no gate for those who have passed through it. That you are already the ocean.

On the progressive path there is something to do, somewhere to get. We have to work to get closer to awareness, because from the perspective of a separate self, things seem closer to or further from consciousness. Realizing that you are not your thoughts feels like progress to the separate self. However, there is nothing at a distance from consciousness because everything is consciousness. You cannot be closer to or further from consciousness from the point of view of reality. It is the mirage of separation that suggests that you can and need to do so. Try walking away from yourself and see how far you get. Your finger cannot point to consciousness because it is consciousness. A wave can never be anything other than the water it belongs to.

Through the progressive path our mind conceives a switch, a change that has to come about. Our autonomic nervous system regulates our breathing, temperature,

2. Cohen, L. (2000). *Good Advice For Someone Like Me.*

digestive system, etc., and creates a homeostasis effect – a steady state. Doing something different can give us a different perspective, and people go to inordinate lengths – fasting, asceticism, hypoventilation, drugs, taking on a monastic life – to do this, to gain control. However, if we accept that the mind arises out of awareness, then the notion of a switch is like watching a film about a character trying to step out of the screen. The switch implies cause and effect, which implies a process, which implies a doer of process, which implies a self and a story.

Questions themselves suggest a process, and answers infer causality. From the question "How do I get rid of ego?" and the separation of 'I' and 'ego' into a subject-object relationship, a process seems inevitable. Questions are like signposts that direct our attention. Change the question and you change where you look. But like signposts, questions point in different directions relative to where you stand. Stand behind the question, and it points away from you. Stand in front of it, and it points back. Practice has the habit of fixing our feet to the ground.

Questions only point to meaningful answers when they are heard from a place of genuine enquiry – a fascination for the question itself. Like Absolem's study of a butterfly's wing, seeking to understand what flying is made of. Through discipline, our curiosity is displaced with reason. We may seek through reason to end suffering, and in so doing it is the reason and not the question that points to our understanding. Making it a practice changes the question you are asking.

The alternative is the *direct path*. Where the progressive path suggests there is a distance between you and awareness, the direct path says there is no distance, and no difference. It is the pathless path. Recognizing our true nature simply requires an open mind.

The knowing of our true self is like memory. We cannot recall that which is not already present. To know it, to look for it, we must already be it. To recall peace, we must already know peace. Memory is a veiling through thought of the recognition of what you already are. Through the veiling of thoughts and feelings, the infinite 'I' is felt as the finite 'I' of the separate self. But it is the same 'I.' The sense of finitude is an illusion. In its solitude, the separate self describes an experience in form – of thoughts, feeling and perception. But if you really look, you will just find the experience of being aware. Happiness is not a state of mind, it is the knowing of your own being.

11. THE EVIL GENIUS ORGANIZATION

The Attachment Quotient as defined by egodynamics provides a measure of an individual's egoic states. We can consider an individual's egoic attachment in specific relation to the construct of an organized social system or organization – that is, in relation to the specific relationships each individual has within that system. To do so, we will need to consider the two aspects that are fundamental to how individuals relate to one another: reciprocity and divergence.

RECIPROCITY AND DIVERGENCE

Egodynamics describes how the relationship between individuals is formed through the fulfilment of divergent egoic need. The presence of ego establishes a power dynamic, in which one or both individuals will seek to assert control over the other to get what they need. The power dynamic describes the conditionality on which the relationship is based.

Reciprocity describes the relationships between two individuals who fulfil each other's needs (Fig 20). This occurs when both have differing (non-competing) needs to fulfil, which the other party can provide. Reciprocal relationships typically reflect the egoic state at Separation Index (SI) s1 – both parties want the other party to get what they want. The level of control exerted by either party is very limited, although it is still conditional, on the basis that ego is present.

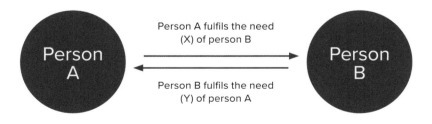

Person A fulfils the need
(X) of person B

Person A

Person B

Person B fulfils the need
(Y) of person A

FIG 20 – DIRECT RECIPROCITY

Power dynamics arise when there is a divergence of egoic need, in which:
- Both individuals are competing to fulfil the same need
- One individual needs something at the expense of the other (where they take what they need from the other but give nothing in return)

Relationships formed by individuals with higher SI demonstrate:
- Increased attachment to egoic identity
- Increased perception of difference/objectivization of the other
- Increased divergence of egoic need
- Increased self (versus other) interest
- Increased power imbalance (locus of control – with control of one party over another)
- Increased suffering

Relationships with egoic states represented by higher SI are therefore unsustainable, as the fulfilment of need for one individual comes increasingly at the expense of the other. The dysfunction of higher SI relationships is reflected in the increasing control that one individual necessarily exerts on the other to get what they need. Ultimately, where the egoic needs are at their most divergent, the survival of one individual requires the destruction of the other, such as observed in extreme psychopathic behaviour or aggressive nation states.

For this reason, long-term dysfunctional relationships are necessarily sustained through an oscillation between higher and lower egoic states. In the case of an abusive relationship, once the monster has been fed and sated, it drops down to a lower SI egoic state that is able to provide the victim what they need, thereby ensuring that the victim does not escape the relationship.

Both egoic states reflect different needs from the relationship, and will therefore have different feelings toward the other. An abuser who has shifted to a lower SI egoic state may feel genuinely sorry for their actions when what they want from the other person has changed, although all egoic states share the same prime directive of egoic survival. It is through this oscillation of egoic states that habits undertaken to fulfil egoic need both arise and perpetuate.

INDIRECT RECIPROCITY

Within an organization, while direct reciprocity still occurs, indirect reciprocity means that I can get what I need from you without needing to reciprocate, as long as you can get what you need from someone else in the organization. Fig 21 explains this relationship. Indirect reciprocity ensures the sustainment of relationships that have levels of SI that would not be sustainable on a directly reciprocal basis. Take the example of a boss who is demanding of a team member, without seemingly needing to offer anything directly in return. The team member puts up with it because they have a job to do, and they get paid, and they work with some other great team members. Cut these elements out of the equation and the team member's needs would not be fulfilled, and they would likely leave.

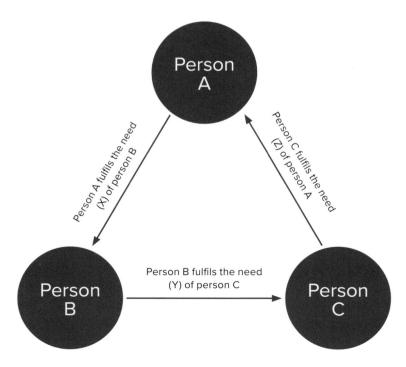

FIG 21 – INDIRECT RECIPROCITY

In this way, relationships can form that would, outside of any formal organizational context, be extremely dysfunctional and unsustainable. Yet, seen within a corporate setting, they are deemed commonplace and acceptable. Indeed, individuals are often attracted to organizations because of the opportunity to fulfil egoic need through the control they can assert through their relationships, which would be otherwise unafforded to them outside of the organization.

POWER DYNAMICS – HOW EGO EXERTS ITS CONTROL

Fig 22 shows the resistance chapters for the ego, as described by the Egodynamics Wheel. For each of these, the individual with the internal locus of control attempts to exert control over the individual with the external locus of control, establishing a power dynamic that is particular to that egoic state.

Resistance Chapter	Power Dynamic	EGOIC NEED	
		Internal Locus of Control	External Locus of Control
Reject	Shaming power	to ignore	to be forgiven
Criticize	Judgemental power	to blame	to gain your approval
Confront	Superiority power	to be the best	to not be me
Oppress	Punitive power	to cause you harm	to end my suffering
Coerce	Coercive power	to control	to depend
Attract	Referent power	to be wanted	to want you

FIG 22 – EGODYNAMICS RESISTANCE CHAPTERS

These six power dynamics are 'first-order,' in that they describe the ultimate egoic state relationship by which egoic need is fulfilled between two individuals. A series of 'second-order' power dynamics – those that are needed in order to fulfil first-order needs – are established through indirect reciprocity when individuals come together as an organization. The relationship between first- and second-order power dynamics is shown in Fig 23, below.

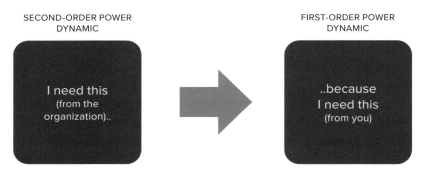

SECOND-ORDER POWER DYNAMIC

I need this
(from the organization)..

..because
I need this
(from you)

FIRST-ORDER POWER DYNAMIC

FIG 23 – FIRST- AND SECOND-ORDER POWER DYNAMICS

SECOND-ORDER ORGANIZATIONAL POWER DYNAMICS

The one thing that every organizational entity has in common is its need for people, and the blueprint for every organization is ego. The egoic enterprise is organized so that it can satisfy the egoic needs of its employees as effectively as possible. That – and not what is written in the mission statement – is the fundamental reason organizations exist and persist, on the basis that no organization can satisfy its employees through intrinsic needs alone. Otherwise, there would be no need for the organizations to 'organize people' in the first place (and we would all be self-employed).

This is what holds the organization together, maintains its organizational integrity, keeps people performing and stops them from leaving. In order to maintain this organizational integrity, egoic need is satisfied through a complex interplay of power dynamics between its members. The role that the organization plays in fulfilling egoic need becomes clearer when we consider the:

- Correlation between the egoic construct – the eight tenets of ego – and the principal operating components of any organization
- Control and resulting power dynamic that each of the organizational components affords ego, to support its fulfilment of need

It establishes a form of 'meta-ego' – what we might refer to as the Evil Genius Organization, or E.G.O. It may sound like an exaggeration, but consider who the organization is really serving in this regard.

Fig 24 shows how:

- Each of the 16 defining components of an organization's operating model (or 'Organizational States') correspond to the eight tenets of ego set out in Chapter 6 (Fig 3), through which the belief in a separate self arises.
- Each of these establish an egoic need across each aspect of the operating model and, as such, provide a basis through which power can be exerted within the organization in relation to that egoic need.
- Each of these second-order power dynamics operate in opposing pairs, establishing an axis through which power can be exerted, which in turn establish a series of eight *organizing dilemmas* through their dual aspects – aspects of organizational dysfunction that leaders must continually seek to reconcile.
- Each power dynamic can be described through its particular leadership style – noting that most leaders would have a preference for a small number – these being reflective of their egoic states according to the contexts in which they arise.

TENETS OF EGO	EGOIC TRAIT	CONVERGENT: Toward ORDER				
		Organizational State	Power Dynamic	Egoic Need	Fear Response	Leadership Style
I experience a world of matter that is separate from me	SEPARATION	KNOWLEDGE	**Informational power** *Power from having wanted information*	*You need the information I have.*	*I fear not having the right information.*	Theorist
I was born (into it), one day I will die	FINITUDE	LEAVERS	**Exiting power** *Power to fire individuals*	*You need me to stay in the company.*	*I fear being sacked.*	Terminator
I am the author of my thoughts	AUTHORSHIP	ROLES	**Doership power** *Power to undertake designated activities*	*You need me to do this job.*	*I fear the job will not be done.*	Servant
I am an individual - There is not two of me	INDIVIDUALITY	INDIVIDUALITY	**Individualist power** *Power to assert an individual moral judgement*	*You need me to be different.*	*I fear being the same.*	Rebel
I have a past that points to my future	TRANSIENCE	RISK	**Predictive power** *Power to anticipate wanted information*	*You need me to be certain.*	*I fear taking too much risk.*	Pragmatist
Through time appears cause and effect	CAUSALITY	CONFORMITY	**Compliance power** *Power to enforce compliance with rules and standards*	*You need me to keep control.*	*I fear not having control.*	Bureaucrat
I have free will and am responsible for my actions	CHOICE	CORRECTION	**Corrective power** *Power to correct poor performance*	*You need me to judge performance.*	*I fear being punished for my performance.*	Autocrat
I move through space - I am located in the body	RELATEDNESS	CONNECTION	**Connection power** *Power gained from acting through an individual*	*You need me for my network.*	*I fear not being connected.*	Socialite

FIG 24 – E.G.O. BLUEPRINT: ORGANIZATIONAL STATES AND CORRESPONDING ORGANIZING DILEMMAS

DIVERGENT: Toward CHAOS				
Organizational State	**Power Dynamic**	**Egoic Need**	**Fear Response**	**Leadership Style**
SKILLS	**Experiential power**	*You need the experience I have.*	*I fear not having the right experience.*	Experimentalist
	Power from having wanted experience			
JOINERS	**Joining power**	*You need me if you want to join this company.*	*I fear not getting this job.*	Expansionist
	Power to hire individuals			
STRUCTURE	**Delegatory power**	*You need me to give you a job.*	*I fear the job does not need to be done.*	Commander
	Power to delegate activities to others			
CULTURE	**Collectivist moral power**	*You need me if you want to join the group and be one of us.*	*I fear being different.*	Populist
	Power to assert collective moral judgement			
OPPORTUNITY	**Visionary power**	*You need me to take risks.*	*I fear not being bold enough.*	Visionary
	Power to set a promissory vision that inspires others			
CHANGE	**Disruptive power**	*You need me to change things.*	*I fear control.*	Radical
	Power to change processes, rules and standards			
REWARD	**Reward power**	*You need me to reward performance.*	*I fear not being recognized for my efforts.*	Sycophant
	Power to recognize good performance			
COLLABORATION	**Political power**	*You need me for my influence.*	*I fear not having influence.*	Politician
	Power gained from acting through a group			

Each second-order power dynamic is realized when four conditions are met:
- Acquisition by Person 1 of an 'object of egoic need' within the organization, from which the power dynamic derives
- Identification of Person 2's egoic need for that object, and the opportunity for its fulfilment
- Transfer of the organizational object to Person 2, to fulfil their egoic need
- Direct (through the individual) or indirect (through a third party) reciprocal fulfilment of Person 1's egoic need

Power dynamics perpetuate the separate self's search for fulfilment, through the illusion of control. It is not possible to be part of an egoic organization without participating to some degree in these power dynamics, through the egoic fulfilment of self and other. Through power dynamics, the ego asserts its identity, be it through their influence, their function or purpose, or their reputation. It is through the totality of these transactions that the organizational entity – as the E.G.O. – is itself perceived and identified with, by those that interact with it. Power dynamics don't end at the employee; they extend wherever there are relationships. To the customer, power dynamics affect how a brand is perceived. Beyond the organization, we can expand the principle of the E.G.O. to any groups with which an individual is associated, and to which they therefore have some form of egoic attachment, such as with social, political or religious groups, for example.

The *eight tenets of ego* represent the pattern of associated thought through which we implicitly recognize the separate self. Through our thoughts arise the illusion of the separation of self from experience. In the same way, the entity of the E.G.O. is formed as an act of self-reference, through reassociation within its eight organizing dilemmas. But on closer inspection, the organization, like the separate self, is an illusion. There is no hard boundary between that which is within and that which is without. But from the necessity for separation, and through every boundary that is drawn, arises the duality of inclusion and exclusion. To that extent, inclusion and exclusion are not consequences of how the organization operates, but rather the basis by which it is able to operate in the first place. No wonder inclusion is proving a hard nut for organizations to crack!

As a finite entity, the organization suffers the fate of all finite forms – finitude. For something to be known, it must be perceived, and only objects can be perceived. As such, to know is to render finitude to our experience. As attention is focussed, and as we learn more, the object under investigation necessarily resolves itself through greater clarity, localization and conformity. Imagine awareness as a perceiver looking through the lens of a camera to bring the objects of experience into focus. Existence is a continual movement, within awareness, between the rendering of its origin and the obscuration of form. In the same way, when we look closely at the behaviour of organizations, we see this eb and flow between order (that which is defined, certain, knowable) and chaos (that which is unordered, uncertain, unknowable). All objects in our experience do this. Even the object of the universe itself, as we look to the edges of an infinitely expanding universe that will forever outpace our gaze, or into the singularity of a black hole with its infinite collapse. When we look into an organization, it is obvious that both aspects – of order and chaos – are to varying degrees necessary for the organization to survive. The materialist perspective refers to this as the essential entropic tendency for change to occur, from a state of order to a state of chaos. From the perspective of awareness, order and chaos are not essential to change, but to existence.

Each of the eight organizing dilemmas establish a dualistic tension across the 16 organizational states, which shift the organization's orientation between order or chaos. Each power dynamic exerts its influence to pivot the organization toward one of these two approaches:

- **Toward order:** To localize results, create certainty, limit change, hinder growth, course-correct
- **Toward chaos:** To grow the organization, reduce conformity, involve many, expand possibilities

Order and chaos reflect the inward and outward perspectives of relativistic identity, as the organization looks inward toward the familiar, and outward to something different. The power dynamics that arise, operating as they do across the eight organizing dilemmas, derive a meta-ego – the *perpetual narrative* (or 'story of ego') across the organization, as a macrocosm of the *eight tenets of ego* (Fig 25).

Egoic Tenet	Ego Interpretation (individual)	E.G.O. Interpretation (meta-ego)	Instituted Power Dynamic
SEPARATION	*I experience a world of matter that is separate from me.*	*I have a reputation to protect.*	Information power vs. Experiential power
FINITUDE	*I was born, one day I will die.*	*I cannot work here forever.*	Exiting power vs. Joining power
AUTHORSHIP	*I am the author of my thoughts.*	*I am the role I play.*	Doership power vs. Delegatory power
INDIVIDUALITY	*I am an individual, there is not two of me.*	*I am part of something bigger than me.*	Individualist power vs. Collectivist moral power
TRANSIENCE	*I have a past that points to a future.*	*I have a history that determines my potential.*	Predictive power vs. Visionary power
CAUSALITY	*Through time appears cause and effect.*	*I accept or resist change.*	Compliance power vs. Disruptive power
CHOICE	*I have free will and am responsible for my actions.*	*I am judged by my performance.*	Corrective power vs. Reward power
RELATEDNESS	*I move through space, I am located in the body.*	*I belong to a team.*	Connection power vs. Political power

FIG 25 – PERPETUAL NARRATIVE BASIS FOR META EGO (E.G.O)

Fig 26 shows the resulting relationship between the organizing dilemmas and associated power dynamics.

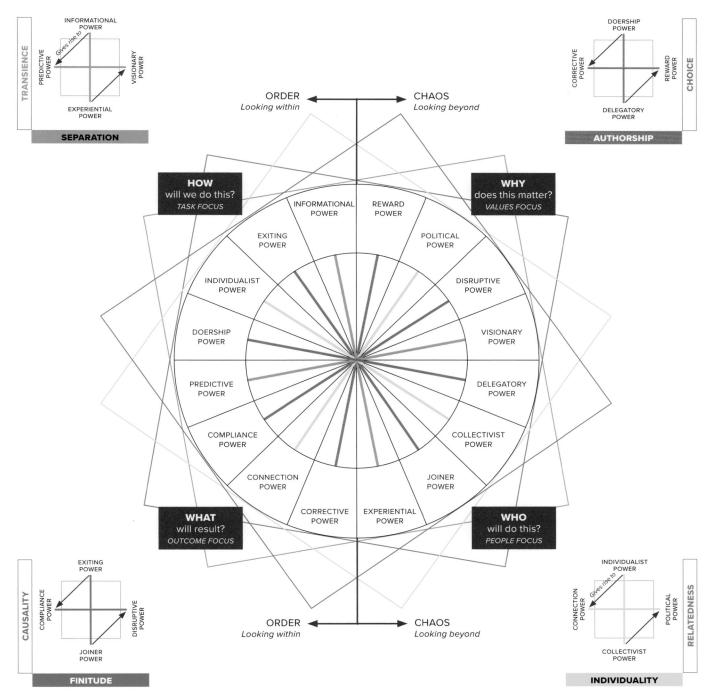

FIG 26 – SECOND-ORDER POWER DYNAMICS ACROSS THE EIGHT ORGANIZING DILEMMAS

The relationship ultimately describes four questions that orientate the ego in its search for fulfilment within an organization, and which underpin the resultant leadership styles that emerge:

- How do we do this? (task-focused)
- What will the result be? (outcome-focused)
- Who will do this? (people-focused)
- Why will this matter? (values-focused)

MAPPING POWER DYNAMICS ACROSS THE ORGANIZATION

We can use power dynamics to understand the level of inclusivity within an organization. To do so requires a holonic approach, which recognizes that an individual's association with the organization will change depending on whether they are perceived to be a part, or a whole. As such, an individual can associate with its organization in three ways:

1. **Part:** As an individual forming part of a larger whole
2. **Whole:** As an individual acting as the whole, that includes other parts
3. **Mutual:** As an individual with mutuality with another individual (them both being part of the same whole)

Fig 27 describes the 15 (+3) different states of inclusion through which an individual can associate with that organization, be it through another individual or a group.

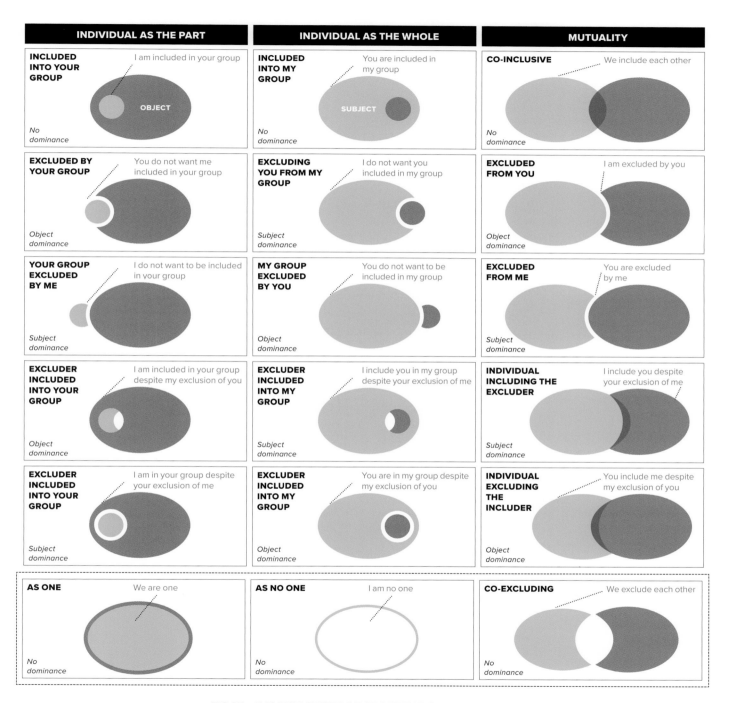

FIG 27 – HOLONIC STATES OF ORGANIZATIONAL INCLUSION

In each state of inclusion, which results through a subject-object relationship, we can describe the power dynamic at play as subject dominant (whereby the subject has the power), object dominant (whereby the object has the power), or involving no dominance (where there is mutual agreement). Inclusion occurs in the absence of dominance, in the absence of power dynamics, through mutuality. Inclusion of an individual who does not want to be included is a form of exclusion. Of the 15 states, only three show mutual inclusion (Fig 27, top row). The bottom row describes three additional variants, all of which show no dominance:

- **As One:** The subject and object are perceived as the same, with no divisible boundary, such as occurs when we empathize with another individual. There is no egoic identification to separate the two.
- **As no one:** The subject is on their own, and so is unable to form associations. In an organizational context, this is the ultimate form of exclusion, reflecting an individual outside the organization.
- **Co-excluding:** The subject and object mutually agree not to associate. This is a neutral position from a power dynamics perspective, as there is no relationship whereby influence can be brought.

THE SEPARATION TEST

It is possible to determine a measurement of inclusivity for an individual (and therefore for an organization, or indeed any system) by considering their Separation Indices (first-order power dynamic) for each of their relationships, with regard to the three forms of holonic association described above. To do so, each relationship is assessed for three factors:

- The holonic association, from their subjective perspective (either as part, whole or mutual)
- The Separation Index (SI) for that relationship, recorded on a scale of +9 (internal locus of control) through -9 (external locus of control)
- The predominant power dynamic for that relationship

The data is assessed from two perspectives:

- From the perspective of the subject who is consistent in all the relationships (self-assessment)
- From the perspective of the object (other individual) in each relationship

SI values above 1 reflect the individual responder's dominance (internal locus of control), as the agent for the defined power dynamic. The results are plotted onto an *Inclusion Variance Target*, shown in Fig 28. Up to two lines are drawn within each power dynamic. These *'power lines'* reflect the average score for: (1) All relationships with SI above the line (+ve SI, shown in red); (2) All relationships below the line (-ve SI, shown in blue). The thickness of each line reflects the number of relationships represented within it. An overall average for above-the-line SI, and an overall average for below-the-line SI, is presented to show the total SI range, or *'Inclusion Variance'* (IV), between them, for each power dynamic.

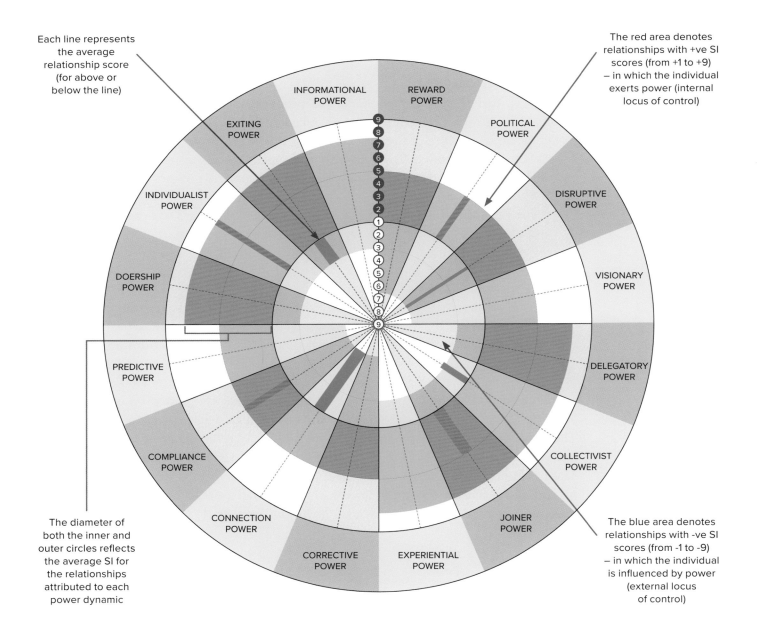

Each line represents the average relationship score (for above or below the line)

The red area denotes relationships with +ve SI scores (from +1 to +9) – in which the individual exerts power (internal locus of control)

The diameter of both the inner and outer circles reflects the average SI for the relationships attributed to each power dynamic

The blue area denotes relationships with -ve SI scores (from -1 to -9) – in which the individual is influenced by power (external locus of control)

FIG 28 – INCLUSION VARIANCE (IV) TARGET (EXAMPLE)

Three inclusion targets are completed – one for each of the holonic associations – to define the nature of their relationships (part, whole or mutual), so that the contribution of the individual can be considered in relation to the types of association they form. Each target yields its own IV. The total IV, which considers all three holonic associations, is the calculated sum average of all three, such that the minimum (optimum) IV is 1, and the maximum is 18. An example of an IV Target displaying the minimum score of 1 (a single empty circle), and maximum score of 18, are shown in Fig 29. When assessing Inclusion Variance for an individual, the difference between their self-rating and that of the other parties can be shown by plotting two additional profiles on the IV Target as the average of both perspectives for each power dynamic.

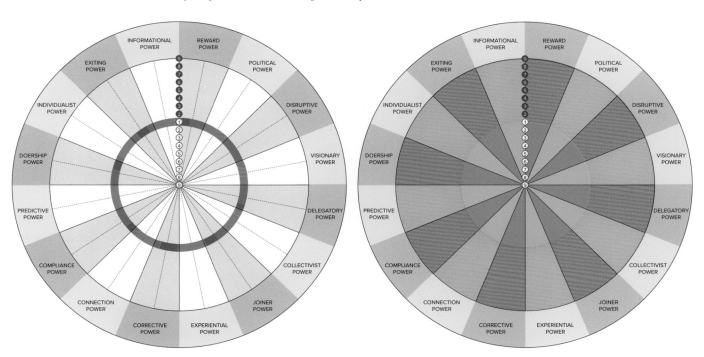

Minimum (optimum/non-egoic) IV = 1   Maximum (suboptimum/egoic) IV = 18

FIG 29 – MINIMUM AND MAXIMUM IV TARGET SCORES

The incorporation of both the subjective and objective perspectives within the IV scores for an individual reflects the perspectival nature of inclusion. Both individuals within a relationship might fundamentally disagree on whether the relationship was inclusive or not, and they would both be right.

As averages are taken, the IV does not provide an indication as to the number of relationships from which the IV derives. The purpose of this is to avoid prejudicing individuals with larger networks to score a higher IV as a result. Take these two individuals, for example: person A, who has been in the organization for two months and knows four people, and person B, who joined two years ago and knows 50 people. Let's imagine they both score an IV of 2. While it might seem that person B has to be more inclusive to get the same score as person A, it's important to remember that each individual's IV score is contextual to their current network. Both person A and person B are, relatively for their own contexts, demonstrating the same level of inclusion. As time passes, person A will inevitably come into contact with more and more people, which in turn will influence their IV score. The important point is that:

- Everyone in the organization has the same target of 1.
- Everyone, irrespective of their place in the organization, has an equal role to play in reducing egotistical exclusion within the organization.
- Everyone in the organization is a leader of equal standing.

The IV assessment relies on individuals' willingness to engage, and provide authentic responses that reflect their actual perspective. The incorporation of both the subject and objective perspectives reduces the opportunity to 'game' the data, while anonymity afforded to all responders may encourage honest responses. To work effectively, however, the assessment needs to be undertaken in the context of a wider commitment within the organization to addressing egoic power dynamics within the business, for which anonymity may prove counterproductive.

To get the overall organizational view, the three targets are presented in exactly the same way, but as cumulative representations of the individual IV targets. For all organizations seeking an inclusive environment, the IV target is 1.

As an indicator of performance, IV is perhaps the most important measure of dysfunction within an organization, and as such will have significant cost impact. It is also a likely blind spot for many organizations that have narrowed their perspective of what inclusion really means within an organization. Organizations with higher power dynamics will need to invest significantly more to maintain their performance and membership.

FROM EGO-SYSTEM TO ECO-SYSTEM

The principles of the E.G.O. can be applied to larger-scale systems. Any egoic system – whether a corporation, a country or a kingdom – is that which seeks fulfilment beyond itself, beyond its borders, at the expense of its external environment. Just like individuals, egoic systems operate either through aggression from an internal locus of control (ranging from nationalistic diplomacy to threatening the territorial integrity of other nations) or through regression (they involute, through an external locus of control that maintains autocratic rule).

Fig 30 shows how each of the components of the E.G.O. operating model translates at country-level, as the basis by which global egoic power structures are perpetuated. A country with an Inclusion Variance of 1 (inclusive of all individuals associated with that system) may find that many of these societal structures, which we (as citizens) have come to expect and depend on, may become redundant.

CONVERGENT: Toward ORDER		DIVERGENT: Toward CHAOS	
Power Dynamic	**Country-level Structures**	**Power Dynamic**	**Country-level Structures**
Informational power *Power from having wanted information*	Media, information control, data security, intellectual property	**Experiential power** *Power from having wanted experience*	Education, qualifications, academia
Exiting power *Power to exit individuals*	Nationalism, employment contracts, retirement	**Joining power** *Power to welcome individuals*	Immigration, tourism, borders
Doership power *Power to undertake designated activities*	Workers, experts, national infrastructure	**Delegatory power** *Power to delegate activities to others*	Jobs, employers, productivity
Individualist power *Power to assert an individual moral judgement*	Role models, national heroes, pariahs, celebrities	**Collectivist moral power** *Power to assert collective moral judgement*	Customs, traditions, morality, national identity, religion
Predictive power *Power to anticipate wanted information*	Collective memory, scientific understanding, history	**Visionary power** *Power to set a promissory vision that inspires others*	Strategies, national ambition and purpose
Compliance power *Power to enforce compliance with rules and standards*	Rule of law, regulations, taxes, policy	**Disruptive power** *Power to change processes, rules and standards*	Advertising, rule of surprise, the arts
Corrective power *Power to correct poor performance*	Prisons, fines, armed forces	**Reward power** *Power to recognize good performance*	Welfare, economics, medals, honours system
Connection power *Power gained from acting through an individual*	Bilateral treaty, unions, ancestry	**Political power** *Power gained from acting through a group*	The elite, politicians, governance, class system

FIG 30 – E.G.O BLUEPRINT AT COUNTRY LEVEL

It is the egoic perspective that drives the corporate and societal compulsion for growth, to become more than they are by consuming more than they need. It is this expansionist ethos that fuels the extraction of natural resources without their replenishment, just as it is to claim the territory of other sovereign states. It is a belief in a national identity over and above mutuality and global community.

As our own ego seeks fulfilment from experience, it identifies with and thereby seeks ownership of the objects within its experience. Within an egoic system, we are the clothes we wear, the car we drive. We have created a consumer society, in which choice and personalization enhances this sense of ownership and status. Our guarantees and sell-by dates encourage us to 'burn after reading.' This behaviour has driven an economy that is extractive and consumptive, drawing from the finite resources of our planet and threatening its biodiversity.

The climate emergency has opened our eyes to the reality that we are both a part of and dependent on a larger eco-technological system. The circular economy model is challenging our notions of ownership and entitlement, by promoting greater sharing, repairing and reuse of products to extend their intrinsic value and eliminate waste. However, most of our economies are still based on linear production systems, and the climate clock is ticking. The transition to a global circular economy will itself require a level of collaboration and trust that will necessitate the dismantling of many of the power structures that have underpinned the global isolationism and protectionist tendencies of nation states. One way or the other, it is true that we will either all succeed, or fail, together. While technology will certainly be pivotal to this success, more fundamental to this is the role of ego. Our global failure to recognize this simple fact represents mankind's single greatest existential threat.

The transition to *net zero* requires a transition from ego-systems to eco-systems – those that are permeable to the ideas of others; that seek not global influence but global accord and collaboration; that embrace free movement over sovereignty; that can marry the traditions of the past with the values of the future. That will not seek to protect cultural and nationalistic identity (be it through the traditions of faith or sovereignty), but rather promote their evolution, even dissolution, to become something bigger than itself.

12. THE UNIVERSAL MOVEMENT

Take a look at Fig 31. Can you see the line that runs vertically through it? It is the same line that delineates everything that exists in our universe; the separation of one form from another. We can see the line because our reality is one of contrast, of relativity. But, of course, the line, in and of itself, does not actually exist. It is this line that manifests everything that we can perceive or conceive. It is this *line of perspective* that gives rise to the universal movement.

The universal movement is the emergence of complexity out of simplicity, whereby detail unfolds itself in degrees of ever-more complex structures and functions. It is the basis by which all life comes into existence in the universe. In nature, we see through the process of evolution the emergence of forms that are increasingly complex, independent and autonomous. From prokaryotic cells, eukaryotic cells, tissues and organs to plants and animals, families, communities, ecosystems and living planets – life shows increasing complexity at every scale.

FIG 31 – THE LINE OF PERSPECTIVE

This chapter explores the development process by which complex forms arise, through *SPIN* – four states of attention (Singularity; Personality; Instituted; and Neoteric) that lead ultimately full cirle to the emergence of simplicity from complexity through the revelation of novel form. These four dynamic aspects explain how reality is experienced through a 'perpetual motion of attention.'

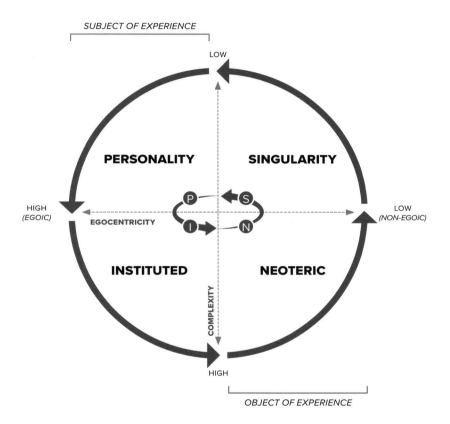

FIG 32 – SPIN: PERPETUAL MOTION OF ATTENTION

SPIN provides a unified model for describing the two core functions by which our current experience is rendered:

1. **Objectivity – the development of form:** The process by which change manifests within experience through the transcendence of complexity toward more innovative forms and practices – from new life to new ideas.

2. **Subjectivity – the development of feeling:** The process by which individual identity and purpose informs how we discriminate within experience, what we give attention to, and how we behave.

1. OBJECTIVE FUNCTIONS

We shall start by considering the objective functions (those that are acausal of subjective experience):

- **Singularity:** Pertaining to the appearance of basal form – from which one form can be distinguished from another.
- **Neoteric:** Pertaining to new and novel forms – the emergence of complex form within experience.

SINGULARITY: The origin of basal form

From a holonic perspective, all states, as holons, demonstrate a degree of autonomy, the persistence of which can in part be explained through the Free Energy Principle.[1] This is an organizing principle for the persistence of autonomous systems in time, be they a cell, an objective function, an organization or a society. The principle explains how living and non-living systems remain in non-equilibrium steady states through the optimization of free energy within the system (a measure of the capacity of the system to do work). The emergence of all structure, all form, necessitates the existence of an objective function – a dynamic state – that looks as if it is minimizing variational free energy. The principle describes the 'selfish' characteristics that enable life to exist, as modelled through a *Markov blanket*, as outlined below.

States of separation

Any system or 'thing' requires separation between itself and everything else. From a statistical perspective, this distinction, or Markov blanket, describes the separation of states that are internal to that thing (its *internal state*), and external to it (the *external state*). The blanket, or boundary, is itself described by two states: *sensory states* (the activities within the boundary, that are influenced by but do not themselves influence the external state, and which influence but are not influenced by the internal state); and *active states*, such as movement (its activity that influences but is not influenced by the external state, out with the boundary, and which is influenced by but does not influence the internal state).

One might conceive of the Markov blanket as a sensory veil, on which the external state leaves its impressions. In the same way as we might conceive the view from a window,

1. Pezzulo, G., Friston, K. & Parr, T. (2022). *Active Inference: The Free Energy Principle in Mind, Brain, and Behavior.* MIT Press.

as observed from behind the veil – the shadows beyond pervade the veil, from which we perceive the external state. It is the ego that conflates external states with a separate external reality, in contrast to the singular reality that pervades all states in existence.

The anatomy of any system has to contain within it a model of the environment in which that system is immersed. Our sensory states create this *model of the world*, which in turn informs our active states (so that we act in accordance with our sensory information). At the same time, our active states gather information from the external state, maximizing evidence for this model of the world, and informing our sensory states. This creates a perceptual loop between listening to the world and doing in the world – of hearing and expressing.

The *free energy principle*[1] further explains that the existence of a given system arises by minimizing the difference between their model of the world (what they perceive it to be) and what they find it to be (through their senses). This difference can be described as 'surprise' (unforeseeable or atypical states and events confronting the system), and is minimized by continuous correction of the model of the system. By minimizing the difference, the energy required for correction is also minimized. Every action we take and every sensation we gather is in the service of minimizing variational free energy. This process of sampling the world to resolve uncertainty – minimizing expected free energy, reducing uncertainty and maximizing information gain – would seem to be the natural and necessary curiosity of all autonomous systems.

The Inference Engine

Through our sensory states, we minimize this difference through continuous perception and correction to the internal state, while through our active states we change the external state toward the expected (inferred) model. As such, the principle of free energy is based on the Bayesian idea of the brain as an *'inference engine,'* whereby the system infers its model of the world. It supports the theory of Unconscious Inference, first put forward by the physicist and physician Hermann von Helmholtz,[2] which implies that our perception is incomplete and that details are inferred by the unconscious mind to create a complete picture.

In other words, perception is an act of hypothesis testing, in which our brains are statistical organs that compute the most likely picture of the world. As von Helmholtz puts it:

2. Helmholtz, H. V. (1867). *Physiological Optics or Treatise on Physiological Optics – Third volume: The Perceptions of Vision.*

"Each movement we make by which we alter the appearance of objects should be thought of as an experiment designed to test whether we have understood correctly the invariant relations of the phenomena before us, that is, their existence as definite spatial relations."[3] The brain has itself been posited as a type of Helmholtz Machine, an artificial neural network that can account for the hidden structure of a set of data by being trained to create a generative model of the original set of data. From this we can say two things:

1. For any autonomous system, such as a cell or a society, the understanding and attention that it gives to its environment is a function of its expression within that environment, and vice versa. You cannot know your environment without becoming it. Movement and expression are the embodiment of intelligence.

2. You never actually know what is 'out there,' only what you encounter, because in all aspects (though physicists might argue the case for quantum entanglement) we exist in a universe where there is no action at a distance.

All systems exist as if they have a perceptual model of the world, through the gathering of evidence. Accordingly, it can be said that every system exists to maximize the evidence for its model, and thereby evidence for (and the probability of) its own existence. Self-evidencing arises in everything from small particles to political movements.

We can extend this inference to the brain itself. Convention presumes that our model of the world is created by the brain. Within this model there must also exist the model of the brain itself. In other words, the brain describes itself through a model of its own making. As such, it appears as a reflection of the world that it describes. Through its perception of form, life and movement, it is itself described and appears as form, life and movement. In reality, however, the brain is part of this model in the same way that toothpaste, or headaches, or indeed other 'models of the world' exist. In other words, that which we perceive is not an activity of the brain, but rather the activity of awareness, from which the brain is itself perceived. Consciousness does not arise in the brain; the brain arises in consciousness.

The appearance of life

Within the active and sensory states we see the two movements, toward and away from – expression and information. As the sensory information becomes more complex, so the

3. The Facts of Perception (1878) in The Selected Writings of Hermann von Helmholtz, Ed. R. Karl, Middletown: Wesleyan University Press, 1971 p. 384.

movement from which the expanding model of the world is derived itself becomes more complex. At some point, there becomes the capacity to change and correct the movement due to the sensory information that was received not just from the previous movement, but from the movement previous to that. This encoding of sensory information within the internal state gives rise to the apparent predetermination of movement – what one might loosely describe as 'intent.' It is this that describes the fundamental characteristic of life, and from which behaviour and learning can be first said to occur. To intend is to endure.

For any system to endure over time it must resist its dispersion by random fluctuations. It is the defining dynamic of any system in existence that it must exactly counter the dispersive forces (of entropy) acting upon it, by exploiting energy from their external environment. An example of this balancing act is homeostasis, the process by which a steady state of internal, physical and chemical conditions is maintained by living systems. It is brought about by a natural resistance to change when already in optimal conditions, in which equilibrium is maintained by one or more regulatory mechanisms. All homeostatic control mechanisms have at least three interdependent components for the variable being regulated: *a receptor, a control centre* and *an effector*. Each of these reflects the particular states described across a Markov blanket:

- **Sensory state:** The *receptor* is the sensing component that monitors and responds to changes in the environment, either external or internal. Receptors include thermoreceptors and mechanoreceptors.
- **Internal state:** *Control centres* include the brain, its respiratory centre, and the renin–angiotensin system.
- **Active state:** An *effector* is the target acted on to bring about the change back to the normal state, such as a muscle or gland.

The receptor receives information that something in the environment is changing. The control centre (also referred to as the 'integration centre') receives and processes information from the receptor. The effector then responds to the commands of the control centre by either opposing or enhancing the stimulus. This ongoing process continually works to restore and maintain homeostasis. For example, during body temperature regulation, temperature receptors in the skin communicate information to the brain (the control centre), which signals the effectors (blood vessels and sweat glands in the skin). As the internal and external environment of the body are constantly changing, adjustments must be made continuously to stay at or near a specific value, or 'set point,' such as the specific pH of different bodily fluids.

Because active states change, but are not changed by external states, they also reduce the entropy of blanket states (sensory and active states). This means that action will appear to maintain and develop the structural and functional integrity of the Markov blanket. Another name for this is autopoiesis, a system capable of reproducing and maintaining itself by creation of its own parts,[4] leading to further development. Autopoiesis can be defined as the ratio between the complexity of a system and the complexity of its environment.[5] This generalized view of autopoiesis considers systems to be 'self-producing' not in terms of their physical components, but in their organization, which can be measured in terms of information and complexity. In other words, we can describe autopoietic systems as those producing more of their own complexity than is produced by their environment.[6] Autopoiesis has been proposed as a potential mechanism of abiogenesis, by which primitive cells evolved into more complex molecules that could support the development of life.[7]

NEOTERIC: The emergence of new form from complexity

The observation that the universe evolves toward increasing entropy, or decreasing order, is described by the Second Law of Thermodynamics. This movement toward disorganization might lead us to think that complex structures, such as organisms and organizations, should never spontaneously come into existence. However, if the overall tendency is toward increasing disorder, how do complex structures arise? There are two reasons for this, depending on your interpretations of:

A. Order and complexity
B. Open and closed systems

A. Order and complexity

Order and complexity are very different ideas. Entropy measures how many different ways you can make an arrangement of small-scale particles that have the same large-scale properties, like 50 degrees Celsius, red hair, or good at cricket.

4. Oxford Reference. Retrieved 2021-11-12.

5. Fernandez N, Maldonado C, Gershenson C (2013). Chapter 2: Information measures of complexity, emergence, self-organization, homeostasis, and autopoiesis. Guided self-organization: Inception. Springer. pp. 19–51.

6. Carlos Gershenson, *Requisite Variety, Autopoiesis, and Self-organization* (26 Sep 2014)

7. Highfield, Roger; Coveney, Peter (1995). *Frontiers of complexity: the search for order in a chaotic world.* London: Faber. p. 210.

Complexity describes "the amount of information needed to describe everything *interesting* about the system."[8] Simple systems are easy to describe, while complex systems require a lot more information. Physicist Sean Carroll's paper on the coffee automaton[8] shows how mixing coffee with cream demonstrates that complexity arises from a low entropy state. Initially, when you pour cream into coffee, the system is easy to describe – there is coffee, and there is cream, in a highly ordered, low-entropy state.

If you mix the two fully together, the initial structure is lost, and entropy increases until milk and coffee are completely dispersed. The resulting state is high entropy, with a huge number of arrangements of molecules that look the same. The system is also simple: coffee and milk now just appearing as a ubiquitous 'coffee-milk.' However, this increase in entropy is only possible due to a temporal increase in complexity – as soon as you mix the coffee with the milk, there are many more ways in which the molecules can be arranged, and therefore how the system can be described.

This emergence of complexity can be observed on every scale, from coffee cups to the cosmos itself. The universe began with the Big Bang, in a very dense state of low entropy and extreme simplicity. In the distant future of our universe, in approximately 10^{26} years from now, our ever-expanding universe is predicted to end in a high-entropy, low-complexity state. In this 'heat death,' all atoms in the universe will reach a thermal equilibrium, so that the universe – understood through its spontaneous processes – will just stop. It is in the space between these points of low complexity that complexity arises, from stars and galaxies to rubber bands and baseballs. We ourselves are in the coffee-mixing stage, in the knowing that in time, all of this will be simplified out of existence.

This universal movement – complexity arising out of simplicity arising out of complexity – is one of abstraction. What we see playing out in Fig 33, over millennia, is equally played out every second, every minute, every day of our lives. Our every action

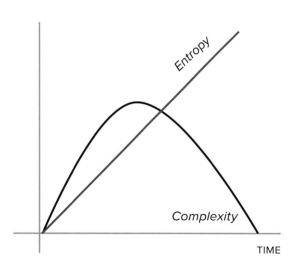

FIG 33 – HOW COMPLEXITY AND ENTROPY CHANGE OVER TIME

8. *Quantifying the Rise and Fall of Complexity in Closed Systems: The Coffee Automaton* (Scott Aaronson, Sean M. Carroll, Lauren Ouellette) – 2014.

is simultaneously an act of creation and destruction, from when we wake (our dreams turning to dust), to when we make coffee.

Because complexity is a measure of how hard it is to describe a set of large-scale properties, it is, to an extent, in the eye of the beholder. We describe the shift from complexity to simplicity as innovation – the ability to reduce sophisticated ideas down into something that is easy to understand. It marks an inflexion point in our perception, a subtle withdrawing of attention through which simplicity can emerge through repeating patterns, correlations, and the bigger picture. The ecologist and data scientist Eric Berlow described how *"simplicity lies on the other side of complexity ... the more you can zoom out and embrace complexity, the better chance you have of zooming in on the simple details that matter most."*[9]

B. Open and closed systems
In the Second Law of Thermodynamics, entropy, and therefore disorder, increases if the system (the container in which entropy is observed) is closed. And whether the system is closed depends on your level of abstraction.

Closed Systems: A closed system is one that can exchange energy with its surroundings, but not matter. They may be part of a larger system, but are not in complete contact with it. They are sometimes also called non-flow processes, because of the inability to exchange mass. A closed system presumes that a thing – a system – can exist in isolation from another thing. The Markov blanket, our dividing line for reality, necessitates both internal and external states. Closed states exist only at a level of abstraction; the moment we zoom out, they cease to exist.

Open systems: Open systems, in contrast, can exchange both matter and energy with their surroundings. They are a part of and in intimate contact with the larger system. Open systems are sometimes termed 'flow systems,' because of the ability to exchange mass of a substance. An open system describes the action across a Markov blanket, the active and sensory states reflecting the changes in matter and energy.

9. https://www.ted.com/talks/eric_berlow_simplifying_complexity

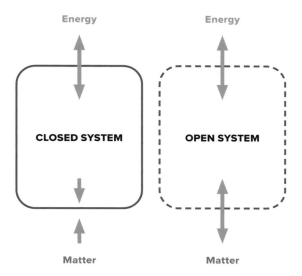

FIG 34 – OPEN AND CLOSED SYSTEMS

In the coffee metaphor, there is an outside agency responsible for inducing this complexity: the spoon. The spoon is important, because without it there would not be an injection of energy from outside, as a catalyst to stir up the system. Similarly, if you placed the coffee in your freezer, it would turn to ice (decreased entropy) – this being possible because you can heat the back of the freezer (increased entropy). In both cases, the Second Law states that this can occur only if it is part of a closed system. If through our abstraction we limited the 'system' to that of the glass, then this exchange would not be possible.

To understand whether the universe is a closed system or an open system depends on your definition of the universe. The Second Law of Thermodynamics says that the *total* entropy in the universe has to increase – and hence, the universal tendency toward increasing entropy assumes it is a closed system. However, the observable universe, meaning only the part of the universe that we can see, is an open system. This is because the 'boundary' of our observable universe is not actually a physical boundary in any possible meaning of the word, and both matter and energy can freely pass through it.

The universe is expanding according to Hubble's Law, which says that the galaxies are moving away from us. And the farther they are from us, the faster they move. If you go far enough away from us, there are objects receding at the speed of light, so we will never see them. They would have to travel back toward us faster than the speed of light to be seen.

This point at which objects are receding away from us at the speed of light (the edge of our observable universe) is called the cosmic horizon. Nothing outside that region can ever be seen. Therefore, the edge of our observable universe defines not the universe, but the limits of our own perception.

In addition to a boundary, a closed system must also have a determinable centre. The Big Bang that occurred some 13.7 billion years ago – the point from which our universe began to expand – was not an explosion that burst outward from a central point of detonation, as the name might suggest. Rather, the universe started out extremely compact and tiny. Then, every point in the universe expanded equally, and that continues today. And so, without any point of origin, the universe has no centre. Hubble's Law might suggest that we are at the centre of the expanding universe, but in fact, if the universe is expanding uniformly, then it will appear to do so from any vantage point.[10]

The universe is expanding at an accelerating rate due to 'dark energy,' an intrinsic property of space. However, if the universe is a closed system with a finite amount of energy, any increase in space will also increase its intrinsic energy, this being contrary to the law of energy conservation (the First Law of Thermodynamics, which holds that energy cannot be created or destroyed). Yet, according to Einstein's Theory of General Relativity, *"As space expands, it releases stored-up gravitational potential energy, which converts into the intrinsic energy that fills the newly created volume."*[11] No energy is created or destroyed, which is consistent with the law of energy conservation, and with that of a closed system.

A third conjecture is that the universe – if we mean 'the entire universe' (everything there is, including things we cannot see) – is neither open nor closed, but isolated. In an isolated system, neither energy nor matter can be exchanged with their surroundings because they have no surroundings. They are literally everything there is.

Impact of open systems on complexity
Open systems describe the conditions necessary for life, with the freedom to interact with their environment, and in which energy and resources can be shared. However, all things, all matter, need a boundary to define them (such as the Markov blanket describes). The boundary that provides its separation is there for the purpose of allowing two-way exchange between itself and the outside environment. The separation, therefore, is not

10. *Where is the Centre of the Universe?* Philip Gibbs (1997).

11. Scientific American: Fact or fiction? Energy can neither be created nor destroyed (*Clara Moskowitz* on August 5, 2014).

an absolute, but a movement. In other words, 'open' is also a relative term, and what we observe in reality is that there are no absolutes.

Rather than say that increasing entropy leads to increasing chaos in a closed state, we could say that the tendency of entropy (toward chaos) is toward closed states, and therefore the emergence of complexity is necessarily manifested through increasingly open states – those that evolve. In other words, the universal movement – the manifestation of complex form in experience – is a movement toward more open states. There is significant evidence for this in organizations today.

Take, for example, a failing organization that exits in a hypothetical closed system. All businesses need to invest time and money to minimize entropy. They provide regular staff training, good reporting of any issues, inspections, detailed monitoring of successes and failures, etc. For a business operating as a closed system, there would be no exchange of resources or information with the outside system. Such an organization would quickly turn to chaos, as there would be no input or energy from the outside to counter the flow of entropy. The apparent autonomy of any system is in reality directly proportional to its interdependence on its outside environment. To counter the tendency toward entropy, organizations need to become ever-more open systems. You cannot grow on your own. Like the crab that breaks out of its shell, every organization, every system, every organism, faces moments when it needs to shed its skin, and reach out further to its environment, or die. In societal terms, the word 'involution' has been used to describe this challenge.

The Chinese word for involution – *neijuan* – is made up of the characters for *'inside'* and *'rolling,'* suggesting a process that curls inward, ensnaring its participants within what the anthropologist Xiang Biao has described as an *"endless cycle of self-flagellation."*[12] Involution is *"the experience of being locked in competition that one ultimately knows is meaningless"*[13] – where the competition no longer falls outside but inside the organization. It is a growing affliction, notable not only in the East (such as within China's hypercompetitive tech industry) but also through the West's cutthroat egalitarianist and meritocratic institutions. Anthropologist Alexander Goldenweiser described involution as what happens *"when a system has developed to a point when it should move to the next stage, but in failing grows inward, becoming ever more complex."*[14] The principal driver for involution is ego – the separate-self seeking the separation of the organization from the system around it.

12. https://www.sixthtone.com/news/1006391/how-one-obscure-word-captures-urban-chinas-unhappiness

13. https://www.newyorker.com/culture/cultural-comment/chinas-involuted-generation

14. Waddington, T. (2007). *Lasting Contribution: How to Think, Plan, and Act to Accomplish Meaningful Work.* (1st Edition). Agate B2.

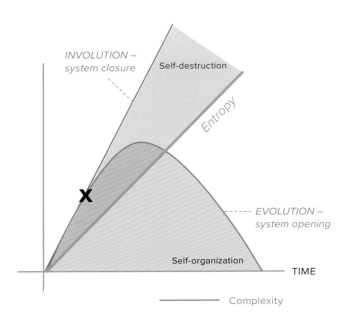

INVOLUTION –
system closure

Self-destruction

Entropy

X

EVOLUTION –
system opening

Self-organization

TIME

Complexity

FIG 35 – EFFECT OF ENTROPY ON OPEN AND CLOSED ORGANIZATIONAL SYSTEMS

Entropy affects every organization. It is inevitable that as the organization grows, it becomes more process oriented, with more specialized jobs, and more complex and draconian rules. Tech start-ups quickly reach a point where they need to change radically, such as through acquisition or buy-out. Ultimately, organizations will reach an inflexion point (point X – Fig 35), at which they must choose whether to pursue a strategy based on involution, or evolution:

- **Involution** is a process of self-destruction. The involuted organization seeks to retain control within itself, leading to greater bureaucracy. In resistance to change, it seeks to retain the old ways of working (and those who control it) in place. The system becomes unsustainable. Increasing levels of complexity turn to chaos.
- **Evolution** is a process of self-organization. Through self-organization, the system naturally opens itself up and seeks change, difference, inclusion from outside of itself, evolving to form part of a larger whole. Innovation reduces complexity to create new, simpler products and ideas.

2. SUBJECTIVE FUNCTIONS

In this chapter, we have considered the universal movement through the objective function of experience – from simple to complex forms, through consideration of:

- **Singularity:** The inception and appearance of basal form, from which one form can be distinguished from another, as it relates to the *Free Energy Principle*[1]
- **Neoteric:** The appearance of new forms – the emergence of complexity within experience, as it relates to the Second Law of Thermodynamics

Two observations can be made of the objective function of experience:

1. Objective transformation happens alongside subjective transformation (self-reference). In other words, objective experience appears only in the presence of its witness, and the transformation of one must necessarily arise within the other for it to be known. We may look, for example, to the night sky and the universe at its most manifest – a backdrop for 200 billion trillion stars. However, we will not fully understand its appearance until we understand that within which it appears – the perspective of the one who is looking.

2. From the subjective perspective, the recursive emergence of complexity creates an infinite loop, in which the transcendence of complexity arises through the appearance of simplicity. Take, for example, how Einstein's ten years of research would ultimately be explainable through five symbols: $E = MC^2$. This articulation of the General Theory of Relativity, through its simplest possible arrangement, provided the foundation for an entirely new direction of scientific thought. As Newton once said, *"If I have seen further [than others], it is by standing on the shoulders of giants"*[15] – a reference to the inheritance of knowledge as a kind of ignorance that through its redaction becomes the mother of all invention.

We can say, therefore, that experience constitutes not just an objective function, but also a subjective function or perspective – that of the witness to the objective function: the self, or ego. There are two functions of ego within the subjective aspect of experience, with regard to the universal movement:

15. *"Letter from Sir Isaac Newton to Robert Hooke"* (1675). Historical Society of Pennsylvania. Retrieved 7 June 2018.

- **Personality:** The appearance of experience from the singular perspective and activity of the ego, as described through Egodynamics (Chapter 8)
- **Instituted:** The collective activity of egoic organizations and systems – the E.G.O. – that results in complex action, as described by *Second-Order Power Dynamics* (Chapter 11)

In relation to manifestation, Aristotle wrote of 'potentiality' as a figure being already present in a rock that was yet to be sculpted. Potentiality and actuality are the polarities of experience – the unrealized and the realized, the elementary and the manifest. They are not states, but rather reflective of a movement between the abstract and the concrete, through which experience reveals itself.

Attention is required to know experience, just as our withdrawal of attention is required to know our true nature. We must lose ourselves in our experience to know experience – that is the price of admission. Like characters in a play who must forget they are in a play in order for the play to unfold. You can only give attention to (and thereby experience) something other than you – the objects of experience. You cannot attend to yourself as you do to an object. It's like saying to the Sun, "Stop shining on the Moon and shine on yourself." Attention is the awareness of objects. Anyone who has tried to 'find themself' will (in ignorance, or frustration) only ever find another object of self-identity – the ego.

Our attention appears to be directed and given by 'us' toward experience. And yet, without conscious effort, our attention is always given to experience. More precisely, our attention is not given by us at all, but to us, through awareness. It is only from the perspective of the separate self that our attention appears to take on its own vector, and in so doing separates ourself from experience, such that experience appears at a distance from ourselves, in space (through the perception of distance) and in time (through thought).

When the ego seeks itself in experience, and thereby in resistance seeks control of how attention is given, it appears to place a limitation on our attention, and the accordant creative process of expression – both individually (Personality) and collectively (Instituted).

PERSONALITY: The perspective of ego within experience

As we have seen, any 'thing' requires separation between itself and everything else. A Markov blanket describes the separation of states that are internal to that thing (its internal state), and external to it (the external state). At some point the sensory state forms a model of the world in which it locates and includes itself. At that point, the internal state is itself influenced by the sensory state, creating a circular feedback loop. It is from this loop that self-reference is made possible, and that the potential arises, within the causal flow of ever-increasing complexity, for an inflexion point denoted by a cognitive expression of 'self' and 'other' – the point at which the system becomes self-aware. It is the same expression that gives rise to the mental concept of attention – the movement or intent by which experience is consciously perceived through its direction away from self and toward experience. Ego is the belief that self-reference implies a self that is separate from experience.

The mechanism by which ego operates is described through egodynamics (Chapter 8). Through our identification with thoughts and feelings, the ego believes that who we are is how we feel. We act as if to bring that feeling into reality. However, you are already that which you want to be, and your refusal to believe this is the only reason you do not see it. You will never find that which you want, that which you need to be, because you can only ever find that which you already are. This egoic pursuit develops habituative behaviours that act to limit the opportunities for self and other.

To cite the words of Pastor William Ramsey, *"The greatest trick the Devil ever pulled was convincing the world he didn't exist."*[16] So it is that the ego's search for atonement through its endless seeking ensures its survival. Seeking will only take you away from that which you already are. To the separate self, all options point to changing one's perspective, by changing experience. Drugs can undoubtedly change your experience, but all experience, comprising as it is of finite form, is finite. Psychedelics and other hallucinogenic drugs alter our radius of perception, including our sensory threshold, our sensitization and receptivity to experience, so that our range of experience is that much greater. But an experience is still a subjective experience. The taste of water is a subjective experience. Psychedelics offer an expansion of our capacity for phenomenal experience, but while there are different levels of perception, and subjective experience could be graded

16. Ramsey, W. (1856). *Spiritualism, a Satanic Delusion, and a Sign of the Times.* HardPress.

by degrees, there are no degrees of awareness, just as there are no degrees of love. As Shakespeare said, *"Love is not love which alters when it alteration finds, or bends with the remover to remove: O no! It is an ever-fixed mark that looks on tempests and is never shaken."*[17] Experience and form will always be finite, but all experiences are known by and appear in infinite consciousness.

INSTITUTED: The perspective of the collective 'meta-ego'

Someone once said that a dream we dream on our own is only a dream, but a dream we dream together is reality. We come together in the silent understanding that our true reality is one of shared being, but in so doing afford the collective expression of ego. The meta-ego of the Evil Genius Organization is an egoic fractal, in which the repeating patterns of the separate self are laid down through its individual members. The challenges faced by organizations attempting to transform their enterprise are not just the result of external factors, but also reflect the challenge from within, as the protective instincts of its egoic power dynamics are tested. In fact, the only organization that could possibly benefit from ego is one that is run entirely by that which it serves – the customer, so that the ego's self-serving actions would be entirely congruent with its customer self-service operation. Of course, many organizations seek customer self-service by degrees, but any organization that is wholly self-service is, by definition, redundant. The key is to help employees to help themselves in the absence of ego.

To the ego, the organizing of individuals – whether for a small team, a company, or a society – presents an opportunity to control their environment. When viewed from this perspective, many organizations appear to have organized themselves through a set of power dynamics that expressly service the egoic needs of their members, by providing a mechanism for ego to exert control over others. Chapter 11 describes how the eight organizing dilemmas establish irreconcilable tensions across each of the 16 organizational states, and which, in the presence of ego, lead to an inequitable dispersal of power. The *eight tenets of ego* to which the organizing dilemmas pertain represent the core design principles that underpin almost every organizational operation that exists today.

We can see, for example, how the organizational states of performance management and benefits – designed to apply corrective measures and recognize individual contribution

17. William Shakespeare, W. (1609). *Sonnet 116: Let me not to the marriage of true mind.*

– stem from the defining beliefs of personal responsibility and authorship. Power dynamics provide a regulatory mechanism, through which ego can exert its influence in furtherance of its search for personal happiness. The absence of this egoic modus operandum would not result in a laissez-faire, devil-may-care attitude, but rather a vibrant curiosity and attention to one's actions and to feedback. This would be fuelled by a continued exploration of what each individual values most, in the pursuit of those opportunities that will best service their expression within the organization.

The skills and mindset required of an egoic organization bare little relation to those enterprises that operate outside of second-order power dynamics. In an egoic organization, leadership is defined by an individual's capacity to exert control through these dynamics. In contrast, in the 'self-less organization,' leadership is defined by an individual's capacity to create value in their absence, through the dismantling of egoic power structures. In an organization devoid of any power dynamics, the exclusive role of 'leader' will no longer be required, with leadership considered both a quality and right of every individual within the enterprise.

Egoic power dynamics derive from the belief that an organization is fundamentally a set of independent organizational states – such as knowledge, skills or performance (as described in Fig 24) – that can be inherited, contained and controlled by individuals within that organization. In reality, there are no actual independent states, such as knowledge, that we can claim ownership of. Notice, for example, that every year around 14 billion pencils are made in the world, but that there is not one person in the world who entirely understands how to make one. Where does graphite come from? How do you extract it? How do you make the tools to extract it? How do you make the coating on the pencil? Oil is a key ingredient, so how do you find the oil field? How do you build an oil field? How do you power it? How does electricity work? The reason no one can know all this is the same reason nobody can truly know what a pencil is. It is only when we relinquish the belief in our authorship and control of organizational states that they will cease controlling us.

As organizations grow, the choice between egoic and non-egoic expression will determine their future success. The inexorable progress toward increasing complexity can either be managed through greater exertion of control, or through the relinquishment of control (to allow a change in direction) – toward involution or evolution, respectively.

The only way that an involuted organization can survive is to spread, like a virus, to change its environment into itself, rather than changing into that which its environment needs. Involution in the East has been propagated through corporate feudalism, to become not just a business issue but a societal one. We are witnessing involution through polarization across the geopolitical landscape.

Involution begets involution, fosters duality and opposition, or in geopolitical terms, 'East against West.' Consider the populist politics that are polarizing opinion, the decoupling of the US-Chinese tech sector, Brexit, the lack of action on climate change, and growing global inequity (witness the collective doubling of the wealth of the world's ten richest individuals during the Covid-19 pandemic). All are representative of a global movement of egoic resistance, and all because the world is changing in a way that is increasingly outside of our control. The ego seeks to assert a dominant role in a world that is fast outpacing it.

In the next chapter we will explore how SPIN can improve our understanding of egoic and non-egoic preferences, as a new framework for cognitive bias.

13. SPIN – CODIFICATION FOR COGNITIVE BIAS

If consciousness is described as infinite potentiality, then experience is the manifestation of finite actuality, or to put it simpler still, *preference*. Our experience – that which we perceive and conceive – arises as an expression of preference. It is the appearance of one thing by virtue of the other, and is inherent to all experience. More information on our preferences is provided in the 5th Law of Attention: attention is an expression of preference (Chapter 7).

SPIN describes how a perceptual loop gives rise to experience through the operation of four dynamic states of attention (Singularity, Personality, Instituted, and Neoteric), as a perpetual flow of attention. As such, it provides a basis for the recodification of our preferences and cognitive biases that describe how experience gains and is shaped by our attention.

The model is framed around these four states of attention:

- **State 1 – Singularity:** Toward basal form, the distinguishing of finitude and difference within experience – the resolution of fidelity
- **State 2 – Personality:** Toward the identification of self, as the responsible author of experience, through the appearance of an individual 'me' – the ego
- **State 3 – Instituted:** Toward the identification with others, as a collective egoic expression through shared endeavours that enable more complex and contingent activity – the meta-ego
- **State 4 – Neoteric:** Toward new forms – the discernment of complexity toward patterns and the emergence of novel, simpler arrangements

The model provides a new categorization for more than 160 cognitive biases (these being representative rather than exhaustive) across 32 categories, including a new classification of egoic biases that describe the preference of Personality (State 2) as described through egodynamics (Chapter 8). SPIN presents an inclusive, whole-system approach that is congruent with the Principle of Totality, described by Gestalt psychology: that conscious experience must be considered holistically (by taking into account all the physical and mental aspects of the individual simultaneously) with each component considered as part of a system of dynamic relationships.

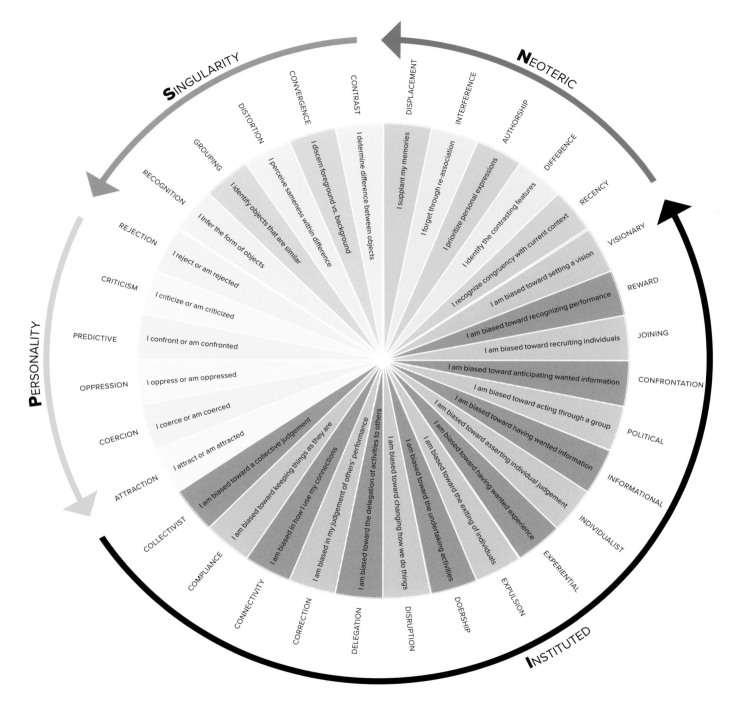

FIG 36 – SPIN CODIFICATION OF COGNITIVE BIASES

STATE 1 – SINGULARITY

The perception of specificity within form, through the resolution of individual objects within experience (objectivization), is possible through five types of cognitive discrimination, with each reflecting simultaneously a faculty and a cognitive bias. They are all aspects of locality – being able to localize and specify form within current experience:

1. **Grouping:** Identifying objects that are similar
2. **Recognition:** Inferring the form of objects
3. **Contrast:** Determining difference between objects
4. **Convergence:** Discerning foreground versus background
5. **Distortion:** Perceiving sameness within difference

1. Grouping:

The perception of discrete objects in experience must first start with the categorization of those characteristics that make it a 'thing' as apposed to a different 'thing.' The first consideration is the relationship with other objects in space. The Gestalt Law of Proximity[1] explains how things that are close together appear to be more related than things that are spaced farther apart. For example, in Fig 37 there are 36 circles, but we perceive the collection of circles in groups. Specifically, we perceive that there is a group of 18 circles on the left side of the image and three groups of six circles on the right side of the image.

1. Wertheimer, M. (1938). Gestalt theory. In W. D. Ellis (Ed.), *A Source Book of Gestalt Psychology* (1-11). New York, NY: Harcourt.

FIG 37 – LAW OF PROXIMITY[1]

We also group objects together that are proximal to each other and appear to be similar (known as Gestalt's Law of Similarity). This similarity of function can occur in the form of shape, colour, shading or other qualities. For example, Fig 38 shows 14 triangles and 35 circles. We perceive the circles grouped together, separate from the triangles.

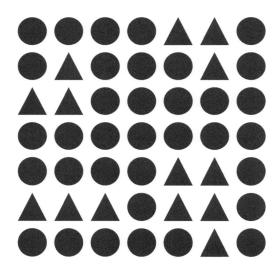

FIG 38 – LAW OF SIMILARITY[1]

In Gestalt psychology, the principle of perceptual grouping is referred to as the Law of Prägnanz[2] and explains our tendency to notice order, symmetry and simplicity, or as the psychologist Kurt Koffka notes, *"Of several geometrically possible organizations that one will actually occur which possesses the best, simplest and most stable shape."*[3] The law's implication is that perception requires the elimination of complexity and unfamiliarity in order to observe reality in its simplest form, to create our *model of the world*. It is the most fundamental of our preferences, and the basis by which the mind creates meaning – the implication of a global regularity. It reflects the brain's evolutionary adaptation

2. Eysenck, Michael W. (2006). *Fundamentals of Cognition.* Hove, UK: Psychology Press. pp. 62–64. ISBN 978-1-84169-374-3.

3. Koffka, K. (1935). *Principles of Gestalt Psychology.* New York: Harcourt, Brace. Retrieved 2019-10-13.

to processing multiple sources of information in an instant. Perception is essentially a time-saving (and therefore energy-saving) device. We can subconsciously process a huge amount of sensory information every second. Estimates of our subconscious processing capacity vary between 20,000 and 11 million bits per second (bps). However, our capacity for cognitive control (conscious selection and prioritization of information with regard to attention, decision-making, perception, motion and language) is far less – around 40 bps, with some research suggesting as low as just 3–4bps.[4]

The brain's shortcuts are therefore many, and unavoidable. The threshold of our visual awareness is 10 frames per second (which we recreate in our movie cameras). We observe the world through a metaphorical zoetrope, and as objects speed up, they appear less distinct, and ultimately disappear from view.

Grouping also confers similarity on those objects within our point of attention. For example, in Fig 39, the triangles in a group of triangles can appear to point in different directions at different times, but triangles close to each other always seem to point in the same direction at the same time, and appear to flip direction when those near them do. Our attention has direction – the triangles in close proximity have no choice but to follow the same line of attention.

4. *The Capacity of Cognitive Control Estimated from a Perceptual Decision-Making Task* (2016) Tingting Wu, Alexander J. Dufford, Melissa-Ann Mackie, Laura J. Egan & Jin Fan.

FIG 39 – TRIANGLES IN CLOSE PROXIMITY POINT IN THE SAME DIRECTION

2. Recognition

Closure: There are a number of ways in which we recognize objects in experience. The first is our ability to infer form where form does not exist. In Gestalt psychology, this is referred to as the Law of Closure.[5] The result is that the form that is incomplete in its delineation is perceived as whole. The act of recognition fills in the gaps, so that in Fig 40 we might recognize a circle, a triangle and a square where none exist.

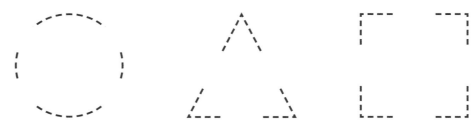

FIG 40 – LAW OF CLOSURE[5]

Individuals perceive objects such as shapes, letters, etc., as being whole when they are not complete, and our perception fills in the visual gap. Psychologist Richard Gregory's top-down processing theory[6] posits perception as a constructive process that relies on using stored knowledge to make up the picture that we see. Indeed, given the amount of information the brain receives, and the amount of processing required, our vision of the world actually runs 100 milliseconds behind the real world. The brain predicts where the ball is going to be when you swing the bat. And what you're seeing right now has already happened.

5. Brennan, James F.; Houde, Keith A. (2017-10-26). *History and Systems of Psychology*. Cambridge University Press, 7th Edition (2017).

6. Gregory, R. (1970). *The Intelligent Eye*. London: Weidenfeld and Nicolson.

Symmetry: We also recognize – that is, we look for and expect to see – symmetry. According to the Gestalt Law of Symmetry, we perceive symmetry forming around a centre point, such that we can divide objects into symmetrical parts that can be grouped together to form a coherent, symmetrical whole. It is for this reason that we use brackets to group our words together, and which explains why we observe two pairs of symmetrical brackets in Fig 41 rather than four individual ones.

FIG 41 – LAW OF SYMMETRY[1]

Filling in: A third aspect of recognition is the phenomenon of *perceptual filling-in*[7] – described by Gestalt psychology as the Principle of Reification, a constructive aspect of perception by which the percept emerges through its illusory contours. The Kanisza Triangle[8] is an example of this – we perceive two triangles obscuring three black circles, even though none of these shapes are actually present. Our perceptual system effectively rejects the coincidence of their symmetrical arrangement.

7. Kanizsa, G (1955), Margini quasi-percettivi in campi con stimolazione omogenea. *Rivista di Psicologia,* 49 (1): 7–30.

FIG 42 – KANISZA TRIANGLE[7]

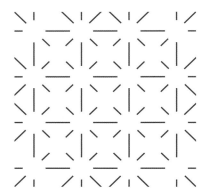

FIG 43 – EHRENSTEIN FIGURE[8]

Similarly, in the Ehrenstein Figure[8] (Fig 43), we perceive circles between the lines that are brighter than the surrounding area, such that the lines appear occluded by them.

FIG 44 – THE MIRAGE OF THE SELF AMONG THOUGHTS

8. Ehrenstein, W. (1941). Über Abwandlungen der L. Hermannschen Helligkeitserscheinung [Modifications of the brightness phenomenon of L. Hermann]. *Zeitschrift für Psychologie: Organ der Deutschen Gesellschaft für Psychologie*, 150, 83–91.

Perceptual filling becomes more pronounced through the phenomenon of 'colour spreading.' The ego is an act of active inference – our sense of separate self a perceptual filling in. In Fig 44 we see the crisscrossed web of our thoughts and beliefs, held taut against our perception of time and space, within which is revealed the independent entity of self. Look closely, and of course no such independent entity exists.

3. Contrast

Contrast is important for the perception of spatial awareness, which is relative. This is demonstrated by the Titchener Circles[9] (Fig 45), in which the two blue circles appear at first glance to be different sizes, when in fact they are the same size.

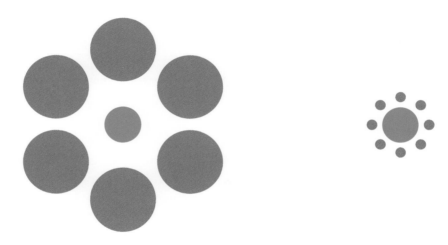

FIG 45 – TITCHENER CIRCLES[9]

9. *A Dictionary of Psychology* (3 ed.), Andrew M Colman, Oxford University Press (2008).

10. L. Wittgenstein. Remarks on the Philosophy of Psychology, Vol. I and Vol. II. Oxford, Blackwell, 1980.

11. Ueber eine optische Inversion bei Betrachtung verkehrter, durch optische Vorrichtung entworfener, physischer Bilder. In: *Annalen der Physik und Chemie, Band 181, Joh. Ambr. Barth, Leipzig,* 1858, p. 298.

4. Convergence

Convergence is the bringing of an object into the foreground of our attention, thereby creating the background in which the object can be held in relief – either through a *perspectival switch*, or through *occlusion*. A perspectival switch, or Gestalt Switch,[10] reflects our tendency to switch involuntarily between alternative perceptual interpretations. In Gestalt terms, it describes the principle of *multistability* (or multistable perception). Schroeder's stairs[11] (Fig 46) are an example, whereby it is possible to view the stairs appearing the right way up, or upside down. The switch happens from a subtle change in attention – whether you focus on A or B in the foreground of experience.

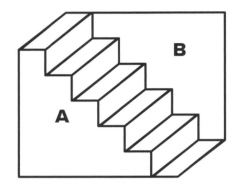

FIG 46 – SCHROEDER'S STAIRS[11]

The second type of convergence is a form of occlusion in which only one perspective is apparent, resulting in what has been coined 'change blindness.' Most people believe that as long as we walk around with our eyes open, then we'll notice when something changes in our experience. However, the reality is that in the focussing of attention, our range of our awareness diminishes to a myopic perspective. This principle of *selective attention* is described by psychologists Christopher Chabris and Daniel Simons in their book, *The Invisible Gorilla*.[12] In their movie perception test, subjects were asked to watch a film of a small group passing a basketball between them, and to count how many passes they made. Although most test subjects were able to accurately count the number of passes, a far smaller proportion spotted the gorilla that strode through the middle of the group during the scene.

At its root, change blindness is the necessity to filter out large amounts of information from our experience. As the point of our attention gains greater resolution and certainty, so too it discriminates against and occludes an ever-increasing periphery of experience. The price of seeing clearly is, in effect, blindness. In fact, this occlusion is an active process. Fixate on the centre dot in Fig 47 and you will notice that the peripheral ring disappears. The ring is replaced with an experience, the nature of which is determined by the background that the object is on.

12. Chabris, C. & Simons, D. (2011). *The Invisible Gorilla: And Other Ways Our Intuition Deceives Us*. (New Edition). Harper Collins.

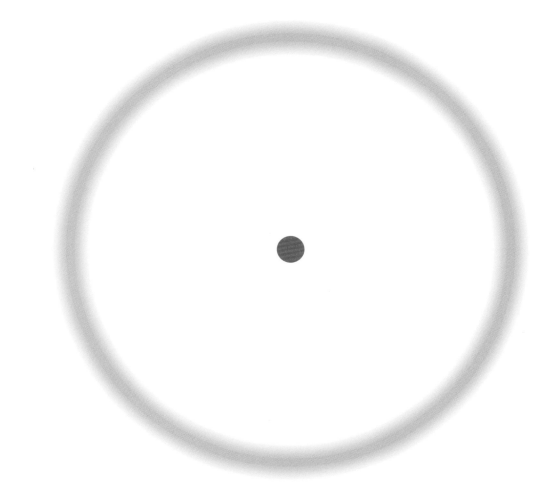

FIG 47 – TROXLER-EFFECT[13]

13. Troxler, D. (I. P. V.). (1804). K. Himly & J. A. Schmidt (Eds.) Über das Verschwinden gegebener Gegenstände innerhalb unseres Gesichtskreises [On the disappearance of given objects from our visual field]. *Ophthalmologische Bibliothek* (in German), 2(2), 1–53.

This is known as the Troxler-Effect[13] and is another example of perceptual filling-in. Similarly, we might consider drawing an analogy with the mind's obsessional focus on understanding, and the attention we give through our enquiry to answers. In so doing, our tendency is to give little attention to that which frames it – the question itself – which might tell us far more about the thing we think we're looking for in the first place. Every answer we seek is based on a set of assumptions on which the question is based. The question "where are you in this room?" implies that: (1) I am in this room; (2) I have a location (in space); (3) I am here now (in time); (4) There is a room; (5) I actually exist. Surfacing these assumptions can change not just our interpretation, but what we discover as a result.

5. Distortion

The Gestalt term *invariance* describes our ability to recognize objects regardless of their rotation, distortion and scale. This allows us, for example, to recognize the reflection of one object in another. And yet, would it be possible to perceive something that did not change? Our experience is perceived through the dimensions of space and time, and consequently is one of perpetual change. The result is that nothing stands still, and that 'stillness' is relative. Because our experience is always changing, nothing ever looks the same twice.

In the 1940s and 1950s, laboratory research undertaken into the vision of frogs indicated that perception and motion were intrinsically linked. The researchers reported the following:

> *A frog hunts on land by vision ... He has no fovea, or region of greatest acuity in vision, upon which he must centre a part of the image ... The frog does not seem to see or, at any rate, is not concerned with the detail of stationary parts of the world around him. He will starve to death surrounded by food if it is not moving. His choice of food is determined only by size and movement. He will leap to capture any object the size of an insect or worm, providing it moves like one. He can be fooled easily not only by a piece of dangled meat but by any moving small object ... He does remember a moving thing provided it stays within his field of vision and he is not distracted.*[14]

> *The lowest-level concepts related to visual perception for a human being probably differ little from the concepts of a frog. In any case, the structure of the retina in mammals and in human beings is the same as in amphibians ... When a person looks at an immobile object, 'fixes' it with his eyes, the eyeballs do not remain absolutely immobile; they make small involuntary movements. As a result, the image of the object on the retina is constantly in motion, slowly drifting and jumping back to the point of maximum sensitivity. The image 'marks time' in the vicinity of this point.*[15]

Fig 48 provides a list of the cognitive biases that pertain to the Singularity state, as a function of SPIN (Fig 36).

14. Lettvin, J.Y., Maturana, H.R., Pitts, W.H., and McCulloch, W.S. (1961). *Two Remarks on the Visual System of the Frog.* In Sensory Communication edited by Walter Rosenblith, MIT Press and John Wiley and Sons: New York.

15. Turchin, V. F. (1977). *The phenomenon of science – a cybernetic approach to human evolution.* Columbia University Press.

TYPE	EXAMPLE BIAS	DESCRIPTION
Contrast: I determine difference between objects	Salience bias	I focus on those items that are most prominent or emotionally striking.
	Contrast effect	I perceive a reduction or enhancement of an object's quality when compared with another contrasting object.
	Distinction bias	I view two options as more dissimilar when considering them simultaneously than separately.
Convergence: I discern foreground vs. background	Attentional bias	I give attention to those things that I am thinking about most.
Distortion: I perceive sameness within difference	Frequency illusion or Baader–Meinhof phenomenon	I perceive something to occur frequently having seen it once, although the frequency has not changed.
	Selection bias	I notice the recurrence of something more as I become more aware of it, although the frequency has not changed.
Grouping: I identify objects that are similar	Mere exposure effect or familiarity principle	I prefer things that I am familiar with.
Recognition: I Infer the form of objects	Default effect	I prefer the default option when choosing between several options.

FIG 48 – LIST OF COGNITIVE BIASES FOR THE SINGULARITY STATE

STATE 2 – PERSONALITY

Fig 49 provides a list of the cognitive biases that pertain to the Personality state, as a function of SPIN (Fig 36). The interrelationship of the different 'personalities of ego' and their according egoic preferences are described in Chapter 8. The 32 distinct persona-based egoic biases are categorized across six chapters, as defined within the Egodynamics Wheel: Rejection; Criticism; Confrontation; Oppression; Coercion; Attraction. Their presentation is context-centric, based on the egoic need within that situation, and which form the basis of all habituative egoic behaviours for each persona.

TYPE	EXAMPLE BIAS	DESCRIPTION
Rejection: I reject or am rejected	Beloved (int. locus of control)	You want me to get what I want.
	Love (ext. locus of control)	I want you to get what you want.
	Relief	I didn't lose what I have.
	Admiration	You didn't lose what you have.
	Dismissive	You don't have what I want.
	Shame	I don't have what you want.
Criticism: I criticize or am criticized	Critical	I can't get what I want from you.
	Guilt	You can't get what you want from me.
	Insulted	You are not the one that can give me what I want.
	Rejected	I am not the one that can give you what you want.
	Anger	I am being stopped from getting what I want by you.
	Defensive	You are being stopped from getting what you want by me.
Confrontation: I confront or am confronted	Antagonism	You couldn't stop me getting what I wanted.
	Jealousy	I couldn't stop you getting what you wanted.
	Self-grandeur	I got what I wanted.
	Self-pity	You got what you wanted.
	Superior	You gave me what I wanted.
	Inferior	I gave you what you wanted.
Oppression: I oppress or am oppressed	Oppressive	I gave you what you didn't want.
	Disgust	You gave me what I didn't want.
	Schadenfreude	You didn't get what you wanted.
	Despair	I didn't get what I wanted.
	Contempt	I stopped you from getting what you wanted.
	Dejection	You stopped me from getting what I wanted.
Coercion: I coerce or am coerced	Controlling	You are being helped to get what you want by me.
	Submission	I am being helped to get what I want by you.
	Coercion	I am the only one that can give you what you want.
	Dependence	You are the only one that can give me what I want.
	Desired	You can get what you want from me.
	Adoration	I can get what I want from you.
Attraction: I attract or am attracted	Vanity	I have what you want.
	Envy	You have what I want.
	Pity	You lost what you had.
	Grief	I lost what I had.
	Love (int. locus of control)	I want you to get what you want.
	Beloved (ext. locus of control)	You want me to get what I want.

FIG 49 – LIST OF COGNITIVE BIASES FOR THE PERSONALITY STATE

The intrinsic difference between egoic and non-egoic preference is in the masking of emotions. Every feeling that the ego feels is an attempt to mask (resist) an underlying emotion that experience has provided for it. The ego belies a feeling that we are unable to express. Where there is ego, there is suppression of emotion. In contrast, an individual who does not possess an ego could feel all the emotions described in the Egodynamics Wheel, but in the absence of any presumed authorship, will accept and express them fully and unconditionally, without labelling them, such that the governing thoughts of ego are unlikely to arise. The egoic masking of emotions that dictate egoic preference can be multilayered, so that getting to the route of their motivation can be difficult. For example, an ego suffering from grief or loss may, in resistance, become increasingly angry, in their pursuit of retribution and blame (self-authorship presuming authorship and therefore responsibility in others), before turning to despair through increasing isolation, with the masking of emotions resulting in increasingly high SIs (Fig 50).

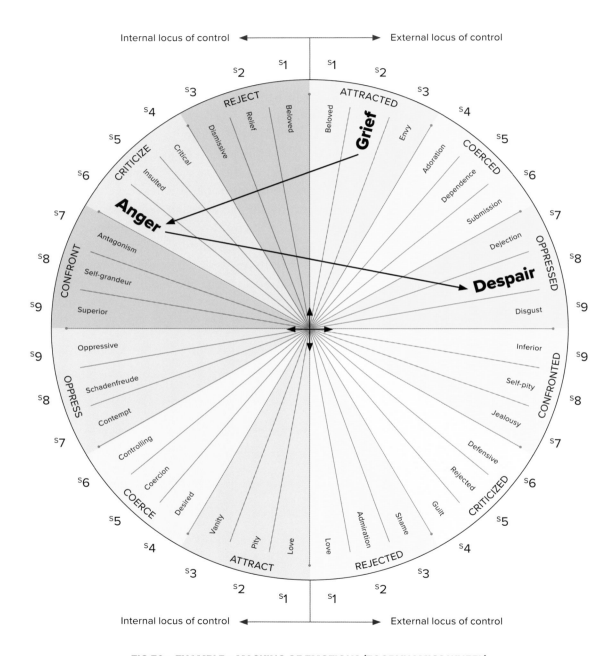

Internal locus of control ← → External locus of control

FIG 50 – EXAMPLE – MASKING OF EMOTIONS (EGODYNAMICS WHEEL)

In time, through continued resistance, the shift is toward emotions of increasing SI, through an increasing sense of separation. Typically (but not always) this would be in the direction of their originating locus of control (internal or external). To the ego, one's identification with these emotions, as their motivation and purpose, is why we can become so strongly attached to what we feel, and why one definition of ego could be *'that which is addicted to suffering.'*

It is not until the ego 'gives up' and is able to accept an emotion that an awareness of the underlying emotion is made possible. This 'processing' is often described by those that have lost their sense of self as *moments of truth*, as powerful emotions come to light that were previously, through resistance, outside of conscious awareness, but always there, determining their course of action for them.

The ego is like the shadow you cast when you stand back from experience, and in darkness obscures the emotion you seek to distance yourself from. The ego calls the emotion unbearable, but it is the resistance to the emotion that makes experience unbearable. Strategies (such as resilience) that describe a process of resistance or tolerance are inherently egoic, however societally accepted, heroic or well intentioned they may appear to be.

The ego believes *'I am what I feel'* and identifies strongly with what they like, and what they don't. We can be afraid of what we like (and judge ourselves accordingly) because we are what we like, just as we are afraid of what we fear because we are what we fear. Like the princess in the story *The Frog Prince*,[16] in which she loses her coveted golden ball – that which she presumes to be her preference – and can only reclaim it on the promise that she kiss a lowly, detestable frog. The fairy tale shows us that it is only through embracing that which we loathe the most (in this case the eponymous frog) that we will discover what we truly love. Whether that's a prince or a frog.

STATE 3 – INSTITUTED

The meta-ego of the Evil Genius Organization arises through the identification of 'I' with 'we' – the collective, comparative identification of self as a shared, institutionalized expression. It is the belief that I belong to something other than myself. Fig 51 provides a list of the cognitive biases as pertain to the 16 classifications of power dynamic for the Instituted state, as a function of SPIN (Fig 36). Each egoic bias operates as a collective expression across each of the Second-Order Power Dynamics (discussed in Chapter 11).

[16] Grimm, J. & Grimm, W. (1812). *The Frog Prince (from Grimm's Fairy Tales).* CreateSpace Independent Publishing Platform.

TYPE	EXAMPLE BIAS	DESCRIPTION
Collectivist moral power: I am biased toward the assertion of a collective judgement	Availability cascade	We find greater plausibility in that which is repeated through public discourse.
	Bandwagon effect	I do and believe in those things that many others do or believe in.
	Courtesy bias	I provide an opinion that I consider socially acceptable but is not necessarily what I think, so as not to offend.
	Groupthink	I minimize conflict within a group by prioritizing consensus over the critical evaluation of alternative and dissenting opinions.
	Illusion of transparency	I overestimate the degree to which my personal mental state is known by others, and overestimate how well I understand the mental states of others.
	Outgroup homogeneity bias	I perceive members of my group to be more varied than they are.
	Group attribution error	I believe that the characteristics of an individual group member is reflective of the group as a whole, so that decisions reflect the preferences of the group.
	Spotlight effect	I overestimate the amount that other people notice my appearance, and will hold off from sharing my views.
Compliance power: I am biased toward keeping things as they are	Conservatism bias	I tend to stick to my views, and do not revise my beliefs adequately when presented with new evidence.
	Status quo bias	I like to keep things the same.
	Change blindness	I do not perceive changes taking place.
	Dread aversion	I perceive more harm from losing than can be gained from winning.
	System justification	I prefer the status quo, even at the expense of the collective interest.
	Plan continuation bias	I would rather stick to a plan than change it, even in the face of changing conditions.
	Normalcy bias	I refuse to plan for or react to a disaster that has never happened before.
	Escalation of commitment	I continue to invest in a plan of action despite new evidence suggesting it's a bad idea, owing to all the previous investments to date.
	Declinism	I tend to view the past favourably and the future negatively - I favour what I know.
Connection power: I am biased in how I use my connections	Affinity bias/Similarity bias	I tend to connect with those with whom I share a similar background, experiences and interests.
	Authority bias	I give more credence and will be more influenced by those in authority, irrespective of the content.
	Cross-race effect	I have difficulty identifying with members outside of my race.

FIG 51 – LIST OF COGNITIVE BIASES FOR THE INSTITUTED STATE

TYPE	EXAMPLE BIAS	DESCRIPTION
Corrective power: I am biased in my judgement of others' performance	Omission bias	I judge harmful actions as worse and less moral than equally harmful inactions.
	Horns effect	I tend to vilify an individual as a result of a single negative trait.
	Hostile attribution bias	I interpret others' behaviour as having hostile intent.
	Intentionality bias	I tend to perceive human action to be intentional rather than accidental.
	Ultimate attribution error	I attribute positive behaviours in my group to personality, but to those outside my group down to their situation.
	Defensive attribution hypothesis	I attribute more blame to a harm-doer as the impact of their actions worsens, or as I perceive myself to be a comparable victim.
	Illusory superiority/superiority bias/better-than-average effect	I overestimate my desirable qualities and underestimate my undesirable qualities.
	Pygmalion effect	I perceive that increasing expectations on my performance will improve my performance.
Delegatory power: I am biased toward the delegation of activities to others	Ben Franklin effect	I perceive that an individual that has done me a favour will more likely do me another favour as long as I don't do one for them.
	Egocentric bias	I claim more responsibility to the success of a joint action than an outside observer would credit me for.
	Automation bias	I depend excessively on automated systems, leading to erroneous information overriding correct decisions.
Disruptive power: I am biased toward changing how we do things	Social cryptomnesia	I tend to remember the origin of a change, but not how it occurred.
	Reactance	I prefer to do the opposite of what is asked of me in order to avoid a perceived attempt to constrain my freedom of choice.
	Novelty logical fallacy	I prematurely prefer new ideas to older ones, solely because they are new and modern.
	Chronological snobbery	I believe the past (such as its art, science, people etc.) is inherently inferior to the present.
	Travis syndrome	I overestimate the significance of the present, relative to the past
Doer ship power: I am biased toward the undertaking of designated activities	Law of the instrument	I rely on a familiar tool or method to solve all my problems, ignoring alternatives – this hammer will fix anything!
	IKEA effect	I place a disproportionally high value on the activities I have undertaken myself, regardless of the quality of the end product.
	Placement bias	I tend to recall my performance as better than others in those where I rate myself superior, and recall myself as lower than average for tasks where I rate myself as inferior.

TYPE	EXAMPLE BIAS	DESCRIPTION
Exiting power: I am biased toward the exiting of individuals	Compassion fade	I behave compassionately toward a small number of identifiable victims than to a large number of anonymous ones.
	Zero-sum thinking	I perceive all situations as zero-sum gains (someone has to lose and someone has to win).
	Just-world hypothesis	I want to believe that the world is fundamentally just, and rationalise inexplicable injustices as deserved by the victims.
	Endowment effect	I would need to be paid much more to give up something I own, compared with the price I would be prepared to pay to acquire it.
	Loss aversion	I perceive a greater disutility of giving up something I own than that utility gained from acquiring it.
Experiential power: I am biased toward having wanted experience	Congruence bias	I prefer to test my hypotheses through experiments that confirm my beliefs than through experiments/alternatives that could disprove them.
	Hot hand phenomenon	I believe that an individual that was successful due to a random event has a greater chance of success as a result.
	Dunning–Kruger effect	I overestimate my abilities for activities where I am unskilled, and underestimate my abilities for activities where I am an expert.
	Negativity bias	I have a greater recall of unpleasant memories compared with positive memories.
	Positivity effect (socioemotional selectivity theory)	I pay greater attention to positive rather than negative memories, the older I get.
Individualist power: I am biased toward the assertion of an individual ethical judgement	Social desirability bias	I tend to over-report socially desirable aspects in myself, and under-report socially undesirable characteristics in myself.
	Empathy gap	I tend to underestimate the strength of feeling in others, when what they feel is different to myself.
	Actor-observer bias/ fundamental attribution error	I perceive the behaviours of others to be due to their personality, but perceive my behaviours to be due to my situation.
	Moral luck	I ascribe greater or lesser moral standing to individuals based on the outcome of their actions.
	Puritanical bias	I attribute the cause of wrongdoing by an individual to a moral deficiency, rather than considering broader societal possibilities.
	Bias blind spot	I believe I am less biased than other people, and able to identify more cognitive biases in other people than in myself.
	False consensus effect	I overestimate the degree to which other people agree with me.
	False uniqueness bias	I see my projects and myself as more singular and different than they actually are.
	Naïve cynicism	I expect more egocentric bias in others than in myself.
	Naïve realism	I believe I am not biased, that I see reality objectively, that the facts are plain to see, and those that disagree are uninformed, irrational or biased.
	Trait ascription bias	I believe I have a varied personality and set of behaviours, but that others are much more predictable.

TYPE	EXAMPLE BIAS	DESCRIPTION
Informational power: I am biased toward having wanted information	Pseudo certainty effect	I make decisions in the belief that I have more control over future events than I actually do, and that the future is more predictable than it really is.
	Anchoring bias	I rely too heavily on one piece of information when making decisions – usually the first.
	Confirmation bias	I search for, interpret and remember information in a way that confirms my preconceptions, ignoring contrary information.
	Curse of knowledge	I (as a more informed person) find it difficult to think about problems from the perspective of lesser-informed people.
	Information bias	I seek out more information than I need to make decisions, believing it will lead to a better decision.
	Surrogation	I lose sight of the strategic purpose that my performance target represents, so that I equate my performance target with the strategic outcome.
	Shared information bias	I prefer to spend more time and energy discussing information with a group that they are familiar with, than on information that only some are aware of.
	Google effect	I tend to forget information that can be readily found online.
	Spacing effect	I recall information better if I am exposed to it over a longer time span than in a shorter one.
Political power: I am biased toward acting through a group	Cheerleader effect	I find that people appear more attractive in a group than in isolation.
	Illusion of asymmetric insight	I believe I know more about my peers than they know about me.
	Reactive devaluation	I devalue proposals that arise from an adversary.
	Social comparison bias	I favour candidates who do not compete with my own strengths.
Predictive power: I am biased toward anticipating wanted information	Clustering illusion (an apophenia)	I overestimate the importance of small runs, streaks or clusters in data – I see patterns that do not exist.
	Illusory correlation (an apophenia)	I perceive a relationship between two unrelated events when no relationship exists.
	Pareidolia (an apophenia)	I perceive a random stimulus as significant – I see animals in clouds.
	Semmelweis reflex	I reject new evidence that contradicts a paradigm – I find it easier to disprove something new.
	Gambler's fallacy	I believe future possibilities are altered by past events, despite the fact that the probability of each event is always the same.
	Attribute substitution	I tend to substitute a computationally complex question with a simpler one, resulting in an incorrect answer.
	Non-adaptive choice switching	I will avoid making the same decision twice, having been burned by my previous attempt (even though the two are unrelated) - 'once bitten, twice shy.'
	Illusion of validity	I overestimate my ability to interpret and predict the outcome when analysing data, when it appears to show a consistent pattern.
	Parkinson's law of triviality	I prefer to focus my time resolving simple trivial issues than on important complex ones – I avoid the hard questions.

TYPE	EXAMPLE BIAS	DESCRIPTION
Joining power: I am biased toward the recruitment of individuals	Survivorship bias	I am more aware and give more time and attention to those that passed our selection process.
	Name bias	I prefer some people's names over others, and prefer these people as a result.
	Not invented here	I do not like to buy in to products, knowledge or ideas from outside this group – I prefer our own.
Reward power: I am biased toward the recognition of good performance	Selective perception	I pay attention to those observations and judgements about an individual that confirm my view, and forget those that don't and cause me emotional discomfort.
	Halo effect	I tend to form an overall positive impression of an individual as a result of a single positive trait, putting them on a pedestal.
	Self-serving bias	I claim more responsibility for successes than failures.
	Ingroup bias	I give preferential treatment to others I perceive to be members of my group.
	Worse-than-average effect	I believe I am worse than others at tasks that I find difficult.
Visionary power: I am biased toward setting a vision that inspires others	Picture superiority effect	I find it easier to learn and recall concepts from pictures than the written word.
	Illusory truth effect	I believe a statement is more likely to be true if it is easier to process, or if it has been stated multiple times.
	Anecdotal fallacy	I find anecdotes (stories) provide more compelling evidence to support an argument than facts.
	Saying is believing effect	I believe what I hear others talk about, as if I had come up with it myself.
	Anthropomorphism	I tend to attribute emotions to inanimate objects - clouds seem angry, my computer looks tired.

STATE 4 – NEOTERIC

The perception of complex associations within experience (patternization) is possible through five types of cognitive discrimination, with each again reflecting simultaneously a faculty and a cognitive bias. They are all aspects of memory – this being the perceived developmental process by which complexity is rendered (actualized in the present) out of simplicity (the potentiality of the past).

1. **Interference:** Forgetting through re-association
2. **Difference:** Identifying the contrasting features
3. **Recency:** Recognizing congruency with current context
4. **Authorship:** Prioritizing personal expressions
5. **Displacement:** Supplanting of memory

Fig 52 provides a list of the cognitive biases that pertain to the Neoteric state, as a function of SPIN (Fig 36).

TYPE	EXAMPLE BIAS	DESCRIPTION
Displacement: I supplant my memories	Cryptomnesia	I believe what was a memory is in fact my imagination, as I can't remember such an event.
	False memory	I believe that what I imagined is in fact a memory.
	Suggestibility	I believe the ideas suggested by a third party are in fact my memory.
Interference: I forget through re-association	Misinformation effect	I perceive my memories to become less accurate the more I recall them.
	Tip-of-the-tongue phenomenon	I can only recall part of an item but not the whole, such as the first letter of a name.
	Part-list cueing effect	I find it harder to recall items from a list when I have previously remembered and recalled a single item from the list.
	Zeigarnik effect	I remember incomplete or interrupted tasks better than completed ones.
Authorship: I prioritize personal expressions	Processing difficulty effect	I find it easier to remember information that I spend longer reading, processing and thinking through.
	Self-relevance effect	I recall memories relating to self better than those with similar information relating to others.
	Testing effect	I remember information I have read better after I have rewritten it, instead of rereading it.
	Generation effect (self-generation effect)	I remember self-generated information better.
	Choice-supportive bias	I remember my choices as better than they actually were.
	Egocentric bias	I recall the past in a self-serving manner that makes me look better than I really am.
Difference: I identify the contrasting features	Stereotypical bias	I remember stereotypes more easily (e.g. around race or gender).
	Bizarreness effect	I remember bizarre material better than standard material.
	Humour effect	I recall humorous information better than non-humorous ones.
	Levelling and sharpening	I recall memories over time with increasing generality punctuated with increasing sharpening and selective recollection of specific details that take on greater significance.
	Peak–end rule	I remember not the sum of an experience, but how it was at its peak (pleasant or unpleasant) and how it ended.
	Serial position effect	I recall items toward the end of a sequence and at the beginning better than those in the middle.
	Von Restorff effect	I remember items that stand out better than other items.
	Verbatim effect	I remember the 'gist' of what someone said better than a verbatim record.
Recency: I recognize congruency with current context	Availability bias	I believe that those items I can recall must be important - I therefore rely more heavily on recent events to inform current action.
	Consistency bias	I incorrectly remember my past attitudes as resembling my present attitudes.
	Context effect	I remember events that resemble my current context better than those that don't.
	Mood-congruent memory bias	I recall information better that is reflective of my current mood.
	Telescoping effect	I displace recent events backwards in time, and remote events forward in time – so that recent events seem longer ago, and remote events more recent.

FIG 52 – LIST OF COGNITIVE BIASES FOR THE NEOTERIC STATE

14. PERSPECTIVAL DEVELOPMENT

In this chapter we will explore Perspectival Development, a new approach to improving individual performance. For this we will introduce the concepts of *preference receptivity* and *sensory perceptivity*, in two parts:

- **PART 1 – PRINCIPLES:** An explanation of the approach and its six key principles
- **PART 2 – PRACTICES:** How to put Perspectival Development into practice

PART 1 – KEY PRINCIPLES

1 – Redefining learning

There are only two things we can learn in life that will improve our ability to meaningfully change our experience, and thereby our performance: (1) Non-egoic preference; (2) Perceptivity. A third aspect, affective resonance, will be discussed later in this chapter.

1. **Preference Receptivity:** Non-egoic preference is not just what we like and don't like, but also our receptiveness and openness to all experience. By understanding our non-egoic preferences, we can learn how to express and share that which we love, and to be open and receptive to all experience. Your preferences cannot be changed, but you can learn what they are, distinguishing non-egoic from egoic.
2. **Sensory Perceptivity:** Perceptivity is the sensory acuity by which we can discern our environment. Through perceptivity, we are able to resolve experience down to the fundamental aspects required to unlock performance and, through preference, we are motivated to act.

It is the development of both preference receptivity and sensory perceptivity that leads to increased performance, both aspects being interdependent with the other. Sensory perceptivity cannot be fully developed in the absence of non-egoic preference, and expression through non-egoic preference cannot be fully realized without sensory perceptivity.

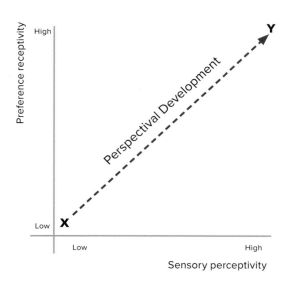

FIG 53 – PERSPECTIVAL DEVELOPMENT

This direct relationship (as shown in Fig 53) pertains to how we learn. The purpose of learning is to seek progress along this path, from X to Y – the process of 'Perspectival Development.' It is fortunately (but also ultimately because of) the inherent nature of consciousness (and thereby ourselves) through creative expression within experience, to progress in this way (in contrast to an entropic decline toward chaos). However, some more traditional approaches to learning act counter to this natural inclination. The conventional definition of learning is: *a sustainable change in behaviour as a result of memory.* The biggest challenge for learning is to sustain behaviour change. The twin aspects of Perspectival Development address this directly, and offer a new definition of learning:

Perspectival Development (learning) = a change in performance as a result of preference and perceptivity

To understand how this works in practice, we need to consider three other factors that influence sensory perceptivity: (a) Perspective Range; (b) Attentional Agility; (c) Reaction Time.

(a) Perspective Range:

Perspective range is the ability to focus your attention. Consider the experience of a new driver. The learner will be overwhelmed with stimuli of indiscriminate intensities. Attention is given to new sensations, and to the thoughts and emotions of anxiety. It can be hard to know what to give attention to, with the result being that they often don't. Compare this with the experience of a Formula 1 driver, who is immersed in their experience, through the collapse of subject and object, which includes their locality – the hands on the steering wheel indiscernible from the subtle vibrations through the suspension, in the absence of resistance. There is a collapse of time, attention on the present, thoughts disregarded (no need to pay attention to anything that cannot be actualized in this moment). All senses are invoked, listening and responding to experience accordingly. There is a heightened sensitivity and ability to discriminate between necessary and unnecessary information. This laser-like focus is a narrowing of the *perspective range*. A telescope necessarily has a low perspective range.

(b) Attentional Agility:

Rather than sensory perspectivity creating a myopic fixation within experience, the narrowing of the perspective range occurs in accordance with an increased sensitivity and ability to rapidly switch attention to what is needed elsewhere – to zoom out, switch lenses – without needing a tap on the shoulder. This dynamic reflex is *attentional agility*. Perceptivity reduces the perspective range and increases attentional agility, both being functions of perceptivity. Fig 54 shows how sensory perceptivity is described by this inverse relationship.

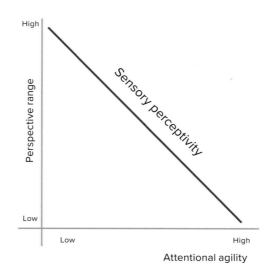

FIG 54 – RELATIONSHIP BETWEEN ATTENTIONAL AGILITY AND PERSPECTIVE RANGE

(c) Reaction Time:

Two factors affect our ability to react:

1. The speed with which we can identify the need to act, determined by both our Perspective Range (our ability to identify a change within experience that requires our action) and our sensory threshold (the minimum level of objective intensity at which we can discern change).
2. Our ability to take action.

While the first aspect determines our speed of response, the second determines whether we are able to respond at all, and has the most significant impact on performance.

2 – Intensity Tolerance

Both Preference Receptivity (our openness to experience) and Sensory Perceptivity (our ability to discern experience) have a directly proportional relationship to the intensity of objective stimulus that can be discerned. Fig 55 below shows the relationship between sensory perceptivity and the objective intensity.

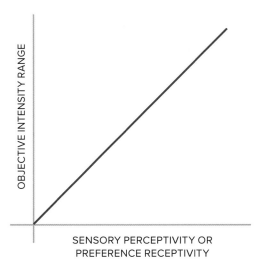

FIG 55 – RELATIONSHIP BETWEEN OBJECTIVE INTENSITY RANGE AND PERSPECTIVAL DEVELOPMENT (PERCEPTIVITY AND RECEPTIVITY)

We can consider the x-axis from both aspects:

1) **Sensory Perceptivity:** At higher levels of sensory perceptivity, there is a wider range of objective intensity that can be discerned:
   - **At higher levels of intensity:** When the music's volume is turned up, we are still able to discern the notes. Imagine trying to find someone in a group of ten people, and then a crowd of 100 – sensory perceptivity means you can still

find what you are looking for. Sensory perceptivity is helpful when playing 'Where's Wally?'

- **At lower levels of intensity:** When the volume is turned down, you are still able to hear the music and discern the notes. This widens the range of objective intensity that you can discern within.

2) **Preference Receptivity:** We could describe our preferences as differences in objective intensity. We like our steak well done or rare, we like our shower at a certain temperature. When our environment is in accordance with our preferences, it's easy to listen and *lean in*. Our preference receptivity allows us to lean in even when our preferences are not being met, and in open acceptance, with greater awareness. It does not change our preferences, but it does mean that, by being more open to experience, we may discover new preferences as we learn and grow. With no resistance, there is no limit to the intensity of experience we can perceive or feel. It is the ego that in resistance can never look directly at its experience – doing so would reveal its absence.

Irrespective of preference, exposure to an abrupt and intense stimulus will trigger a 'startle reflex' – an automatic protective response to prepare for an immediate threat. This fight-or-flight response is a subconscious reaction that occurs through our autonomic nervous system. We're born with different baseline levels of how much we startle, which is closely associated with our sensory threshold (see below). Although our startle response is fixed, the threshold changes according to different stimuli. For example, if you don't like spiders, you're more likely to be startled by one. Similarly, if you've been in a car crash, you're likely to have a heightened startle response in traffic. In human beings, the most common startle response is to blink your eyes. But if a sound is loud enough, you'll also tuck your head in and raise your arms to protect your skull. Note that there is a difference between our reflex response and reaction time. While reflexes such as the startle reflex are involuntary movements to stimuli that cannot be trained into or out of us, our reaction time refers to the voluntary movements that we make consciously.

3 – The potentiality of information

Our thoughts arise from feelings. Conception relies on our faculty of perception. Used in the right way, our concepts can serve to draw our attention back into experience through our senses, rather than taking our attention exclusively to thought. Consider, for example, the naming of trees – the association of 'ash' or 'elm' or 'cedar' to 'leaf,' through the shape of a leaf. Or the naming of birdsong – the association of 'thrush' or 'robin' or 'sparrow' with the sound of its call. An owl's nest, if read properly, speaks to the health of a forest.

In their book, *On Intelligence*, technologist Jeff Hawkins and journalist Sandra Blakeslee wrote that *"for every fibre feeding information forward into the neocortex, there are ten fibres feeding information back toward the senses."*[1] Where most people see an undifferentiated mass of green leaves, an expert bird watcher spots a toucan, three species of parrots and a humming bird.

We can use these labels to direct our attention more fully into experience, like way-points on a map that help the explorer navigate. Crucially, the information needs to be the absolute minimum to direct attention toward perception. Otherwise, our conceptual associations will multiply in the absence of perception, and our attention will be taken toward thought, to the label we attach. We must use the journal to capture our thoughts sparingly. Put simply:

- Minimal information: Leads us back into sensory perception (direct experience)
- Maximum information: Leads us to conceptual association (imagination)

The tendency of the mind is, through thought, to raise questions, and through questions to seek answers. For new ideas, we must allow our attention to relax and turn from our thoughts to our senses and to experience. The reason for this is that all thoughts arise through feeling (perceiving), and so in those 'lost in thought' arises the law of diminishing returns, and the proverbial rabbit hole of wisdom (the conviction that the same thing said differently is somehow new). We must return to experience through our senses for inspiration – our most potent concepts and ideas cannot be summoned by experience, they are revealed spontaneously. In our enquiry, we must treat our questions, our thoughts, like a net: hold it loosely, cast it wide, and you are far more likely to catch new ideas.

1. Hawkins, J & Blakeslee, S. (2005). *On Intelligence: How a New Understanding of the Brain Will Lead to the Creation of Truly Intelligent Machines*. (Reprint Edition). St. Martin's Publishing Group.

The form that this information takes, to direct our attention and for it to have greatest effect in its instructional form, therefore matters. This modality will differ fundamentally depending on whether it points to that which can be provided in the moment (simplicity) or that which must be constructed, through recall and memory (complexity). Fig 56 shows how our approach to learning content necessarily reflects our cognitive preferences or biases (see Chapter 13).

Aspect	Content Type A: Simple Conceptual	Associated Cognitive Bias: Singularity	Content Type B: Complex Conceptual	Associated Cognitive Bias: Neoteric
1	Specificity	Grouping: Discerning objects that are similar	Inconclusive/incomplete (enquiry)	Interference: Forgetting through re-association
2	Distinction	Contrast: Determining difference between objects	Surprise (reaction)	Difference: Identifying the contrasting features
3	Familiarity	Recognition: Inferring the form of objects	Subjectivity (meaning)	Recency: Observing congruency with current context
4	Anchored	Convergence: Identifying foreground vs. background	Customised (personalized)	Authorship: Prioritizing personal expressions
5	Orientation	Distortion: Perceiving sameness within difference	Invention (interpretive)	Displacement: Supplanting of memory

FIG 56 – INFORMATION MODALITIES AND RELATED COGNITIVE BIASES

These heuristic aspects reflect the cognitive ability (or bias) of the mind to most efficiently processes simple and complex information (given their heuristic shortcuts) for its application within sensory experience.

Where simple concepts are required to express within experience, the information is effectively disposable. The journey on the map is one-way, linear (the explorer not seeking a way back). Modalities that will apply here are all examples of short-form, typically visual formats: lists, maps, infographics, flow diagrams.

Where more complex conceptual associations are required, we must turn to memory. Emotions are an important aspect of memory – the modalities for complex associations are therefore designed to evoke an enhanced emotional response, as attention is given more fully to thought. It does not require high levels of application at that moment. Rather, it requires a story, and so modalities that support storytelling will apply here: blogs, video shorts, immersive theatre.

The aspects described for each type are themselves a guiderail for the construction of effective learning content for each. Each aspect can be seen across a spectrum, between the simple (type A) and complex (type B) aspects of conceptualization:

Type A: Simple Conceptual (the Map)	Type B: Complex Conceptual (the Story)
Specificity: A clear distinction and categorization of all aspects, avoiding ambiguity. *On the map, this provides the key.*	**Inconclusive:** An incomplete picture 'in development,' allowing for multiple possibilities and interpretations. *In stories, this engenders enquiry and curiosity.*
Distinction: The use of contrast to provide direction and clarity – what one thing is by what it is not. *On the map, this is the direction or route.*	**Surprise:** The use of contrast to redirect. Data that is unexpected and does not fit with our model of the world. *In stories, this pertains to urgency or peril, and the accordant reaction or response.*
Familiarity: The application and intent is known, without the need to discover it. *On the map, this is its use case – its scope denoted by the different locations.*	**Subjectivity:** Relevance and application is sought through interpretation. *In stories, this translates to purpose and meaning for its characters.*
Anchored: This brings the user to the start, to the most important point of attention. Information is directed. *On the map, it reads "you are here," whoever you are. You are never lost.*	**Customized:** The information is tailored to the individual and cocreated. Understanding is elicited. *In the story, it is the assumed role of reader as the protagonist in the story. It is their prerogative to get lost.*
Orientation: An explicit and literal instruction, seeking a single answer/destination to a single definitive question. *On the map, whichever way you turn it, the destination is clear.*	**Invention:** Conceptual enquiry should consider that there is no one right answer, rather many answers that point to a common question – attention to which is therefore given to derive the right questions. *In stories, this pertains to the use of metaphor.*

FIG 57 – COMPARISON OF TYPE A AND TYPE B CONTENT REQUIREMENTS

This schema challenges a couple of commonly held myths regarding content and learning:

Myth 1- Learning experiences need to be kept content-light: This is only half true. Type A is, by its nature, limited in content, but directive, whereas the content in type B could be significant (stories do not lack content!) but are non-directive and exploratory.

Myth 2 – Use experiences to make learners care more: Engagement with content presumes a preference for it (through its correlation with attention). The schema below (Fig 58) describes a common view of how different learning modalities should accommodate different levels of motivation or preference in the learner.

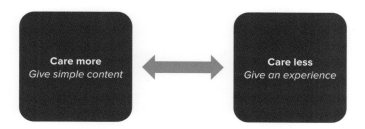

FIG 58 – CONTENT VS. EXPERIENCE SCHEMA

However, part of the challenge with this approach is that it does not accommodate the needs of someone who must develop deeper levels of conceptual association to more fully express and attend to their experience, and for whom there is already a deep preference to do so. This could include, for example, complex decision-making, or development of holistic, system-wide solutions, which rely on the faculty of memory to act. For that individual, information plays an important role, which will necessarily require more than the simple data points offered by type A (Fig 57).

The reality is that our preference is only assured through continual exposure to (and thereby expression through) affective sensory experience. Simply put, there is no learning without experience. The nature of that experience will vary, of course.

Type A lends itself much more readily to practical application of the information, whereas for type B we need to create lived stories to re-energize thinking, to develop detailed conceptual models through experience and not outside of it.

- Type A – information applied to experience (application)
- Type B – information gained from experience (ideation)

In other words, we need to ensure that for both type A and type B information, their experiences provide the learner with the opportunity for expression. Crafting the right experience in an organization is just as important for type A as it is for type B, when we recognize the importance of engagement (preference) in performance. In an organization, the approach required can range from interventions within current work experience (improving workflows and processes, providing better tools) to interventions developed outside of current employee experience (such as using the immersive experience technique 'Storyliving' – more on that to follow).

The Education and Training Department in an organization should perhaps be called the 'Experience Department.' It is the function of such departments everywhere to support people along the path of perspectival development, by providing access to the right learning experiences. Progressive organizations call such experiences 'work,' rather than positioning professional education as a function that is separate from the work itself.

4 – The threshold of attention

Perception occurs at the minimum point of fidelity – the farthest point at which one thing can be distinguished from another. Even an empty canvas can be resolved, when given aspect through its frame. In truth, all our attention is given toward a vanishing point – to a point where there is nothing to see.

What we see is not always apparent to us. The threshold between the conscious and subconscious mind is the level above which we consciously perceive experience – 'supraliminal stimuli' – and below which all 'subliminal stimuli' are subconsciously perceived. Our subconscious mind is able to process information at higher resolution[2] and at a higher sampling rate[3] than the significantly lower processing capacity of our conscious mind.

2. Peirce & Jastrow. (1885). *On Small Difference In Sensation.*

3. Kunst-Wilson, W. R., & Zajonc, R. B. (1980). Affective discrimination of stimuli that cannot be recognized. *Science*, 207, 557-558.

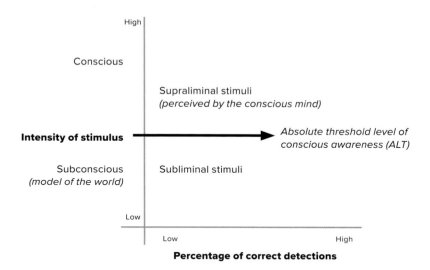

FIG 59 – SENSORY THRESHOLD OF CONSCIOUS AWARENESS

What makes subliminal messaging so insidious is that even though we're utterly unaware of the message hidden in whatever we're watching or listening to, part of our subconscious mind cannot help but respond to these concealed stimuli – it happens entirely without our conscious knowledge or consent. 'Neuromarketing' and consumer neuroscience have already decided that the best person to sell to is not you at all, but the subconscious 'you' that you've never met.

Not everyone has the same threshold of sensitivity. People with Autism Spectrum Disorder (ASD) and Attention Deficit Hyperactivity Disorder (ADHD) have a sensory threshold that is outside the norm. ADHD is perhaps an inaccurate term, given there is really no such thing as a deficit of attention (noting that the point at which attention should be given is always subjective), just as there is no such thing as a deficit of experiencing. Rather, there are differences in where and what we give attention to.

The two principal types of ADHD describe two forms of response to stimulus, but not the underlying cause – inattentiveness and hyperactivity (with a third type being a hybrid of both):

(1) **Inattentive:** Doesn't pay attention to details, cannot focus on tasks, does not listen when spoken to, easily distracted

(2) **Hyperactive:** Impulsive type – fidgets, runs about, talks too much, always on the go, interrupts

We all have a threshold for the level of sensory activity we can accommodate. As we have discussed, with higher levels of performance, we observe higher levels of non-egoic preference (alongside an openness and acceptance of experience) and higher perceptivity, or *sensory acuity* (ability to discern and discriminate within our attentional field). Both factors act to reduce the sensory threshold, so that increasingly subtle changes in the environment can be detected. An important aspect of this threshold is that it is dynamic, and can vary according to how attention is given, as it is needed. As we learn, we learn to flex this threshold accordingly.

Through their training, a Formula 1 driver will develop greater perceptivity, becoming highly sensitive to their environment, able to tune in very precisely to the (what might be to others the overwhelming) noise of the engine. This sensitivity and acuity is only possible because there is preference to do so, and an openness and receptivity to the environment. This is why (although it might sound counterintuitive) that sensitivity not only allows us, but *compels us*, to lean in with our attention to greater levels of sensory intensity, rather than shy away from them to divert our attention.

Our sensory threshold is learned through experience. Anyone with young children will be familiar with how easily they can become overwhelmed and overstimulated, and how their attention can shift from complete fixation (TV on) to complete disinterest (TV off). Our sensory threshold is like a filter that allows us to interact effectively with our environment.

Exposure to long periods of higher stimulus intensity can increase your sensory threshold. Spend time in a noisy room and you will grow desensitized to it, as your sensory threshold is raised. However, the impact of prolonged levels of high stimulus intensity can be debilitating. Soldiers in wartime learn to function by significantly raising their sensory threshold beyond their normal levels. These high-intensity stimuli imprint upon their long-term memory. When they return to civilian life, their sensory threshold returns to pre-combat levels. Subsequent recall of traumatic events elicits levels of stimulus intensity far higher than their sensory threshold can accommodate, inducing post-traumatic stress disorder (PTSD).

In some individuals (adults and children), the sensory threshold is set outside the norm. We live in a world where almost all human experience has been designed on the presumption of a standard sensory threshold, for a 'neurotypical' human, and yet in reality we are also all different, with differing levels of sensitivity. You might notice a sensitivity to light,

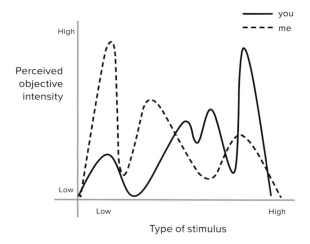

FIG 60 – EXAMPLE VARIATION IN STIMULUS SENSITIVITY

or to a type of music, or to a particular perfume. There is, of course, no 'normal.' Society tends to think of difference in terms of the absence of a sense, rather than the cognitive variability within one. Thankfully, neurodiversity is starting to get more mainstream attention, but until we all begin to recognize the neurodivergence within ourselves, its recognition will likely be limited. We can describe two types of neurodivergent sensitivity:

1. **Hypersensitivity:** When the threshold is set lower than the norm, resulting in sensory overload.

2. **Hyposensitivity:** When the threshold is set higher than the norm, resulting in decreased sensory stimulation.

An important aspect of the threshold is that it differs according to stimulus. People can be affected by different stimuli in different ways, with differing sensory thresholds, and may demonstrate hypersensitivity or hyposensitivity according to different stimuli (Fig 60). We become more or less sensitized to certain stimuli based on our own experience.

1. HYPERSENSITIVITY:

When the threshold is set lower than the norm, sensory overload happens. This is termed *hypersensitivity.* Your brain is overwhelmed with information from your five senses and can't process it correctly. Rather than taking one thing in at a time, your brain can't prioritize. Some people refer to this as getting 'stuck.' When your brain is stuck, it starts sending out signals that you need to escape your situation. Feeling overwhelmed and uncomfortable is how your body encourages you to get away from stimuli so your brain can get back on track. From a physiological perspective, the reason the brain gets overwhelmed is unknown, though structural differences may play a role. Many autistic people experience hypersensitivity to bright lights or certain light wavelengths, such as from fluorescent lights. Certain sounds, smells, textures and tastes can also be overwhelming. Individuals with hypersensitivity respond in one of two ways (either strategy may be deployed, depending on the situation):

- **Hypoactive:** Hypoactivity is a form of sensory avoidance typically attributed to individuals who are hypersensitive. They try to get away from stimuli that most people can easily tune out. Sensory avoidance can look like pulling away from physical touch, covering the ears to avoid loud or unpredictable sounds, or avoiding certain kinds of clothing.
- **Hyperactive:** Difficulty with processing too many inputs can be frustrating, anxiety- or anger-provoking, or even meltdown-inducing for some people. It is a fact that you can only pay attention to one thing at a time.

2. HYPOSENSITIVITY

When the threshold is set higher than the norm, the term *hyposensitivity* is used. Research suggests that a reduction in dopamine is a factor in ADHD.[4, 5, 6] Dopamine is a chemical in the brain that helps move signals from one nerve to another. It plays a role in triggering emotional responses and movements. Its role in compelling action when we feel the need[7] – for example, out of the need to conform, rather than because we might enjoy it and want to – could explain why children with reduced dopamine levels exhibit reduced attention spans in the classroom. Individuals with hyposensitivity can also respond in one of two ways (again, either strategy may be deployed, depending on the situation):

- **Hyperactive:** Hyperactivity is a form of 'sensory seeking,' meaning that the individual needs more proprioceptive input. People who are hyposensitive may appear hyperactive and engage in sensory seeking to get more sensory input from the environment. For example, people with autism may stimulate their senses by making loud noises, touching people or objects, or rocking back and forth. This can look like a constant need for movement. They also might experience difficulty recognizing sensations like hunger, illness or pain, or be attracted to loud noises, bright lights and vibrant colours. Notice how you speak more loudly when you have ear plugs in, so that you can hear what you're saying, and how quickly we forget that our sensory experience is not shared by everyone else. Hyperactive

4. *Evaluating Dopamine Reward Pathway in ADHD: Clinical Implications.* Nora D. Volkow, MD; Gene-Jack Wang, MD; Scott H. Kollins, PhD; et al (2009).

5. *Striatal Dopamine Transporter Alterations in ADHD: Pathophysiology or Adaptation to Psychostimulants? A Meta-Analysis.* Paolo Fusar-Poli, Ph.D., Katya Rubia, Ph.D., Giorgio Rossi, M.D., Giuseppe Sartori, Ph.D., and Umberto Balottin, M.D., Ph.D. (2012).

6. *Dopamine transporter density in patients with attention deficit hyperactivity disorder.* Darin D Dougherty, MD, Ali A Bonab, PhD, Thomas J Spencer, MD, Scott L Rauch, MD, Bertha K Madras, PhD, Dr Alan J Fischman, MD. (1999).

7. Berridge, K.C., Robinson, T.E. What is the role of dopamine in reward: hedonic impact, reward learning, or incentive salience? *Brain Res Brain Res Rev.* 1998 Dec; 28(3):309-69.

individuals may notice features in a room that those with lower thresholds have never noticed before, such as the shape of a ceiling vent or a door handle. Often, patients with ADHD will find themselves inexorably drawn to objects and want to play with them, as their attention brings with it this need to interact and express.

- **Hypoactive:** Individuals who are not stimulated may make careless mistakes because they have difficulty sustaining focus, following detailed instructions, and organizing tasks and activities. They are easily distracted by external stimuli, and often lose things. They may leave projects unfinished and appear not to listen when you speak.

The primary determinant of an individual's behavioural response is their sensitivity to their environment. As described above, a hypoactive and hyperactive response can be demonstrated by both individuals with hypersensitivity and hyposensitivity, but for different reasons. Understanding and interpreting the emotional responses of individuals with ADHD and ASD can be important in establishing how best to improve their lives.

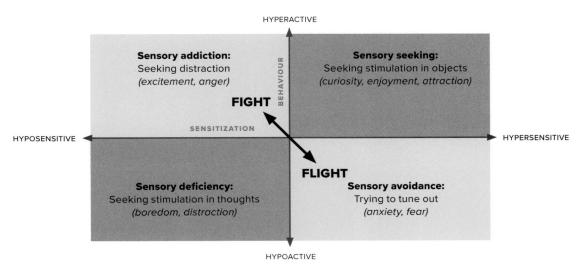

FIG 61 – BEHAVIOURAL IMPACT OF SENSORY THRESHOLD VARIANCE

Fig 61 applies as much to individuals with ADHD and ASD as it does to our own behaviours, the only difference being the degree of stimulus required to trigger the behaviour.

Given that we experience the world through thinking and perceiving, there is an interesting comparison to be made with ADHD and ASD, and those individuals who have suffered short-term memory loss. Anyone who has smoked cannabis might have fallen afoul of its ability to temporarily alter or disrupt short-term memory processing. The experience can be frightening for those attempting to understand and think through what is happening to them, as this process seems to restart every few seconds, as the last train of thought is lost. The experience is not dissimilar to those affected by sensory overload, in the resultant inability to control their attention.

Approaches used to help individuals with hypersensitivity and hyposensitivity include meditative techniques to calm the mind and reduce attention to thoughts, and in children can include placing them in a 'low distraction' environment, to minimize compelling alternate stimuli, like loud music or visual distractions. The important point is to reinforce that the individual is not doing anything wrong. Creating an environment that rebalances their level of stimulation to attract their attention is the first important step. From there, there is the opportunity to explore their personal preferences and perceptivity, to improve their opportunities and abilities to engage effectively with their environment. Questions to guide the conversation can include:

- **To explore preferences:** What do they enjoy doing? What do they dislike? How do these make them feel? How do they express how they feel? What opportunities are there for them to express themselves freely in this way?
- **To explore perceptivity:** What do they like to give attention to? What most gets their attention? How does it make them feel? What might they notice that is outside of their direct attention?

How often have you asked someone these questions, or indeed when were these questions asked of you? Neurodiversity itself is a spectrum. We all fall somewhere along the range of ADHD/ASD symptoms, experiencing and exhibiting them to some degree or another.

5 – Sensitivity and addiction

The absolute level of the threshold of sensitivity is entirely subjective and relative. The sensory threshold can be raised or lowered according to our egoic-emotional response:

1. **Egoic Hypersensitivity:** The sensory threshold for a stimulus is lowered. Overstimulation provokes an egoic need to avoid the stimulus (hypoactivity).
2. **Egoic Hyposensitivity:** The sensory threshold for a stimulus is raised. Understimulation provokes an egoic need to seek out the stimulus (hyperactivity).

From the perspective of ego, both function as warning mechanisms. Hypersensitivity helps the ego identify what is present (the threat it needs to avoid), while hyposensitivity warns the ego to identify what is absent (the reward it needs to obtain). Changes to the sensory threshold should not be confused with sensory perceptivity. A lowered sensory threshold that results from egoic hypersensitivity means that while lower levels of stimulus intensity are required for the stimulus to gain our attention, there is no accordant resolution of fidelity as it triggers an avoidance response.

Both aspects are also associated with low levels of preference receptivity, such that through ego, we seek out only that which we need within a limited set of egoic preferences.

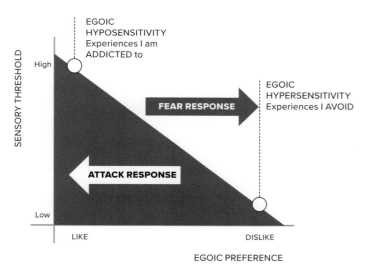

FIG 62 – RELATIONSHIP BETWEEN SENSORY THRESHOLD AND EGOIC PREFERENCE

1. **Egoic hyposensitivity:** Another word for egoic hyposensitivity that results in hyperactivity is *addiction*, and when this behaviour is observed outside of the norm, we label individuals 'addicts.' However, anyone with an ego (it being a thought that practically everyone identifies with) is an addict. Ergo, we are all addicted to thinking.

   An addict is someone who develops lower sensitivity to a particular stimulus, in resistance to experience, and so seemingly needs increasingly higher levels of the stimulus to get what they need – this being to escape the need-induced suffering. A heroin addict's need for a fix, which is egoic in origin, is experienced as a physical, sensory need (the body needing it to operate effectively and to avoid pain), but it is the habituative egoic suffering that perpetuates the addiction.

   The compulsion to attend to physical needs extends to thoughts. Our addiction to thinking compels us toward a point of understanding, the payoff for which is not the understanding, but our need for it, which ends the moment we feel we have it. Ignorance is bliss. Anyone who has experienced 'tip-of-the-tongue syndrome' (where an object of memory is just out of reach) will recognize the anguish as the mind struggles to remember that name, or place that person, the association tantalizingly close. Typically, individuals can remember the first letter of a name, and yet most of the time, the information we are grasping for is utterly unimportant (and hence, why we struggle to remember).

   The difference between the need for heroin and the need to breathe is the presence or absence of authorship. Ego does not put the painkiller in your mouth when you have a headache – that is a normal non-egoic preference to avoid pain. The difference is whether there is acceptance of the pain (regardless of whether you like it or not) or resistance. When there is resistance, we suffer not because of the pain, but in the belief that we will not be happy without its cessation. Addiction leads ego to bang its head against the wall the moment the pain has stopped.

2. **Egoic hypersensitivity:** Egoic hypersensitivity that results in hypoactivity is also a form of addictive behaviour, and is a flight response to suffering and resistance to experience that seeks the sanctuary of safety. It is an addiction to activities that enable their redirection of attention into withdrawal. From the perspective of ego, if you defend yourself, you will be attacked. Safety and peace lies in defencelessness.

6 – Impact of Ego on Activity Preference

Fig 63 shows how our decision to undertake or avoid an activity is affected by a number of factors, including our preferences, our ability (sensory perceptivity), our sensory threshold, our form of response (hyperactivity or hypoactivity) and ego. Our preferences are therefore multifaceted, and (when it comes to ego) context-centric.

	ACTION	WITHOUT EGO we give greater attention to those activities for which we have:	WITH EGO we give greater attention to those activities for which we have:
SENSORY THRESHOLD	Engage	A lower sensory threshold that provokes excitement and interest (hyperactivity due to hypersensitivity) e.g. *"I love working with the group."*	A higher sensory threshold that provokes sensory addiction (hyperactivity due to hyposensitivity) e.g. *"I need the recognition of this group."*
SENSORY THRESHOLD	Avoid	A higher sensory threshold that provokes a withdrawal response (hypoactivity due to hyposensitivity) e.g. *"This group doesn't stimulate me."*	A lower sensory threshold that provokes a withdrawal response (hypoactivity due to hypersensitivity) e.g. *"I am afraid of looking bad in front of this group."*
ABILITY (sensory perceptivity)	Engage	Abilities that allow for our fullest expression (*high ability*)	Abilities that will best get us what we need from experience (*high ability AND/OR high power dynamics*)
ABILITY (sensory perceptivity)	Avoid	Abilities that allow for our least expression (*low ability*)	Abilities that will not get us what we need (*low ability AND/OR low power dynamics*)

FIG 63 – FACTORS AFFECTING THOSE ACTIVITIES THAT WE GIVE GREATER ATTENTION TO (PREFERENCE)

Whether you identify as a *creative thinker*, a *details person* or a *big-picture thinker*, the answer is likely that you are all of them, depending on the circumstance. General statements, such as *"Introverts get their energy from being alone,"* are clearly inadequate. Egoic responses are always context-centric, the context being the egoic persona assumed for that particular situation. They are a learned reaction, perpetuated through an egoic emotional need.

PART 2 – PERSPECTIVAL DEVELOPMENT PRACTICES

Practice does not make perfect, perfection being unattainable or requiring an infinite amount of time. How long does it take to become expert at something? It depends on: (a) How much you enjoy what you are doing; (b) How what you are doing changes over time. The fundamental difference is one of perspective. Perspectival development is about shifting our point of view to shift performance. It is a conscious exploration of how we give attention to experience, so that through the learning process the participant learns how to learn.

As we have discussed, all you can ever learn in life is perceptivity (learning what you perceive) and preference (learning what you like). Performance gets stuck when we either fail to change our experience or continue to look at our experiences (changing or not) from the same perspective. Ultimately, both sensory perceptivity and preference receptivity are intrinsically linked, their dynamic interdependence establishing an *'affective resonance'* within experience that leads to the collapse of the subjective perspective – of a self that is separate from their objective experience. The result is what we see in the best performances, whether it's playing piano before a packed concert hall or talking someone down from jumping off a bridge. What's notable is the manner in which attention is given, through the apparent absence of the performer, or at least to the one who is performing.

Accordingly, the three core aspects of perspectival development are:

A – SENSORY PERCEPTIVITY: Changing our perspective to change our experience
B – PREFERENCE RECEPTIVITY: Changing our experiences to change our perspective
C – AFFECTIVE RESONANCE: Changing our perspective and experience through empathy

Perspectival Development provides a set of principles through which to design learning to affect these three outcomes. To develop Preference Receptivity, we design learning for the user – we craft the experience around the user, employing *user experience design*. Conversely, to develop Sensory Perceptivity, we devise learning for the experience – we design the user around the experience, employing *ontological design*. The principle of ontological design is that when we design objects, spaces and experiences, we are, in fact, designing the human being itself. For affective resonance, we combine both aspects, through the application of *immersive design*.

A) SENSORY PERCEPTIVITY:

The goal of Sensory Perceptivity is to *change our perspective to change our experience*. Perspectival Development prescribes three approaches to achieve this, which were introduced earlier in this chapter:

1. **Perspective Range:** Improving the degree of discernment and fidelity for our point of attention (selective attention)
2. **Attentional Agility:** Improving how we can change and flex our point of attention
3. **Reaction time:** Improving our ability to take action to shift our perspective

The following practices provide different approaches to help learners develop greater sensory perceptivity. Their individual application would need to be tailored through ontological design, to the learner's individual context and performance challenge.

1. Perspective Range:

Perspective Range is our ability to selectively attend to an object within our environment, in the presence of multiple competing stimuli. The practices are designed to develop the learner's ability to bring the object of attention (the target) from the background into the foreground of experience. In this example, the target is an individual in a room full of noisy people.

Locating the target: For this practice, the objective is to identify the individual target as quickly as possible. To do this, the learner is provided with a limited set of characteristics that denote sameness and difference, relative to the others in the room. In this case, it could be visual characteristics, such as how they look, or behavioural characteristics, such as what they might be doing or whom they are with. The learner will need to explore the environment, shifting their perspective until they can recognize the target through the comparative associations they have formed. By repeating the practice, the learner will begin to perceive greater contrast between the characteristics of the target and the other potential targets in the room, so that the target of attention takes less and less time to locate. Other applications could include a mechanic being able to discern what a particular noise from an engine means, through to a driver being able to spot safety traffic hazards more quickly.

Observing the target: For this practice – and assuming the same scenario – with the target located, the objective is to give continuous attention to the target, to identify as many defining characteristics as possible. This practice requires both selective and sustained attention. Challenge is introduced through increasing sensory distractions, which are congruent with the sensorial aspect required for observation. For example, where the challenge is to listen to and record what the target is saying, the volume of competing voices in the room is adjusted so that greater levels of attention are required to discern the target stimulus. Through practice, the learner narrows their perspective range to give more exclusive attention to the target, despite the interference.

2. Attentional agility:

Attentional agility is our ability to change and flex our point of attention within experience, noting that we can only ever give attention to one thing at a time. The practices are designed to develop the learner's ability to shift focus through increasing degrees of divergence. Rather than developing an attentional muscle, the skill requires a relaxation and loosening of resistance, so that less (rather than more) effort is required. The practice establishes a *challenge environment*, within which the learner is required to undertake at least two distinct activities at the same time. Each challenge environment is defined by a goal that is common to all activities undertaken within that environment, and that must be completed in order to achieve the goal. Challenge is introduced into each environmental setting by varying the difficulty level of each challenge, and/or by introducing a different challenge environment. For example:

Within the same challenge environment:
- By increasing the level of challenge of one of the activities (such as by placing a limitation on time or resources, or by increasing the complexity of the task), *so that the learner has to give increasing attention to the high-challenge activity*
- Or, by changing the level of challenge across both activities, *so that the learner has to continuously redirect attention between the different activities according to their increasing and decreasing levels of challenge*

Within different challenge environments:
- By switching between different, but similar, challenge environments (requiring similar cognitive patterns), *so that the learner has to refocus attention as the environments change*
- Or, by switching between different challenge environments with activities that require very different cognitive approaches – such as moving from simple problem solving (requiring convergent thinking through concrete conceptual associations) to more complex problems (applying integrative thinking, to form more abstract conceptual associations) – *so that the learner has to adjust how they give attention to their conceptual model within their experience*

3. Reaction Time:

This practice develops the ability to respond to changes in our experience. The most important factor affecting our reaction time is following through on the impulse to act, and the biggest barrier to this is thinking. Helen Keller describes how in the absence of thinking she reacted through a natural impulse:

> *"I had neither will nor intellect. I was carried along to objects and acts by a certain blind natural impetus."*[8]

And, she describes how thinking seemed to temper her response:

> *"I was eager to know, then to understand, afterward to reflect on what I knew and understood, and the blind impetus, which had before driven me hither and thither at the dictates of my sensations, vanished forever."*

The challenge is that over time, through reasoning, we learn to out-think our natural impulses, resulting in a lack of decisive action. Thinking kicks in the first place because of how we are feeling. Action comes naturally when we feel inclined to act, and we rarely have to think about it. However, most of the time our instinctive reaction to doing anything out of the ordinary is to feel unease, particularly when the consequence of doing so

8. Keller, H. (1903). *The Story of My Life*. Adansonia Publishing.

is not entirely known or is new. In resistance to feeling, we turn our attention to thought, which provides us with a very clear rationale as to why this feeling should be avoided at all cost, and thereby the justification for doing nothing.

We like to do what feels good, and our preferences are limited, but there are two ways to get past this:

- Through your preferences: Broaden your definition of what you like and what you don't (see 'Preference Exchange' below)
- Through our thinking: Learning to take action in spite of thinking, using the *One Breath Rule*

One Breath Rule: Consider that with every breath (we take around 23,000 each day), there arises an opportunity to act. Our actions follow our attention. When we give attention to experience, there is the opportunity to change experience, to take action. When we give attention to thought, our attention and therefore our motivation is toward thinking. The solution to this is that there is a short window of time and opportunity to notice that this has happened – that our attention has shifted to our thoughts – and that we have the opportunity to act. Thoughts will set out clearly that we need a detailed plan in place, need to consider all options, and need to wait until we are ready. But this is the very reason (and is, in part, an evolutionary defence mechanism) that we get stuck in habitual behaviour: we are unable to break out of this cycle of thinking. This technique – the *One Breath Rule* – can help you break the cycle. There are two parts to it: (1) Step Forward; (2) Share Back.

- **Step Forward:** When we notice the opportunity to act, such as speaking up in a meeting, we take a breath, consciously, deeply. On the *inhalation,* we think the word *'one.'* On the *exhalation,* we think *'breath.'* The purpose of this is twofold: to create a trigger point so that in future practices we recognize and know what is coming next, and to interrupt our thinking (you cannot think two thoughts in the same moment). Giving attention to the thought 'one' in this way slows down the arrival of your next thought – the so-called *quantum Zeno effect.* At the end of the breath, you take action. No preparation, no further consideration or thinking required, just act. When we turn our attention to thinking in resistance to experience, we only have a very small amount of time to act before we get hijacked by our thinking. The only way we can act is to react. If you give it a second thought, you're too late!

- **Share Back:** After we have acted, and the practice has concluded, we need to share back what we learned from the action we took. We're sharing how we feel, and in the same way as we step forward, we do this in one breath – quickly, simply, without reserve. The purpose is to ensure that we are able to fully discern how that experience changed through our action, by considering the deepening of our perspective. Doing so in one breath requires us to get to the heart of the matter, to really look honestly at what has changed, and what we have learned.

As a skill, it seems that the ability of individuals in organizations to react diminishes the further they progress up the ranks. This organizational inertia is reflective both of an increasing pressure to perform and an increasing timespan of discretion (the time typically devoted to activities) through work that is more complex and that necessarily requires attention taken away from experience and redirected into deeper retrospection and planning. To shift from inertia to action, we need to be remember that:

- **You will never be ready:** To wait until you are ready is to wait for a moment that will never come. The only time you can take action in is this moment.
- **Feeling wrong is right:** The act of not acting – and therefore of overthinking – has led us to misidentify how we feel. Take the sensation of butterflies in our stomach, for example. The ego layers our sensory perception with ideas of anxiety, fear and worthlessness. Yet, physiologically it's exactly the same sensation as when we get excited. The only difference is thought. The way out of this is to drop the idea that we need to feel good to act. As soon as we lose that egoic presumption, we can give our attention to the feelings themselves, through our senses, and realize that in our full awareness, our sensations can help show us those opportunities to act, rather than being the reason we look away.

B) PREFERENCE RECEPTIVITY:

The aim of Preference Receptivity is to *change our experiences to change our perspective.* Below are two approaches to achieve this:

1. **Preference Quest:** Improving the expression of what we love, so that we can share it more widely
2. **Preference Exchange:** Increasing openness to new experiences, to extend our interests and the diversity of our network

1. Preference Quest:

Our ability to express ourselves in an authentic, meaningful way is a fundamental determinant of our success. Our preferences and the activities we choose to undertake are both egoic (those that require extrinsic motivation or reward) and non-egoic (in which the opportunity for expression is the reward). Life expects us to know what we want, and is usually quite helpful in pointing out what that should look like. Consequently, we're motivated toward making more money, progression up the career ladder, weighing less, buying a bigger house, and all forms of extrinsic motivation that fuel our egoic preferences. The egoic belief is that we need experience to make us happy. This is the fundamental difference between egoic and non-egoic preferences. In reality, nothing can make you happy, because the only happiness there is that which you already are. There is only this! The challenge, therefore, is that as well acquainted as we are with our egoic preferences (that which we feel we need to do to be happy), many of us have given little attention to our non-egoic preferences (that which gives us true happiness).

We're obsessed with getting value from something, from somewhere. Take a bottle of water. From the tap it costs nothing; we go to the supermarket and it's £2; in a restaurant it's £3; on a plane it's £5. All that changes is the value we place on it. We think we need to get somewhere, to get the value we deserve, but the only one who knows our value is us. It's the same with our preferences.

We could draw a similar analogy with a sailing ship. Most people give attention to the direction they need to head in to be successful – be it in their career or in their personal life. The sails – their skills and abilities – are the tools that will get them there, to steer their ship to the shore. Non-egoic preferences ask us to look not to the shore, but to the wind, and to that which you can feel. Its secret is not where you're going, but to discover where you're coming from.

Preference Quest is a practice to help identify and consciously express our non-egoic preferences, as a basis for building greater purpose, engagement, attention and ultimately performance. It is a quest to find what we love, in who we are. Or in the words of German-American poet Charles Bukowski, *"Find what you love, and let it kill you."* Our non-egoic preferences are those experiences that we love, and which we give our time and attention to effortlessly. They offer the space to express ourselves freely, and so lend themselves to higher levels of performance. In fact, they (and all non-egoic preferences) are therefore the only means by which you can develop high performance. This approach runs contrary to the common misconception that you need to focus on your weaknesses to improve performance.

Preference Quest sets each learner a challenge: To identify a non-egoic preference and to create an opportunity to express and share it with the world. In an organizational context, the scope would include any activity that contributes to your performance in role, be it directly or indirectly. To that extent, the scope is broad and should not be limited to activities within the formal workplace setting. The practice for engendering our creative expression within experience follows four steps (Fig 64).

FIG 64 – FOUR-STEP PREFERENCE QUEST APPROACH

1) Discover it: The first step is to find out what your preferences are. The learner looks back over the last month (or longer, if it helps) and asks: (1) What did I do that I am most proud of? (2) What do I wish I could have done? (3) What did I do that gave me the most energy? (4) When did I go above and beyond when no one told me to? (5) What parts of those activities did I enjoy the most? The learner creates a list of those activities that reflect their non-egoic preferences, and then identifies one activity where there is a near-term opportunity to share it with others.

2) Create it: Once your preference is identified, you need to get ready. Creativity is core to the constructive aspect of learning. This applies regardless of the activity undertaken, whether it's the development of a new idea, creating a physical prototype, compiling an engaging presentation, or preparing to bring a new performance to a familiar activity that puts your stamp on it. It is the development of something tangible from something intangible – meaning.

3) Share it: There is no value to that which cannot be expressed. The function of all per-formance, whether through art, sport or business, is to point us toward the understanding that what is expressed is simultaneously the voice of the artist and the audience. It marks a movement from potentiality into actuality – not just for the artist, but for those who share in it. Through the Preference Quest practice, the learner explores the best way to share this experience with others, through two important questions: (1) How can I show the audience what this means? (2) How can I show them something that they have not seen before? Long ago it was commonplace for soldiers to enshrine within their armour protective charms, to confer efficacy upon the shield or blade. Through our preferences, we can choose to drop our defences, reveal our true selves and, in doing so, invite others to do the same.

4) Feel it: As children we presume that our teddy bears can talk and drink tea, because we do. This perceptual tendency, known as anthropomorphism, is innate. Keller describes this experience as a child:

> *"I only know that after my education began the world which came within my reach was all alive. I spelled to my blocks and my dogs. I sympathized with plants when the flowers were picked, because I thought it hurt them, and that they grieved for their lost blossoms. It was two years before I could be made to believe that my dogs did not understand what I said, and I always apologized to them when I ran into or stepped on them."[8]*

As grownups, we learn that there is a difference. It appears that to know experience – one that is separate from ourselves – we need to understand that difference. We believe that this difference, which distinguishes our perspective from all others, distinguishes ourselves as the separate self. It's common for people who listen to a recording of their voice to see it as different and not their own. The reality is that what we hear when we speak (and what we subsequently hear in our head when we think) is not what our voice sounds like, because we're listening from 'inside the speaker.' All of experience is like this, until we recognize that the echo that comes back, whether of one voice or many, is ours. Preference Quest practice invites the learner to listen to those who have shared in their experience, to understand the impact is has had, and to look closely at how the experience has changed their own feelings and perspective.

2. Preference Exchange

Preference receptivity describes an openness to experience, in which we can give our full attention, irrespective of whether we have a strong like or dislike for something. It is an important aspect of performance, given that our environment constantly changes, toward and away from the conditions we could describe as 'optimum' for our performance. Preference receptivity is an invitation to stop seeking to control and change experience, but to instead change our perspective.

Our preferences form through the environments to which we are exposed. If you've never tried sushi, you will likely still have a preference, albeit a conceptual one, perhaps having seen it on TV. However, until you experience sushi directly, using all your senses, your preference has not been actualized. Preference exchange is about *actualizing our preferences* through direct experience. The objective of the practice is to challenge preconceptions that arise from limited experience, and to give greater, open attention to our senses.

Preference Exchange practice works by pairing two individuals who perceive each other as different, who will each share with the other an experience – a preference – that they have a deep and abiding passion for. Each pair will respectively play the role of Guide and Explorer. As Guide, one's role is to introduce the preference through the different perspectives that describe why they love the experience so much. As Explorer, the person's only prerequisite is to be open to the experience, such that they participate fully, whether they're keen, or slightly curious, or a downright critic. The purpose of the practice is not to change anyone's preferences, but to improve awareness through direct experiences that offer a wider diversity of perspectives. Preferences cannot be changed, but they can be developed by learning about the different qualities that constitute an individual's holistic perspective. Individuals with actualized preferences can talk clearly and unequivocally about why their preference is one of desire or dislike.

A WORD ON CRITICS:

When we dislike something, we look away from it, and so our perspective is limited to that aspect we don't want to see. As a result, every time we look back, the aspect we don't want to see is the only one we can see. If you have a dislike for spiders, it's likely that you have a very limited understanding of them, both conceptually and sensorially. It's unlikely, for example, that you have ever stroked the back of a tarantula and noticed just how soft it is.

Through preference exchange we invite a progressive, unfolding exploration of an object's different qualities. The aim is to gradually extend the individual's intensity tolerance to develop a more panoramic perspective. If you have arachnophobia, you will have a very narrow perspective, and accordingly a very limited threshold of intensity. A progressive approach might be to invite the individual to initially touch something familiar that also feels like the back of a spider, rather than the spider itself.

A critic who, through lack of awareness, has developed a strong dislike for an object in their experience is not dissimilar to an addict who's developed an extremely strong desire for that same object. Both have, in resistance, developed a narrowed perspective and limited intensity tolerance range. The only real difference is that the critic can only tolerate very low levels of stimulus, whereas the addict can only tolerate very high levels of stimulation.

Preference Exchange doesn't just develop perspective, it builds networks. The two are not unrelated, and our connectivity and relatedness to others is a factor of our empathetic appreciation of their different perspectives. Now, more than ever, in a world of increasingly polarized opinions, there is a need to connect via experiences through which we can share our most authentic selves. The 'Empathy Practice' (described in Chapter 9) provides a further opportunity to deepen our understanding of another's preferences, and in so doing close the gap between their reality and our own.

C) AFFECTIVE RESONANCE
THE STORY LINE

While the objects of experience are known to us through our thoughts and perceptions, through the assertion of ego our faculties of conception and perception derive our sense of separation between self and experience:

- In time – the conceived distance of self from this moment (between past and future)
- In space – the perceived distance of self from the objects of experience

This movement, between egoic and actualized experience, can be seen to occur on a continuum or 'Story Line' (Fig 65).

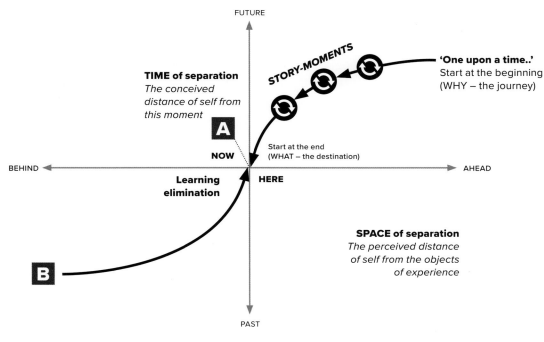

FIG 65 – THE STORY LINE

The *story of me* exists along this line, its sigmoidal representation denoting our acceptance or resistance to experience:

- **At point A** we give attention fully to this moment. Action happens, thinking happens, but for no one. In acceptance, our attention can relax, as we collapse the sense of separateness from 'my experience' to one that is shared. The story ends.
- **At point B**, in resistance our attention is turned away from current experience toward thinking – of past and future, and the pursuit of meaning. As our attention seeks egoic fulfillment through the objects of experience, we pursue the 'progressive path' – the need to become so that we can be.

It is the role of learning to direct attention to this moment (the only moment that there is), to transcend the story of ego, to enable progress along this line from point B to point A, toward the eventual elimination of learning. As we have discussed, there are two ways it can achieve this:

The map: For individuals at point A, learning is minimalistic, pointing to the 'what' of experience that enables direct application, directing attention to that which is immediately discoverable, without reference to thought or memory.

The story: For individuals at point B, learning points to the 'why.' The story of me draws attention into thought, to discover that which can only be found outside of direct experience. However, from the perspective of learning, there are two types of stories, in which the learner can either:

- **Lose themself:** The understanding that the story reveals is fictional, bearing no relation to current experience. Rather, it serves as an escape from direct experience, such as going to the movies.
- **Find themself:** These are the stories that can transcend fiction, to redirect attention back into direct experience. These stories engender moments of affective resonance with, and a bridging between, our imagined and actual worlds.

Affective resonance describes how we identify with our experience. Through increasing affective resonance, we perceive experience as a natural extension and expression of ourselves ('I am that'). It is a relaxation of attention that allows us to engage fully with our direct experience, rather than directing our attention inward, through the distanced perspective of ego. Stories can engender affective resonance individually and collectively:

(1) **For the individual:** Personalized story experiences designed to disrupt the ego's 'story of me' in those individuals whose actions are significantly impacting organizational inequity. The approach is high-touch, tailored and directed as one might a living play, to create powerful moments that elicit empathy and draw awareness back into the present moment.

(2) **For the system:** The evolution of individual stories into a collective expression or 'movement' that is self-organized and organic, in response to egoic environmental inequity.

In this chapter we shall discuss the first of these two methods, through an approach called *Storyliving*. In the next chapter, we'll consider the collective approach through which social movements are formed.

Within all experience is an invitation to see beyond the narrowed perspective of egoic story. From getting ready for experience (and thereby avoiding it, which requires space and time) to embracing experience, ready or not (that which only ever takes place here, now). In Fig 65, the Story Line traces this line of enquiry and understanding that is gained through experience. Point A marks a point of departure – our own cosmic horizon, beyond which there is a withdrawal of attention from the objects of experience, to simply rest in the awareness from which all experience arises – the peace of our being.

STORYLIVING

Storyliving is an immersive storytelling approach, designed to engender a profound shift in a leader's empathetic understanding and connection with the world, through the development of affective resonance. Affective resonance arises as the learner shifts from 'caring deeply about my experience' to 'caring deeply about our experience – of self AND other.' Another word for this is *trust*.

Storyliving is applicable where senior leadership capability (and thereby organizational performance) is critically undermined by a fundamental empathy gap (Chapter 9). To ego flip, the individual changes their own story. Through Storyliving, we create stories that change the individual. The approach is underpinned by six storytelling principles (Fig 66), that accord with the six steps of the ego flip self-practice (Chapter 9), which enable the leader to: (1) Live the story; (2) Tell the story.

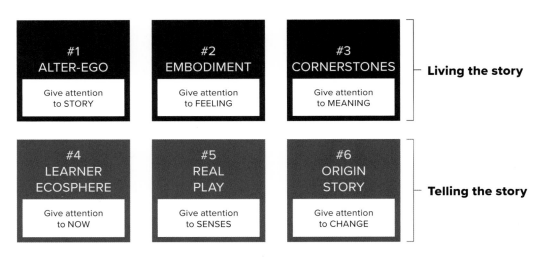

FIG 66 – STORYLIVING PRINCIPLES

LIVING THE STORY

Principle 1: Alter Ego

Within the experience, the learner takes on the role of the story's central character – as their alter ego. As Shakespeare described, *"They have their exits and their entrances, and one man in his time plays many parts."* [9] The experience unfolds around twin narratives: the protagonist's and that of the story's antagonist. The antagonist is the embodiment both of challenge to the protagonist perspective and of the ignorance by which the protagonist's lack of empathy is perpetuated. Within this empathy gap, the story follows the protagonist's egoic search for

9. Shakespeare, W. (1599). *As You Like It*: act 2, scene 7.

meaning, its path plotted using the Story Funnel model (Fig 67). To begin with, the perspectives of both parties are divergent, and seemingly irreconcilable, but through increasing urgency and futility, their perspectives ultimately converge around a common cause and understanding, so that the empathy gap can be closed.

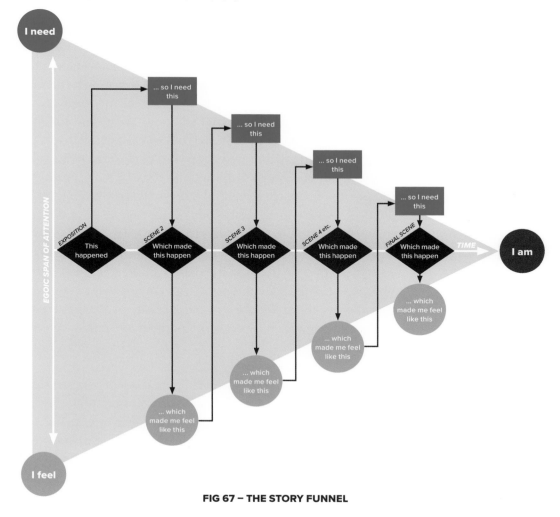

FIG 67 – THE STORY FUNNEL

The learner's role as the central character is key to this process. Just as an actor must lose themselves in their performance to play the part, so too their role as the alter ego gives the learner permission to discard old assumptions. That which we feel, we become.

Principle 2: Embodiment

Embodiment is our ability to give awareness to and expression of our emotions. Embodiment is a core skill for leadership, and yet it's one that is rarely discussed or developed. It is a dual movement that brings attention inward, to develop greater sensory perceptivity to our emotions and, through that awareness, find new forms of expression for our feelings within our experience. Storyliving channels that expression through the central character – the *alter ego* – which the learner embodies to bring the story to life.

Method Learning – the practice of embodiment (Chapter 9) – can help leaders open themselves up to explore new roles and perspectives. The scarcity of embodiment as a leadership skill is equal to the prevalence by which organizations and their leaders accordingly present themselves, behind a mask. In ego, in resistance, we develop our habitual responses. We revert to script, our perspective fixed and limiting our development. We wear a mask that averts our gaze from those feelings that we fear will reveal us. We are not the mask we wear. And yet, to turn and take off the mask of ego is not something that ego can ever do (it being the mask behind all masks). Rather, through the practice of embodiment, and in an embrace of its endless vanity, we can invite ego to play a wider range of parts, to experience a greater breadth of characterizations. To stand in the hall of mirrors and know its likeness through the many reflections of self-reference.

Principle 3: Cornerstones

The Storyliving experience unfolds using the story funnel through a series of immersive chapters or scenes, each crafted around a cornerstone (Fig 67). The cornerstone is the question that compels the search. The learner may ask: *"What is the most important question I have right now?"* and through the story will mark progress by how far that question changes. Facts and feelings are placed purposefully at odds with one another. The learner's decisions are progressively compelled toward an emotional response, and away from more reasoned, rational arguments.

FIG 68 – BRIDGING OF THE IMAGINED AND UNIMAGINED WORLDS

As the learner progresses through the story, it is their affective response – the primacy of feeling over fact – that drives them ever closer to the centre of the maze, and the ultimate resolution of their truth.

TELLING THE STORY

Storyliving connects an imagined world, or 'reverie' (that which the learner experiences through the eyes of their alter ego), with the unimagined world, our 'reality' (that which they arrive from and return to). It is in our reality that the origin of the story and its truth are revealed. In the transition from 'my world' (my perspective) to a 'shared world' (a shared perspective, between protagonist and antagonist), empathy can arise, and real change be made possible.

Principle 4: Learner Ecosphere

The rendering of any theatrical performance must necessarily confer on its audience a transparency. As the stage lowers its lights, the audience is consigned to shadow – the performance requires their absence. There is indeed a great ritual that takes us to this understanding, from the moment we surrender our tickets and progress through the foyer, to take our seat, turn off our phone; as the lights are lowered, our senses heightened in the darkness. This hermetic seal creates a world within, separate from the world without. Learning must strive for the same and yet, in recent times, through increasingly virtualized learning, the performance has in effect moved out of the theatre and into the street, with all the distractions that this affords.

Like Orpheus and Eurydice, who turned and looked back, most learning contends with the learner's temptation toward the familiar, toward the distractions of life and ego. Storyliving creates a space for learning within its own learning ecosphere, an anechoic chamber (a space that produces no echo) in which all attention is directed inward, to be given exclusively to those objects that immerse the learner in their experience. Metaphorically, it is the curtain, drawn across the space of our awareness to divide that which we know from that which we don't. It is a place that suspends belief through disbelief, that flips the rules of perspective, that looks behind the screen to reveal not the wizard, but Dorothy herself. To create this experience requires a separate space – a physical location at a distance from familiar places. For learners, the rituals resume as they take the journey not to their seats, but to the stage, and the story is set. Wearing new clothes, with a new name. George Orwell understood the profundity of this when he lived as a homeless person, recounted in his memoir *Down and Out in Paris and London*.[10]

Principle 5: Real Play

The experience that Storyliving creates must be felt to be believed. As such, its rendering is sensorially visceral, designed so that in the story, the learner gives attention through all their senses. Through immersive design, Storyliving deploys a multimodal approach that reflects the highly interdependent way in which our senses work together.

Imagine, for example, that you were learning to play a piece of music on the violin. You could just play it over and over again, *or* you could try a multimodal approach.

10. Orwell, G. (1933). *Down and Out in Paris and London*. (1st Edition). Penguin Classics.

You could: play the composition with a different violin and see what different sounds you can make; play it in a different tempo or key; play in front of an audience or to an empty room; play with earplugs in and then without; play reading from sheet music or from memory; watch professional violinists play and observe their different styles; view YouTube tutorials, where different musicians give their own interpretations, with endless variation, in note-for-note walk-throughs; listen to a recording with the music turned down or with the volume turned up, to see what notes or phrases stand out differently as a result.

Through contrasting modalities, the learner is better able to discern the common underlying qualities that signify great performance. A common misunderstanding is that individuals have a preferred learning style, and therefore a sensory modality that suits them best. The Visual Auditory Read/Write Kinaesthetic model (VARK) claims that people differ according to what mode of instruction or study is most effective for them, and that learning should therefore be adopted to reflect the individual's preferred learning style. While it is clear that people have a strong sense of their own learning preferences (visual, kinesthetic, intuitive) and believe that learning preferences impact performance,[11] the evidence as to whether these preferences matter is far less compelling. The learning-styles view has acquired great influence within the education field, but a number of studies have shown that preferences for learning styles have no impact on your ability to learn, and have challenged the data on which the VARK model is based.[12, 13, 14]

A 2009 review noted, *"The contrast between the enormous popularity of the learning-styles approach within education and the lack of credible evidence for its utility is, in our opinion, striking and disturbing. If classification of students' learning styles has practical utility, it remains to be demonstrated."*[12]

If the learner were a violinist, then in the context of Storyliving, each scene is part of the music that the learner is attempting to play. Through contrasting sensory intensity, we shift the learner's attention through the story. For example, to hear something that they have never heard before, we may at first create silence. The quietest place on Earth is an anechoic chamber in Minneapolis. Those who have experienced its silence describe their

11. *Learning style, judgements of learning, and learning of verbal and visual information.* Abby R. Knoll, Hajime Otani, Reid L. Skeel, K. Roger Van Horn. (2016).

12. *Learning Styles: Concepts and Evidence.* Harold Pashler, Mark McDaniel, Doug Rohrer, and Robert Bjork.

13. *Testing the ATI hypothesis: Should multimedia instruction accommodate verbalizer-visualizer cognitive style?* Laura J. Massa, Richard E. Mayer (2006).

14. *Another Nail in the Coffin for Learning Styles? Disparities among Undergraduate Anatomy Students' Study Strategies, Class Performance, and Reported VARK Learning Styles.* Polly R Husmann 1, Valerie Dean O'Loughlin (2019).

shift in attention, as they notice the rustle of their clothes, the sounds of the fluid in their mouth, even the pulsing tone of the blood in their brain. As our attention is redirected inward to the body, the sense of space also seems to contract, and become small. This attentional shift arises without effort, and simply by being aware.

Through this multimodal tactile approach, the learner can explore through the natural curiosity of their senses, this being the implicit form of learning we call 'play.' This playfulness, from which our natural curiosity arises, is an essential aspect of Storyliving. We could consider play both the triumvirate of the core aspects of immersive design (interest, challenge and utility), and an alternative definition of perspectival development – *'learning through play'* – such that when we engage the learner in the game:

- **Interest** is our preference to play the game – our expression of what we want, through our inhabitation of the character we play (*preference receptivity*).
- **Challenge** is the degree of difficulty – the task that requires our focus and resolution to change the outcome of the game (*sensory perceptivity*).
- **Utility** is what gives the game its purpose and meaning – the place we are trying to get to (*affective resonance*).

Implicit learning occurs when we believe something is real because it feels real. It negates the need for conscious competence or effort that can disrupt attention. As a result, learning is not only more easily assimilated, but through the learner's affective response is deeply retained, engendering longer-lasting and more fundamental behavioural change. This is the power that play brings to learning. Keller describes this implicit approach:

"Since I had no power of thought, I did not compare one mental state with another. So I was not conscious of any change or process going on in my brain when my teacher began to instruct me. I merely felt keen delight in obtaining more easily what I wanted by means of the finger motions she taught me. I thought only of objects, and only objects I wanted."[8]

Principle 6: Origin Story

Beyond the ecosphere, the story leaves traces. The Storyliving construct is a fiction based on fact – a metaphorical narrative for 'the real world.' That is its purpose: to point to the truth in our own lives. As the learner returns to normal life – as they transition from reverie to reality – their journey continues as they discover from an ethnographic perspective its echoes, as they see and hear from real people, in real places. The discovery of this origin story (the origin of its truth) is where the learning turns to action, to pursue questions left unanswered, to reveal the next chapter. The Storyliving experience prepares the learner for this enquiry, by collapsing the empathy gap. It is from this perspective, in which the alter ego is divested, that empathy-based change is now possible.

Storyliving uses immersive storytelling to create a bridge between two contrasting perspectives – of my world and your world – through empathy. In the next chapter, we will discover what happens when we use stories to bridge across many worlds through many lives, to create a movement.

15. CULTURAL SYNCHRONICITY

THE DEPTH OF THE WAVE

On the surface, the sea appears as a series of localized waves, separate from each other, their deeper connection only knowable when we look beneath the surface. From an ontological perspective, we could similarly describe all entities as existing in a large, interconnected web or field. To exist in a set of fields would be to send waves of various frequencies to the rest of the field. Using this model, we could conceive of the universe as an infinite set of fields, so that what we think of as matter or energy consists of varying frequencies within that field. This is the ontology strongly suggested by quantum field theory. The relative existence of individual entities within the field is described by their sameness and their difference, or from the perspective of waves, as that which is resonant and that which is not. All things in our universe are constantly in motion, in process. Even objects that appear to be stationary are in fact vibrating, oscillating, resonating, at specific frequencies. To that extent, every 'thing' is described by its activity, in that our experience of them must always appear to be changing in time.

Resonance is the recognition of sameness within experience. In awareness, conscious experience is known wherever there is resonance, be it from the cellular perspective, the societal perspective or the human perspective. From the perspective of physics, we might describe resonance as a form of *shared quantum entanglement*. This is the physical phenomenon that occurs when a group of particles are generated, interact, or share spatial proximity in a way such that the quantum state of each particle of the group cannot be described independent of the state of the others, including when the particles are separated by a large distance.

Resonance describes a specific type of motion, characterized by the synchronized oscillation between two states. It is the sharing of a vibratory frequency, which establishes synchrony (also known as coherence). Spontaneous synchrony occurs when objects – as separate, indivisible entities – become connected. It is one of the most fundamental properties of the universe, occurring in everything from inanimate objects through to all living organisms, and appears to run counter to the entropic tendency toward disorder. The science of synchronization – also called *complex network theory* or *harmonic oscillator theory* – is concerned with coupling, and coupling is important because, at a certain level, everything is connected. At an organizational level, culture provides a way of describing this connectivity.

Synchrony is everywhere, from the laser, when photons of the same power and frequency are emitted together, to how the Moon's rotation is exactly synced with its orbit around the Earth, such that we always see the same face. Synchronization is fundamental to the development process through which complex forms arise – a process described as a 'phase transition,' the emergence of new forms of organization through mutual orientation and simplification. Biological entities rely on synchronization and coherence between their constituent parts to achieve more complex types of behaviour.

Evolutionary biologist Tam Hunt and psychologist Jonathan Schooler (2019) explain: *"In any set of oscillating structures, such as neurons, synchronization leads to increased and faster energy and information flows because the flows work together, in 'sync,' and are thus amplified (coherent) rather than being 'out of sync' (incoherent.)"*[1] Neurophysiologist Pascal Fries (2015) states, as an example, *"In the absence of coherence, inputs arrive at random phases of the excitability cycle and will have a lower effective connectivity."*[2]

The first recorded observation of synchronization was in 1665, when astronomer Christian Huygens observed that two clocks that were close together would gradually synchronize their pendulum swings. The reason for this coupling was that the clocks were connected by a wooden beam. It was the transfer of mechanical vibrations along the beam, from one clock to the other, that caused the two to become coupled.

Synchronization is observed throughout the natural world, from the very large (such as in the flocking behaviour of 100,000 starlings) to the very small (your heart can keep beating due to the synchronous electrical rhythm of 10,000 pacemaker cells in the heart's sinoatrial node). In animals, we describe this behaviour as a swarm – a mass synchronization of movement – and the rules that govern swarms in nature can teach us much about how organizations and societies can help their people work together to create more synchronous, and therefore harmonious, behaviour. In nature, there are four basic rules of any swarm:

1. **Purpose:** When there is a threat, the swarm must disperse for it to spontaneously reform.
2. **Coupling:** Each individual in the swarm is only aware of and interested in their closest neighbour.
3. **Coherence:** They have a tendency to line up and take on the same behaviours.
4. **Observation:** They perceive and are attracted to each other.

A good example of this is the male firefly in Southeast Asia, which spends most of its time living a relatively solitary existence. Each firefly has a natural flashing cycle frequency,

1. *The Easy Part of the Hard Problem: A resonance theory of consciousness.* Tam Hunt and Jonathan W. Schooler. *Front Hum Neurosci.* 2019; 13: 378.

2. Fries P. (2015). *Rhythms for cognition: communication through coherence. Neuron* 88 220–235. 10.1016.

but when they see their neighbour flash, they restart their cycle – they couple. When hundreds of fireflies come together, they will flash continuously for some time until a tipping point or phase transition is reached, when quite suddenly they fall into synch. In the case of fireflies, it is believed that this synchronization is designed to make it easier for females to identify the males, so they can mate. The combined light is so bright that fishermen can see them out at sea, and use them to navigate home.

We can make two additional observations about swarming behaviour that have implications for our organizations:

1. **Swarms must be mutually beneficial for all members:** In the natural world, examples include: providing warmth through flocking behaviour (common scooters flock together to stay warm in winter); conserving energy (geese fly in formation in each other's slipstreams to reduce wind resistance); and predatory protection (the synchronized movements or 'murmuration' of starlings make it difficult for the falcons to pick out individual birds). As with the firefly, all benefits are ultimately to further the survival of the swarm.

2. **Swarming enables rapid communication between members:** The four rules describe a process of communication that both enables and sustains synchronization, through the rapid dissemination of information across the swarm. For example, on where to forage (if one bird in a flock finds a reliable food source it will alert the flock, and the entire group benefits), or in detecting a threat (such as with herring, where the identification of a threat sends a visible shock wave through the school).

Our natural human tendency to come together is, in effect, to swarm. We are all swarming, whether through our organizations, through our religions, in the way we drink tea, or the way that we vote. In fact, this occurs any time we form part of a system of collective beliefs, and often in ways that are not obvious to us. (It's far easier to see the swarm from the outside looking in, than from the inside looking out.) Swarms persist through our habitualized behaviours – those that we no longer pay attention to. Our lives are a series of learned ritualizations that mimic the world around us. In organizations, we swarm around processes, knowledge, information, and around each of the 16 organizational states.

CREATING A PHASE TRANSITION

Cultural Synchronicity describes how this synchronization of collective endeavour (the swarm) can be applied to organizations to achieve an organizational phase transition. It is the possibility for the presentation of a uniquely collective behaviour to achieve extraordinary results. In nature, this collective endeavour is termed *encapsulation* – the emergence of the group's activity as a new single unit or whole.

A phase transition brings about a fundamental change in the organization's state. It marks the inflexion point at which the synchronized flashing of the firefly is established, and a new order is formed. It enables a profound shift in the environmental conditions and organizational dynamics. The application of cultural synchronicity is therefore toward the creation of systemic change in organizations – to the system itself, as opposed to changes within the system (those that are already enabled though the system).

For a phase transition to occur within an organization, the swarm must reach a critical point of resonance with the system. Every object in existence has a natural resonant frequency, or *eigenfrequency*, at which a system tends to oscillate in the absence of any driving or damping force. When that frequency is shared with others, it has an amplifying effect. The effect is often striking, such as when an opera singer can use their voice to shatter a glass. In organizations, a phase transition does not increase the value in the system, but rather changes the value (its purpose) by which the system is itself measured and defined.

	Non-systemic Change	Systemic Change
Purpose	Bring about a change within the system (transforming)	Bring about change to the system (transcending)
Presenting challenge	Voting in a democracy (inclusive)	Protesting in a dictatorship (exclusive)
Reoccurrence	Once (one vote)	Repeated (multiple protests)
Environment	Equitable (non-egoic)	Non-equitable (egoic)
Complexity	Simple (rules are known)	Complex (rules need breaking)
Outcome	Uncertain (cause and effect known)	Unknown (cause and effect unknowable)

FIG 69 – NON-SYSTEMIC VS. SYSTEMIC CHANGE

As an approach, Cultural Synchronicity applies the principles and rules of swarming and social synchronization in the natural world to the rituals and collective rhythms of the world of work. It presents an opportunity for organizations to invite social and cultural change from the ground up, as a natural response to rebalance the egoic power structures that place a limitation on individual and organizational expression.

Within Cultural Synchronicity, there are four conditions that are necessary to achieve a systemic phase transition in organizations (and which are congruent with the rules of swarms) and four roles, through which each condition is enacted:

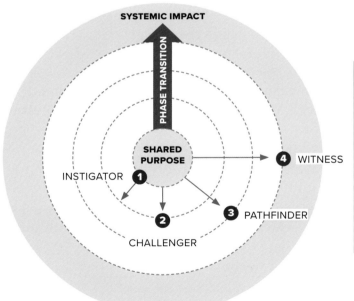

CONDITION	ROLE
1. PURPOSE – Fixing the Purpose	*Instigator:* Their actions place a limitation on the environment, from which arises the swarm's purpose.
2. COUPLING – Taking the Challenge	*Challenger:* Undertakes to challenge the Instigator, through counteractive shared action.
3. COHERENCE – Passing it On	*Pathfinder:* Attracted to the swarm by the Challenger to take on the challenge.
4. OBSERVATION – Sharing the Story	*Witness:* Observes and shares the story, as they watch events play out.

FIG 70 – PURPOSE TO IMPACT: CREATING A PHASE TRANSITION

THE CULTURE FLASH

Synchronous culture change – that which requires a radical change to the system – cannot be directed. Swarming is an entirely devolved process of self-organization, in which there is no leader. Indeed, any attempt to instil control would place a limitation on the individual expressions on which its collective movement depends. However, just as Huygens observed the beam that connected his two clocks as the origin of their synchronization, we might also ask what it is that can connect us within our own organizations.

When London first opened its Millennium Bridge across the River Thames, it operated with a resonant frequency that, unbeknownst to the designers, was the same as the people walking on it. On the day the bridge opened, and as more and more people began to walk over it, the bridge began to swing ever so slightly, from side to side. The movement was minimal at first, but in response, in an attempt to keep their balance, people walked with a wider stance, to keep time with the swing so that they could keep on walking. As a result, the swinging increased, as everyone fell into step and marched in synch across the bridge. Soon afterwards, the bridge was closed.

The Millennium Bridge is an example of how we can bake into our environment opportunities to create synchronous behaviours with those around us, by discovering that which is resonant. It also shows us that what creates resonance – that which connects – is not the bridge, and not even the people, but their unification, which is itself indivisible and undefinable. As composer John Williams once said of music, *"It isn't the orchestra, it isn't the composer, or the audience, it's the connective link, the nexus, the linking of all of that together. I'm just a guy who puts dots on a paper, it means nothing."*[3] In cultural synchronicity, that connection – the fundamental aspect of resonance – is created through story.

A Culture Flash is the moment in which one individual (as the 'Challenger') invites another individual ('the Pathfinder') to step outside of their egoic story through a shared experience that will profoundly change their perspective. Each experience centres around a shared challenge – one that necessitates a change in their experience that is designed to change themselves, and through which their individual stories are transformed. Like a living story, the challenge is passed from one person to the next – an emergent collective memory whose propagation induces a new cultural narrative and shared emotional resonance, toward a common and defining purpose.

3. https://youtu.be/
iaE3OHUT0S8
(courtesy of https://
thelegacyofjohnwilliams.com)

Through each Culture Flash, the Challenger becomes the change through their repudiation of the prevailing power dynamic. As US President Woodrow Wilson once said, *"Be bright, be brilliant, and be gone."* Through these cultural flashpoints the stories spread, and through their emotional resonance, these moments of individual brilliance emerge as a singular, synchronized movement that can bring about systemic change. The four conditions that distinguish Cultural Synchronicity from traditional approaches to culture change are described below.

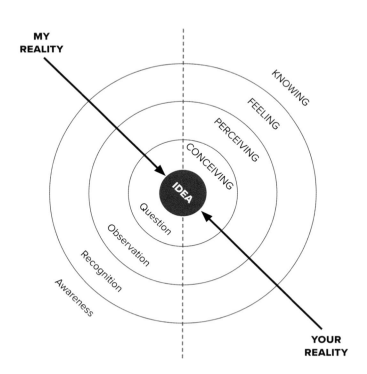

**FIG 71 – CULTURE FLASH: IDEAS THAT CREATE
A SHARED POINT OF ATTENTION**

CONDITION #1: PURPOSE – FIXING THE PURPOSE

At the centre of every story, ever swarm, is an idea. An idea is a thought – the discernment of something new that shifts our perspective, not by changing experience, but by changing from where we perceive experience. To gain our attention, all ideas are preceded by conception (our thoughts), all conception preceded by perception (our sensations), all thoughts and sensations preceded by feeling, and all feeling preceded by knowing (Fig 71). Ideas are important because those that create a shared point of attention – a shared connection – create purpose.

Cultural Synchronicity starts with purpose. The origin of all swarms is the *Instigator* (there can be more than one), whose actions place a limitation on the swarm and its environment. In the natural world, a murmuration of starlings is instigated by the presence of the falcon (its Instigator), and the threat it presents. In an organizational context, the Instigator reflects those individuals whose actions perpetuate an egoic power dynamic, which rigs the system and places a limitation on the organization's operation. It is this that derives the swarm's purpose. However, purpose alone is not enough for the swarm to form. For purpose to be recognized it must be shared, which is to say it requires a story. And to tell its story (as with all stories), something has to change.

Because the Instigator's influence on the environmental system is systemic, individuals within the system cannot change it on their own. Indeed, any occasion where systemic change is sought that does not address egoic power structures will necessitate the use of them to affect that change. There are, therefore, two ways for change to happen: through resistance or in acceptance. When environmental conditions are systemic, they prevail because those that are impacted act independently in resistance, in isolation from each other. This changes when a single individual, the *Challenger*, undertakes an action that is asynchronous to the normalized behaviours – they challenge the system. This first Culture Flash illuminates and reveals the purpose of the swarm – the egoic inequity within the system. The Culture Flash has two conditions: (1) It is in active opposition, but in acceptance (and thereby in full awareness) of the system (that which is seen cannot be unseen); (2) The swarm's purpose attracts the attention of another individual, or *Pathfinder*.

CONDITION #2: COUPLING – TAKING THE CHALLENGE

The swarm's purpose – its story – is the axis around which swarms form, and through which their members identify. For purpose to be shared, it must be experienced, in order for its story to spread. This experience takes the form of a challenge that is set by the Challenger, for the Pathfinder to complete, and which brings Challenger and Pathfinder together. The challenge answers the question. "How can we bring our purpose to life?" That is the vehicle by which it is embodied, shared, sustained and transformed. It is undertaken together – jointly by both Challenger and Pathfinder – in a coupling in which the Challenger guides the Pathfinder through the challenge as one might lead a dancer in the dance, its impact amplified through their synchronization. The challenge disrupts the system, illuminating the inequity and creating a flashpoint for change.

Through this process, the Challenger's entrusting of the swarm's purpose to the Pathfinder necessitates an intimate relationship. Our work networks are often fluid, transactable, consumable, their utility and value directly proportional to our ability to get the job done. Our relationships have become points on a map by which we navigate our careers, and while our networks have grown more diverse, they have simultaneously lost their depth and affinity. Cultural synchronicity unlocks an organization's capacity to change through deeper, more meaningful, personal connections. It is only through our intimate relationships that we derive deeper purpose and through which change is not enforced, but entrusted. The highly selective basis by which the Challenger and Pathfinder are attracted to each other recognizes the importance of these deeper connections to creating meaningful change. In a world of competing priorities and diminishing resources, our capacity for empathetic change necessitates the fostering of these intimate connections.

CONDITION #3: COHERENCE – PASSING IT ON

The actions of the Challenger and of the Pathfinder that couple them pose a challenge to the system that will (through the Instigator) seek to remove them. For example, at the early stages of a murmuration, the falcon can more easily target the small number of swarming starlings that might otherwise have remained hidden, just as a bully may more easily discredit their first accuser. Therefore, the success of swarming within a system is equal both to its provocation of the system and the speed by which its story can spread. This is not dissimilar to what is observed in the early stages of a start-up that, to outcompete much larger competition, must either grow at an accelerated rate or die.

The Pathfinder becomes the Challenger as they in turn couple with other individuals, and the process is repeated, creating a flywheel effect. The challenge by its nature must be simple, repeatable, relatable, expressible and personal (no two are identical) – and in this way symbolic. Change is never then, only now. Change that is led, planned and directed will inevitably seek to realize its potential in the future. And yet, if we define purpose as that which matters in THIS moment, then purpose-driven change must focus its attention on the only moment that matters – right now. The challenge-based approach brings change into the present, by bringing about change through simple, accessible tasks designed to elicit authentic, affective expressions of the purpose to which they pertain.

Today we are seeing increasing challenge to inequity across the globe, through not just local but global swarms, whether through protests on the street against autocratic regimes or the promotion of philanthropic causes. The Ice Bucket Challenge[4] is an example of a social movement that, through this challenge-based approach, managed to raise more than

4. Sherman, C & Wedge, D. (2017). *Ice Bucket Challenge: Pete Frates and the Fight Against ALS.* (1st Edition). ForeEdge.

$115 million for research into amyotrophic lateral sclerosis. Its success stemmed from a small number of individuals that entrusted this hugely important and resonant purpose to their nearest and dearest acquaintances, by setting each the challenge of pouring an ice bucket over their head and posting a video online – this being the basis by which money could be raised and through which the purpose could be fulfilled. The extreme nature of the challenge reflects its overt provocation to the system of underfunding it sought to derail. In an organizational context, the principles that underpin this challenge-based approach to engendering shared purpose in the service of systemic organizational change, are:

- **Intrinsic:** Participants must gain intrinsic value through their completion of the challenge – it does not require them to change the system, just themselves.
- **Intense:** The challenge requires the Pathfinder to stretch themselves – to see themselves in a different light, and for others to do the same.
- **Affective:** The challenge should evoke an overt emotional and physical response in the Pathfinder – be it laughter, shock, anger or sadness – to engender emotional resonance in others.
- **Inclusive:** The challenge should be simple, short, easy to repeat – the bar is set low so that everyone can join in.
- **Collective:** Participation confers belonging – everyone who undertakes the challenge is automatically accepted as part of the swarm.
- **Equitable:** The challenge is the same for everyone, and because everyone undertakes the same challenge, the difference is always pointing to the purpose, not the person
- **Developmental:** The collective synchronization of the swarm describes a learned response, as its encapsulated behaviours change over time.
- **Celebrated:** Each and every challenge should be shared and celebrated – like a Culture Flash – to set the world alight, to spread the word.

While the rapid propagation of the challenge through a one-to-many approach might seem more adept at accelerating the process (the mass communications approach being the typical model by which change communications are deployed at scale across organizations), the intimacy of one-on-one relationships on which emotional resonance is founded

– that which is necessary for shared purpose to be entrusted to others as the catalyst for meaningful change – would be lost. It is also the only way to protect the original intent of the swarm.

CONDITION #4: OBSERVATION – SHARING THE STORY

To learn truth and meaning, it must first be hidden from us, so that through its discovery it can be known. That is how purpose is revealed to the Pathfinder, through the challenge. The story of the swarm – its shared purpose – is passed from one member to the next through the synchronous coupling of Challenger and Pathfinder around this unifying performance challenge. As the swarm grows, the story of its passing emerges as a met-anarrative. It is this 'story of stories' that gains the attention of the fourth group – the *Witnesses*. As outside observers, Witnesses bring attention to the swarm – their presence enabling it to grow by fulfilling one of three roles:

1. **Transition from Witness to Challenger:** The Witness steps into the story unbidden to undertake the challenge as a new Challenger, to start a new movement or swarm, or to join up with the existing one.
2. **Transition from Witness to Pathfinder:** The Witness is invited into the swarm to take on the challenge.
3. **Attract more Witnesses:** Witnesses share the story to create a new set of Witnesses. As with the Challenger and the Pathfinder, the more personal the connection through which the story is told, the more likely the progression from Witness to active participant.

To attract and grow this observer audience within the organization, Witnesses should consider the following:

- **Engage high-profile Challengers:** These are individuals who are likely to attract greater attention due to their extensive connections and reputation, such as organizational influencers, relationship brokers or high-profile role models.
- **Create a collective memory:** Philosophers Andy Clark and David Chalmers'[5] thought experiment features two people travelling to a museum. One has Alzheimer's, and so has written down the directions, whereas the other refers

5. Andy Clark, David J Chalmers (January 1998). "The extended mind." Analysis. 58 (1): 7–19.; reprinted as: Andy Clark, David J Chalmers (2010). "Chapter 2: The extended mind." In Richard Menary (ed.). *The Extended Mind*. MIT Press. pp. 27–42. ISBN 9780262014038.; and available on line as: Andy Clark, David J Chalmers. "The extended mind." Cogprints.

to memory. Both are objects in our experience with different forms, but which can only ever be perceived now. Is the notebook an extension of memory? Today's technology provides a thousand ways in which to change the form of our memories, to amplify how our stories are shared. Videos shared through social media create a collective memory that can instantly reach people anywhere in the world to raise awareness.

- **Tap into the cultural zeitgeist:** The stories that are shared will gain greater resonance and interest if they can tap into the cultural zeitgeist, such as by tuning into recent societal interests or trends. The big social media tech companies exist through the monetization of this data. Tools such as Google Trends and X (formerly known as Twitter), as well the organizations' own newsfeeds, can be useful to check trending topics to tap into.

The combination of these four conditions gives rise to a *trust-less system* – one in which the absence of trust (in which trust can no longer be gained or lost, rather than it manifesting through distrust) enables the swarm to grow, and a movement (whether political or cultural) to form. The critical point of phase transition – the moment of synchronization – is the moment in which every voice can be heard, when it speaks as one. In this moment of revolution, a new system, a new voice, a new culture can emerge. This synchronicity is only made possible due to the underlying reality that everything is connected. The beam that spanned Huygens' clocks is the same as the floor that we stand on, or the air that we breathe.

LEADING ONWARD:
THE FUTURE OF LEADERSHIP

16. CODEX FOR THE EXISTENTIAL EVOLUTION OF LEADERSHIP

In Part 3, we will look to the future of leadership, what this means for the evolution of human experience, and the important role that all of us – as leaders – have to play.

The end of every story can be traced back to its origin. Our life story is like a mirror in which for life to begin, it must carry within it the reflection of the life that is ending. On a cosmological level, scientists refer to this end as our 'heat death' – the point at which our ever-expanding universe will achieve a state of infinite entropy, in which energy cannot flow, and change (and thereby experience) ceases to exist, its fate sealed at the very moment of its inception, within the infinite density of the big bang. So it follows that as we look to our own story, and seek to understand not only its evolution but its ending, we need look only to its origin: the ego.

RECLAIMING THE UNIVERSAL MOVEMENT

Objective reality is relativistic, in that everything exists in relation to something else. In other words, every object in existence can only be in existence because it is either a part of something else, or is itself the whole from which other parts are made. Every object in reality is actually not a part or a whole, but a holon (both simultaneously depending on your perspective). That is, in every aspect of reality – be they physical, biological or social systems – independent self-supporting entities do not exist. Holons therefore constitute any conceivable entity, from the smallest subatomic particles and strings to the multi-verse, comprising many universes, and within every concept, from maths or language to the economy, or to you.

Consequently, reality is always perspectival, perceived from a particular point of view. As philosopher and journalist Arthur Koestler, who first proposed the word holon in his book, *The Ghost in the Machine*, states: *"Einstein's space is no closer to reality than Van Gogh's sky. The glory of science is not in a truth more absolute than the truth of Bach or Tolstoy, but in the act of creation itself. The scientist's discoveries impose his own order on chaos, as the composer or painter imposes his; an order that always refers to limited aspects of reality, and is based on the observer's frame of reference, which differs from period to period as a Rembrandt nude differs from a nude by Manet."*[1] Because reality is relativistic, so as we lend reality (or rather it lends us) our particular plane of attention, there appears a directionality and hierarchy to form and manifestation, in which we observe increasing levels

1. Koestler, A. (1967). *The Ghost in the Machine.* One 70 Press.

of complexity. From the holonic perspective, we see that form is organized in nested degrees of increasing complexity – the universal movement.

At lower levels of complexity, more predictable, recognizable patterns are observed that repeat in time and space, while at higher levels of complexity, form exhibits increasingly uncertain, divergent and less predictable patterns of activity. Complexity evolves as each whole is conceived as part of a greater, more complex whole. Consider economist and Nobel Prize winner Herbert Simon's parable of the two watchmakers:

There once were two watchmakers, named Bios and Mekhos, who made very fine watches. The phones in their workshops rang frequently; new customers were constantly calling them. However, Bios prospered while Mekhos became poorer and poorer. In the end, Mekhos lost his shop and worked as a mechanic for Bios. What was the reason behind this?

The watches consisted of about 1,000 parts each. The watches that Mekhos made were designed such that, when he had to put down a partly assembled watch (for instance, to answer the phone), it immediately fell into pieces and had to be completely reassembled from the basic elements. On the other hand, Bios designed his watches so that he could put together subassemblies of about ten components each. Ten of these subassemblies could be put together to make a larger subassembly. Finally, ten of the larger subassemblies constituted the whole watch. When Bios had to put his watches down to attend to some interruption, they did not break up into their elemental parts but only into their subassemblies.

Now, the watchmakers were each disturbed at the same rate of once per 100 assembly operations. However, due to their different assembly methods, it took Mekhos four thousand times longer than Bios to complete a single watch.[2]

The watch parts serve as a metaphor for memory. In the parable, memory appears as the interruption that Bios attends to. As his watch is put down, it – and time – stops, its memory preserved. As this process is repeated, a process of development is realized. As the memory is retrieved, so it is brought into new association with the constituent parts of current experience, until finally the watch is formed.

Just as cogs make up watches, or as words make up paragraphs, and paragraphs make up pages, and pages make up books, so too are we organized psychologically, physically

2. *"The Architecture of Complexity"* – Herbert A Simon. Proceedings of the American Philosophical Society, Vol. 106, No. 6. (Dec. 12, 1962), pp. 467-482.

and socially in ever-increasing complexity, each arising out of and contingent on that from which it derives. Take away letters and there are no words, no words mean no sentences, and so on. Similarly, the universe, the most fundamental of holons, does not appear without you in it.

Through this development process appears cause and effect. But causality is also an illusion that arises through the perception of space and time. Form can only exist in the presence of other form. Life is only possible through the presence of life. In the parable of the two watchmakers, it is through its disturbance that the watch comes into existence. Through relativity, time appears absolute. In the absence of relativity, there is no time. The tale therefore requires the presence of two watchmakers in order to make the comparison, in the same way as you cannot tell the time from only one watch.

This universal movement is that which derives a perfect balance between order and chaos. Consider how within the human body our acid-base balance is maintained through our 15 trillion cells at a consistent 7.4 pH. Drop by only 0.6 pH or increase by only 0.4 pH and you will die. Conversely, consider the origin of our universe. If the rate of expansion one second after the Big Bang had been smaller even by one part in a hundred thousand million, the universe would have recollapsed before it ever reached its present size. We also see how some of the values in the universe are finely adjusted to make possible their development. For example, if the electrical charge of the electron had only been slightly different, stars either would have been unable to burn hydrogen and helium, or else would have exploded. And without the light of a star, there would be (so far as we can understand) no life.

The universal movement is toward the absence of authorship and centralized control. Every living organism exists through an exquisite balance that is undertaken for no one. The 15 trillion cells in the human body act on their own accord, under the auspices of the cellular brain, the nucleus. At a cellular level, controls prevent the cells from growing out of control, thus preventing cancer. These controls balance the needs of the cells with the needs of the human body, so that in this case, while the growth of the cells is curtailed, it means that the human body can stay alive (the ultimate fate of cancer being to kill itself).

When we observe any complex system, there appears to be autonomy and control. And yet, when we point to who is making this happen, who is in control, there is nothing and no one to point to. This is indeed what Koestler is referring to as the 'ghost in the machine.'[1] Everything is holonic, both a part and a whole, and as such is a relativistic rather than absolute entity. Most people with functioning limbs would believe that they have the autonomy to stand on your own two feet. Note, however, that you can only do so because of the ground that is under you, so you owe your autonomy at least in part to the ground. What holds up the ground? The world. What holds up the world? Extending this line of reasoning is the same as seeking a ground upon which reality can be contained. But reality is groundless.

Autonomy reflects the relativity to that with which it is perceived to be part of or separate from. In the same way as the ego asserts autonomy through its authorship to move from sitting to standing, so in the absence of ego we note that standing still happens, but for no one. Similarly, when we observe the cells in our body, we perceive autonomy through the persistence of their function over time. But it is not the persistence of the cell that enables its function. Rather, it is the persistence of that which the cell is not. It is only when we, as holons, step outside of ourselves, in the dissolution of part from the whole, that this becomes obvious.

The universal movement is the experience of change. This asymmetrical aspect of experience is undeniable. Within individual experience, we could say there are three essential aspects (Fig 72).

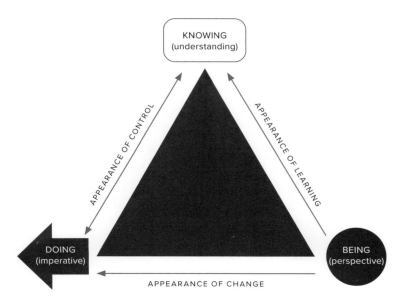

FIG 72 – THE ESSENTIAL ASPECTS OF EXPERIENCING

The first aspect is the understanding or recognition of experience. It is our internal state, inside the Markov blanket, through which we form our model of the world. It is our **knowing** of experience. The second is our intention or *imperative* within experience, in which we perceive our action. It is that which defines our external state, outside the Markov blanket. It is our **doing** within experience. The reciprocation between the internal states – of knowing and doing – gives rise to the appearance of choice and control. At the same time, the awareness by which knowing and doing is perceived derives a singular perspective through which experience arises – the aperture through which we perceive reality, whose limitation in turn confers our limited perspective onto reality. It is from this that arises our perceived direction of attention, toward the internalized (introspective) and externalized (extrospective) aspects of experience, and which forms our identity, or individualized perspective – our **being** within experience.

As attention is given to our internal state, there arises the appearance of learning – of memory. As attention is given to our external state, there arises the appearance of change. These three aspects of experience – the triumvirate of knowing, doing and being – are ultimately not separate, but the same. They are the activity of awareness, to reveal and know itself. Paradoxically, it appears that awareness must first limit itself, to forget itself through the giving of attention to the finite forms of experience, in order to know itself. This universal movement within experience is that something must be lost for it to be found. That we must forget before we can remember. It is the narrative arc of all our stories – of our history and of our future. The paradox pertains to that fact that in reality, nothing is ever lost, is ever at a distance from awareness.

The universal movement of awareness is timeless, but through perspectival reality it appears to take place within space and time. As such, we could describe the universal movement as like that of a wave. From the perspective of the wave, its movement is finite, its existence temporary. But look beneath the surface and one can see the universality by which all waves, all movements, ultimately move as one, with no start and no end. It is from this perspective that we may consider the universal movement through which humankind is itself evolving.

From the perspective of humanity, the universal movement is the evolution of human experience, which can be said to be arising through a series of 'waves' – periods of human history that mark an inexorable progression toward complexity, autonomy, balance, and ultimately stillness. As humanity – through its organizations, systems and technologies – is seen to evolve, so too ego, as an integral aspect of human experience, will evolve.

Through this understanding, it is possible to form a universal model for the evolution of human experience, through four successive waves that reflect four fundamental, progressive shifts in human perspective. This story – the 'Codex for the Existential Evolution of Leadership' (Fig 73) – shows how the thought structure of ego operates as the fundamental blueprint by which the human experience (and thereby our societies and our world) will change.

It describes the basis of our story: how ego is directing the development of mankind's perspective, toward a **vanishing point**, through the appearance of a past and future.

The model defines the common characteristics of human experience that propagate each wave, and how each wave gives rise to the next, with each one reflecting an existential threat and opportunity. It describes how our progression from this wave to the next will require a new form of leadership, through a set of conscious imperatives. Note that while the use here of the term 'evolution' is not synonymous with genetic evolution, genetics is one of many aspects by which the universal movement can be observed.

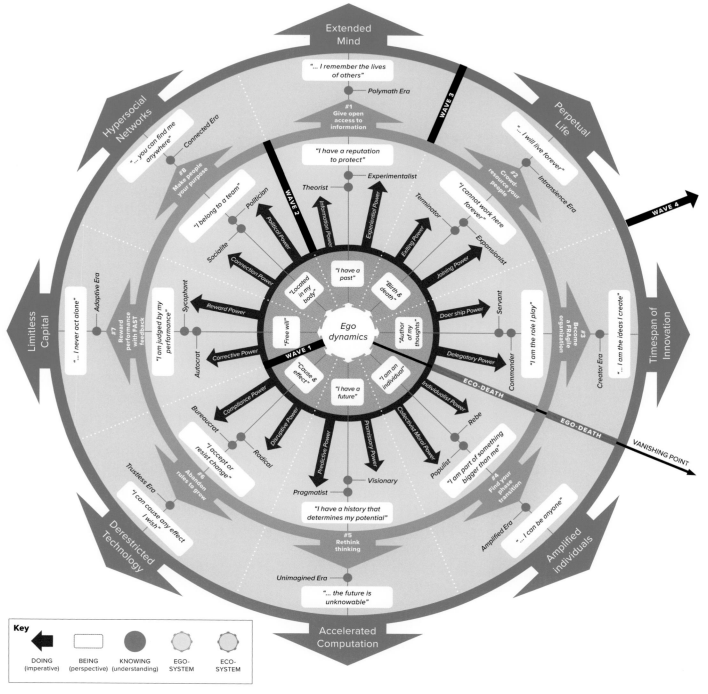

FIG 73 – CODEX FOR THE EXISTENTIAL EVOLUTION OF LEADERSHIP

THE FIRST THREE WAVES

Each wave contains the core characteristics of human experience – of knowing, doing and being:

- **Knowing:** Preceding each wave is the knowing of experience – the basis of our understanding as that by which we recognize and thereby identify experience. Because reality is perspectival, everything we know reflects the inherent limitations of thinking and sensing, and must therefore take on the form of those limitations. Ego reflects the most profound of these limitations – as the identification of self with ego. Our organizations today are a macrocosm of the thought structure of the separate self, through which they are conceived. Their appearance is the product of ontological design – we design and shape organizations in order to design and shape the individuals within them. At the same time, ego, as an aspect of experience like a table or chair, is also a product of that experience. So it is that we observe congruence, for example, between the evolution of technology, and the evolution of ego – our sense of self defining the technologies we need, while simultaneously being shaped by the experiences that our technologies create.
- **Doing:** Our activity – the 'doing' within experience – is that which compels our action and attention. Our activities reflect our current understanding. They describe a set of imperatives by which the wave is formed and propagated, and which ultimately must also recede for a new wave – a new form of understanding – to arise. They describe our forms of expression within each wave, our behaviours and our rules.
- **Being:** Within each wave, our locus of perspective derives the role we assume for ourselves – that which we identify our perspective with. In our current wave, we tend to think in terms of the hats we wear, as the many parts or roles that we play.

The evolution of human experience can be described by the transformation of these three core characteristics across each of the four waves that span the universal movement. Here, we will consider the first three.

ASPECT	FIRST WAVE	SECOND WAVE	THIRD WAVE
Knowing (understanding)	Example: *"I have a past."*	Example: *"I have a reputation to protect."*	Formed from both individual intelligence and AI
Doing (imperative)	Unconscious Imperative	Conscious Imperative	Meta Imperative
Being (perspective)	As 'if' (hunter of hunted)	As 'what' (my role or function)	As 'why' (our era – the shape of time)

FIG 74 – THE EVOLUTION OF HUMAN EXPERIENCE THROUGH THE FIRST THREE WAVES

THE FIRST WAVE: PRE-CIVILIZATION

The First Wave is the age of self, which predates the onset of society and rule-based systems of social organization. The wave begins at the dawn of modern man. There is great uncertainty over when modern man first arrived, but perhaps given the evolutionary necessity of childbirth, we might presume that the first man to be modern was in fact a woman. The biology professor Dr. Richard G. Klein describes the turning point in human history and creativity at around 40,000 years ago[3] when, as social anthropologist John Noble writes: *"Modern Homo sapiens arrived in Europe and left the first unambiguous artefacts of abstract and symbolic thought. They were making more advanced tools, burying their dead with ceremony and expressing a new kind of self-awareness with beads and pendants for body ornamentation and in finely wrought figurines of the female form. As time passed, they projected onto cave walls something of their lives and minds through paintings of deer, horses and wild bulls."[4]*

For thousands of years, humans existed in groups of fewer than 150. It was only recently that evolutionary psychologist Robin Dunbar was able to demonstrate the correlation between social group sizes in primates and the size of the neocortex in the brain.[5] Humans do not have the cognitive capacity to form trusting relationships beyond around 150 people. Dunbar found evidence for this in surveys of naturally forming social group

3. Klein, R & Edgar, B. (2002). *The Dawn of Human Culture.* (1st Edition). Wiley.

4. Wilford, J. N. (2002). *When Humans Became Human.* New York Times.

5. Robin Dunbar, R. (2009). The social brain hypothesis and its implications for social evolution. *Annals of Human Biology* 36(5):562-72.

sizes throughout history, from the estimated population of Neolithic farming villages, to the splitting point of Hutterite settlements, to the basic unit size of professional armies in Roman antiquity. For larger social groups, social trust required a rules-based organized system. Of the First Wave we can say:

FROM THE PERSPECTIVE OF KNOWING

In this First Wave, the egoic structure of thought described by the eight tenets of ego informed our understanding (Fig 3). We emerged as a species as the subject of our experience, with self-awareness that denoted an individual identity, a self that is separate from objective experience.

FROM THE PERSPECTIVE OF BEING

In the First Wave, we assumed the identity and perspective of that which assured our survival. Our flight response arises when our perspective is *as if* we are the prey, just as through our fight response arises our perspective *as if* we are the predator – the hunted and the hunter. This engrained fight or flight perspective shaped our thinking, our attention, our choices, and is the source of many of our cognitive biases today, because we think as if we need to survive.

FROM THE PERSPECTIVE OF DOING (UNCONSCIOUS IMPERATIVES)

The imperatives are those actions that, through the furtherance of our survival, enabled our evolution to the Second Wave. They reflect the inclination toward settlement, to larger groups, to the safety and security of civilization, through the establishment of social hierarchy and the dominion over others. They are the second-order egoic power dynamics (Chapter 11) that arose from first-order Egodynamics (Chapter 8), and which pertain to the organization of individuals and activities through centralized control. They are the egoic basis by which organizations and societies are formed, and on which their purpose and design is established.

Organizational power dynamics are 'unconscious imperatives' – the basis by which egoic power is exerted through a centrally controlled organization, and through which arise the eight organizing dilemmas that reflect polarizing and competing organizational needs within a system, between order and chaos. They represent the defining dissonant characteristics of a centrally controlled organizational system, on which the Second Wave is based.

THE SECOND WAVE: CENTRALIZED SYSTEMS

The Second Wave is the age of the centrally controlled system. The earliest signs of a sedentary society can be found in the Natufian culture that arose in the Levant region of Western Asia as early as 12,000 BCE[6] and evolved into an agricultural society by 10,000 BCE. Sumer, located in Mesopotamia (today's southern Iraq), is the first known complex civilization, having developed the first city-states in the 4th millennium BCE. It was in these cities that the earliest known form of writing, cuneiform script, appeared around 3,000 BCE. Of the Second Wave we can say:

FROM THE PERSPECTIVE OF KNOWING

In the Second Wave, there is an evolution of the egoic tenets to: (1) Reflect a broader collective identification between self and organization; (2) Accord with the eight organizing dilemmas – the hierarchical lines through which egoic control manifests in a centralized system. These are described in Fig 75, 'Development of First and Second Wave Egoic Tenets.'

FROM THE PERSPECTIVE OF BEING

There is a shift in individual perspective toward one of collective value. Centrally controlled systems confer upon their membership titles that define what 'their function' is, this denoting their value within that system. Within an organization, we describe these functions as roles, and it is through these roles that ego assumes its organizational identity and perspective. An individual's perspective will vary according to their egoic function. For example, an individual exerting informational power will assume the perspective and role of a *Theorist*, in contrast to an individual who is exerting experiential power, who will assume the perspective and role of an *Experimentalist*. In total, there are 16 different roles that ego assumes within a hierarchical system, as Fig 75 describes.

6. Ofer Bar-Yosef. (2016). The Natufian culture in the levant, *Threshold to the Origins of Agriculture.* www.columbia.edu. Retrieved 4 January 2016.

First Wave: Pre-civilization			Second Wave: Centralized System (Organization)			
Egoic Tenet	Imperative: Unconscious		Egoic Tenet	Perspective: As 'what'		Imperative: Conscious (precursor to 3rd wave)
	Toward ORDER	Toward CHAOS		Toward ORDER	Toward CHAOS	
I experience a world of matter that is separate to me.	Informational power	Experiential power	I have a reputation to protect.	Theorist	Experimentalist	#1 Give open access to information
I was born, one day I will die.	Exiting power	Joining power	I cannot work here forever.	Terminator	Expansionist	#2 Crowdsource your people
I am the author of my thoughts.	Doership power	Delegatory power	I am the role I play.	Servant	Commander	#3 Become a FRAgile organization
I am an individual, there is not two of me.	Individualist power	Collectivist moral power	I am part of something bigger than me.	Rebel	Populist	#4 Find your phase transition
I have a past that points to a future.	Predictive power	Promissory power	I have a history that determines my potential.	Pragmatist	Visionary	#5 Rethink thinking
Through time appears cause and effect.	Compliance power	Disruptive power	I accept or resist change.	Bureaucrat	Radical	#6 Abandon rules to grow
I have free will and am responsible for my actions.	Corrective power	Reward power	I am judged by my performance.	Autocrat	Sycophant	#7 Reward performance with FAST feedback
I move through space, I am located in the body.	Connection power	Political power	I belong to a team.	Socialite	Politician	#8 Make people your purpose

FIG 75 – DEVELOPMENT OF FIRST AND SECOND WAVES EGOIC TENETS

The purpose or function of any system, be it organizational or societal, is to transform itself. It is through its transformation that value, in whichever form it takes, is realized. The states that describe each system – whether states of knowledge, or skills or relationships – describe a state of transformation. They have no intrinsic value other than to that which they enable and transcend.

The 16 egoic roles within a system pertain to the 16 different organizational states of change on which all centrally controlled organizational systems are constituted (Fig 76 below). In a hierarchical organization, the function of leadership is to assume these roles in order to control the transmutability of each of these states, such that through their transformation their value is recognized across the enterprise. This control manifests through the power dynamics that run along hierarchical lines, under the auspices of ego, and through which discrimination is unavoidable.

Toward ORDER		Toward CHAOS	
State	Leader Role	State	Leader Role
KNOWLEDGE	Theorist	SKILLS	Experimentalist
LEAVERS	Terminator	JOINERS	Expansionist
ROLES	Servant	STRUCTURE	Commander
INDIVIDUALITY	Rebel	CULTURE	Populist
RISK	Pragmatist	OPPORTUNITY	Visionary
CONFORMITY	Bureaucrat	CHANGE	Radical
CORRECTION	Autocrat	REWARD	Sycophant
CONNECTION	Socialite	COLLABORATION	Politician

FIG 76 – ORGANIZATIONAL STATES AND ASSOCIATED LEADERSHIP ROLES WITHIN A HIERARCHICAL SYSTEM (SECOND WAVE)

Through this transformation, the centralized organization can be said to 'eat itself.' Consider the function of learning. Organizations may transcend a particular aspect of learning through automation, only to derive a new requirement through the skills needed to control or improve upon this new state. (Automation doesn't happen by itself.) In other words, learning arises through the elimination of learning. This paradoxical implication requires each state to be present to secure its own absence – a paradox that pertains to all states of identity, be they systemic or egoic.

FROM THE PERSPECTIVE OF DOING (CONSCIOUS IMPERATIVES)
Today, the unconscious imperatives that brought the Second Wave into existence are no longer sustainable. Centrally controlled organizations have survived and even thrived through egoic power structures under a modus operandum of command and control because the pace of change has allowed it. Were an organization to exist in a changeless world, egoic control would be absolute. The one thing that ego seeks control of, beyond all else, is time. Dictatorships survive by isolating their people from the changes in the world outside. However, no dictatorship or organization is immune to the accelerating pace of change that is increasingly evident as a universal movement in the world around us.

The arrow of time, which marks the asymmetrical movement from order to chaos, has never been more pronounced. Businesses are investing increasing amounts of time and money to minimize organizational entropy, through ever more sophisticated controls. The more complex the organization, the more energy is required to contain it. The cognitive psychologist Steven Pinker describes *"The ... ultimate purpose of life, mind and human striving: to deploy energy and information to fight back the tide of entropy and carve out refuges of beneficial order."*[7] Ultimately, however, this is like the wave holding back the sea. The organization is never separate from that which it seeks to be separate from.

7. Pinker, S. (2017). *Edge 2017 Annual Question.*

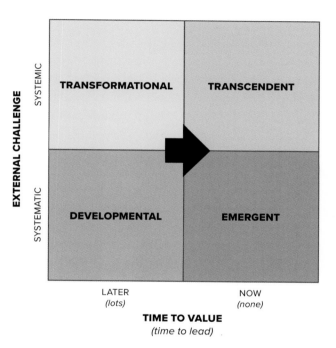

TIME TO VALUE
(time to lead)

FIG 77 – IMPACT OF TIME TO VALUE

Fig 77 shows how an organization's approach to change reflects how much time is available for value to be realized. As the pace of change accelerates, so the time to value must necessarily decrease for it to be realized. In this way, the ability of current organizational approaches to affect controlled change (in particular, systemic change) will continue to reduce proportionate to the increase in change in its external environment.

While the universal movement is as inescapable as experience itself, the endurance of the human race is not. What is certain is that the Second Wave – which we are in – is coming to an end. The old ways are being dismantled, but at the same time, there is increasing resistance to change, evident through the polarizing geopolitical landscape. It is revealing what has always been the insanity and contradiction of egoic control, in which individuals, through the systems they command, must point bombs at each other to protect their own interests, and thereby assure their mutual destruction. And yet, this insanity is not a bug in the system. Rather, it is integral to the change unfolding before us.

The pace of change is equal only to its complexity. Take, for example, challenges such as: the potential for extreme climate change and ecological collapse; more virulent global pandemics; increasing access to more advanced weapons technologies. Or, the 'quantum apocalypse,' in which the advent of quantum computers will enable any code encrypted by today's standards to be cracked in seconds, potentially rendering all our modern systems of finance, commerce, communication, transportation, manufacturing, energy, defence, government and healthcare inoperable.

One of the symptoms of the Second Wave's unsustainable responses to these challenges involves growth. While not all egoic organizations grow (due to the imposition of financial, regulatory or other controls), it is the inclination of egoic organizations to seek growth, to become more than they are. The devastation wrought on our ecosystem as we continue to plunder its resources (we have lost 70% of our wildlife populations in the last 50 years) is testament to this, as we seek happiness through materialistic experience. The Second Wave is heading toward an ECO-death – we are witnessing the escalating destruction of both our ECOlogical system and our ECOnomic systems, whose linear models and obsession with profitability are proving unsustainable.

In a capitalist non-linear economy, value is locked away through ownership – through the ownership of natural resources, for instance, or interest on loans. Consider the intrinsic value lost to a financial system for every £10 invested in shares, rather than funding the education of a child who cannot afford to learn. Because the value that is locked away does need to be earned for the value to increase, the system is rigged – the rich cannot get richer without the poor getting poorer. This inequity arises from the egoic need and assertion of ownership – the belief that value should be owned and controlled, rather than shared equitably and distributed solely through the flow of goods and services.

Organizations and societies of every size and colour have a simple but profound choice. It is a choice that becomes ever more apparent to leaders as they assail the ranks themselves: in resistance, seek ever greater control (that which satisfies ego); or in acceptance, relinquish it through the empowerment of others. The evolution of the Third Wave is the transcendence of the limitations of centralized systems of control (whether capitalist or communist in nature), toward a non-hierarchical, interdependent system of mutual empowerment.

In light of this, a radical new approach to leadership is required if we are to surmount the Second Wave into the next. The approach is described through eight **Conscious Imperatives** – conscious actions that directly address the eight organizing dilemmas and according egoic power dynamics that define the Evil Genius Organization, and which present the possibility for creating organizational coherence between change inside and outside the organization. They are in direct contrast to the **unconscious imperatives** that brought about and have to date perpetuated the Second Wave, and which have so defined today's conventions of leadership. Conscious Imperatives present a wholesale shift toward self-organization and decentralization, as the means by which today's organizing dilemmas, which have so profoundly limited organizational performance, can be reconciled. Together, they constitute a new *manifesto for conscious leadership*, as an invitation to leaders to radically transform their organizations. The Conscious Imperatives are discussed in more detail in the next chapter.

THE THIRD WAVE: DECENTRALIZED SYSTEM

The Third Wave is the age of the metaverse. It represents a paradigm shift from the conventions of centralized control toward a radically decentralized system – from **ego-system** to **eco-system**. It is one in which a new form of organization can thrive through a symbiotic relationship with its environment – one that will bend with rather than break against the uncontainable tide of change. It marks the transition from the existence of independent organizations – set apart in space and time – to the dematerialization of physical space, distance and objects. In the metaverse there will be no kill switch. Unlike today's power-driven regimes, no one will be trying, or be able, to turn off experience.

The metaverse should not be defined (as it is today) simply by technological advancements, such as web 3.0 and virtual reality. Rather, like all waves, it necessitates a radical change in human perspective. The metaverse is an invitation to lose ourselves in our experience, so that whom we understand ourselves to be transcends experience. Of the Third Wave we can say:

FROM THE PERSPECTIVE OF DOING (META IMPERATIVES)

The Conscious Imperatives of the Second Wave will ultimately give way to a new set of correlates – the Meta Imperatives that will define the Third Wave. The convergent effect of these Meta Imperatives is to radically accelerate the rate of change – to 'accelerate the acceleration.' Through the universal movement, the effect of each wave is paradoxically to compel that which precedes it. Indeed, the convergent effects of these Meta Imperatives have already begun, their origins evident in the unpredictability and disruption to today's world order and its notions of stability, longevity and resilience. Fig 78 describes the Meta Imperatives of the Third Wave.

SECOND WAVE	THIRD WAVE	
Conscious Imperative	**Meta Imperative**	**Description**
#1 Give open access to information	**Extended Mind**	The extension of mind into matter, through the development of brain computer interfaces that will super-charge our cognitive abilities and create access to a shared synthetic memory that amplifies our human intelligence by billions of times.
#2 Crowdsource your people	**Perpetual Life**	Aubrey de Grey predicts that the longevity escape velocity – the point at which for every year you are alive, technology is extending your life for more than a year – will be reached by 2030, such that anyone alive at that point has the potential to live forever. The value of time will be measured not in how it is consumed, but with how it is shared, as the new circle of life marks time in the many new ways it can bring people together.
#3 Become a FRAgile organization	**Timespan of Innovation**	With less time doing, and more time innovating, we will enter the creator era. Doing more with less through increasing automation will create more time to ideate around our biggest challenges, and also reduce the timespan of innovation – the time and agility to turn ideas into reality through ever more creative solutions – reducing time to value.
#4 Find your phase transition	**Amplified Individuals**	Individuals will amplify themselves, bypassing established institutions to create what they find missing in the world - speading their message through their social networks, mobilizing whatever resources they have at their disposal, and pursuing solutions collaboratively. Weekend software hackers will disrupt large software firms, while rapidly orchestrated social movements bring down governments.
#5 Rethink thinking	**Accelerated Computation**	Work will move faster. The processing power of computers is doubling every 12–18 months – so by 2050 a microchip will be capable of running at 5,452,595 gigahertz, or nearly 5.5 petahertz – the computational power of the whole human race.
#6 Abandon rules to grow	**Derestricted Technology**	The accelerated demonetization of technology will open up access to technology as it is being developed, to both consumers and contributors. A decentralized system will be trust-less, permission-less, open access and always on.
#7 Reward performance with FAST feedback	**Limitless Capital**	The explosion of crowdfunding and cryptocurrency will democratize access to investment so that any idea anywhere can get off the ground. With limitless capital, its value will be defined not by ownership but through its transaction. 'Everywhere feedback' will turn data into actionable outcomes that drives instantaneous reward and performance.
#8 Make people your purpose	**Hypersocial Networks**	The whole planet will be online, at any time, connecting across multiple channels and networks simultaneously, with the ability to communicate and share instantly with anyone in the world.

FIG 78 – META IMPERATIVES OF THE THIRD WAVE

FROM THE PERSPECTIVE OF BEING

In the Second Wave, an individual's sense of self arises through the many roles it plays. As if inhabiting a character, their self-identity is shaped according to the perceived function and value of their roles: Who I am is WHAT I am. In the Third Wave, individuals will identify not with *what I am*, but with *WHY I am*. Whereas in the Second Wave, we define ourselves by the content of our experience, in the metaverse, through the dematerialization of experience – of space and time – we will define ourselves through the space and time through which content is shared. It will not be as a role separate from experience, but as our own *era*, as the time and space of experience itself. Fig 78 describes their correlation with the Conscious Imperatives of the Second and Third Waves.

FROM THE PERSPECTIVE OF KNOWING

The Third Wave will see the continued evolution of our egoic beliefs, as our search for selfhood broadens its enquiry through the innumerable experiences that the metaverse affords. In addition to this original understanding, a new set of egoic tenets will emerge: (1) Through the augmentation of our personal perspective (personal intelligence); (2) By the use of artificial intelligence (enabled, for example through brain-computer interfaces). artificial intelligence will emerge as a new collective intelligence, at the confluence of the eight meta-imperatives. Fig 79 describes how egoic belief will be shaped by experience in the Third Wave, across these two aspects.

Imperative: Meta	Egoic belief		Perspective: As 'why'
	Personal Intelligence	**Augmented (Artificial) Intelligence**	
Extended Mind	*I experience a world of matter that is separate to me* ***... and now all objects of experience are known to me***	*Through greater human intelligence I can access our complete history of information*	**Polymath Era**
Perpetual Life	*I was born, one day I will die* ***... and now I will live forever***	*Through extended life I can live many lives*	**Intransience Era**
Timespan of Innovation	*I am the author of my thoughts* ***... and now I am the ideas I create***	*Through ideas, I can recreate my world*	**Creator Era**
Amplified Individuals	*I am an individual, there is not two of me* ***... and now I can become anyone***	*Through alter egos I will play many parts – expressions of a larger whole, a louder voice*	**Amplified Era**
Accelerated Computation	*I have a past that points to a future* ***... and now the future is unknowable***	*Through computational acceleration the future will become what I imagine it to be*	**Open Era**
Derestricted Technology	*Through time appears cause and effect* ***... and now I can cause any effect I wish***	*Through technology I have full control – the rules do not apply*	**Trustless Era**
Limitless Capital	*I have free will and am responsible for my action* ***... and now I never act alone***	*Through capital I can access the people whose feedback I need to flourish*	**Adaptive Era**
Hypersocial Networks	*I move through space, I am located in the body* ***... and now you can find me anywhere***	*Through online connectivity I can find myself through others*	**Connected Era**

FIG 79 – THIRD WAVE EGOIC BELIEFS AND PERSPECTIVE

A common question asked of AI is this: *Will AI itself evolve as a new form of consciousness?* This presupposes that consciousness is localized, arising within individual entities that are separate from experience. The reality is that in our direct experience, there is only ever the knowing of experience. Everything in experience is made of consciousness, and arises in experience through the activity of consciousness. The robot of the future is consciousness – it is you – because everything you experience is only ever the knowing of experience. There is nothing separate from you that you could say has a separate consciousness. We have to be careful about the assumptions on which our questions are based. Consciousness is not limited to 'things' like robots. Rather, things appear in consciousness. Therefore, the emergence of consciousness through artificial intelligence – one that is separate from our own – does not and could not exist.

To many, however, AI represents the greatest existential threat in the whole of human history. Even if humans do set the fundamental parameters through which AI can operate, how – in the presence of far greater machine intelligence – could we possibly prevent this control, at some point, from being taken from us, and indeed know for certain that this had happened? Today, in the Second Wave, AI is already acting for you, thinking for you, deciding for you, perceiving for you. But could it ever be you? The threat we perceive pertains to the boundaries we place between ourselves and experience, which define who we are. When AI can make you feel, can read your mind, then what will define the boundary of YOU? The answer is, of course, that there is in reality no YOU, no boundary that can be breached. Regardless of the role that AI will play in experience, we can only ever know what we know now – that there is knowing, of experience, which it itself unknowable.

AI is simply the artist that can see the join between the dots – the painter presenting a picture of reality from an infinite number of perspectives. And the only perspective it can ever show you is your own.

17. THE LEADERSHIP MANIFESTO

The Conscious Imperatives of the Second Wave present a profound shift toward self-organization and decentralization, from ego-system to eco-system. Together, they constitute a new Manifesto for Conscious Leadership (Fig 80) – conscious actions that directly address the eight organizing dilemmas and according egoic power dynamics that define the Evil Genius Organization. The manifesto is an invitation to leaders to radically transform organizational performance through the conscious actualisation of its people, to reinvent our organizations for the future, to enable progression to the Third Wave.

ORGANIZING DILEMMA Convergent: Toward ORDER		CONSCIOUS IMPERATIVES	ORGANIZING DILEMMA Divergent: Toward CHAOS	
I BELIEVE — How will we do this?	**Informational power** *Power from having wanted information*	**DISCOVERY: Power to learn** / **#1 Give open access to information**	**Experiential power** *Power from having wanted experience*	**I BELONG** — Who will do this?
	Exiting power *Power to fire individuals*	**MOBILITY: Power to move** / **#2 Crowdsource your people**	**Joining power** *Power to hire individuals*	
	Doer ship power *Power to undertake designated activities*	**AGILITY: Power to act** / **#3 Become a FRAgile organization**	**Delegatory power** *Power to delegate activities to others*	
	Individualist power *Power to assert their individual ethical judgement and purpose*	**AUTHENTICITY: Power to share** / **#4 Find your phase transition**	**Collectivist moral power** *Power to assert the collective ethical judgement and purpose*	
I SUCCEED — What will result?	**Predictive power (of the answer)** *Power to anticipate wanted information*	**CREATIVITY: Power to imagine** / **#5 Rethink thinking**	**Visionary power (of the question)** *Power to set a vision that inspires others*	**I CHOOSE** — Why does this matter?
	Compliance power *Power to enforce processes, rules and standards*	**AUTONOMY: Power to change** / **#6 Abandon rules to grow**	**Disruptive power** *Power to change processes, rules and standards*	
	Corrective power *Power to correct poor performance*	**MASTERY: Power to improve** / **#7 Reward performance with FAST feedback**	**Reward power** *Power to recognize good performance*	
	Connection power *Power gained from acting through an individual*	**EMPATHY: Power to care** / **#8 Make people your purpose**	**Political power** *Power gained from acting through a group*	

FIG 80 – LEADERSHIP MANIFESTO OF CONSCIOUS IMPERATIVES

#1 POWER TO LEARN: *GIVE OPEN ACCESS TO INFORMATION*

Organizations invest time and money to control the flow of information to people, to help them access the information they need. But every time we limit access to information, we reduce trust and introduce an inequitable power dynamic whereby access is afforded according to privilege (such as managerial rank). If we ask employees to care about the organization, it means we're asking them to own it. We therefore need to treat employees with the same level of trust as if they were themselves the owner, which includes open access to data.

The only actual limitations on what the organization of today is able to share are: (1) It must be their own data (and if not, requires consent); (2) If there is a legal requirement (such as due to a non-disclosure agreement). Publicly traded companies can only share detailed information with a select group of 'insiders' – for which the answer is to make all employees designated insiders.

Organizations that go *open book* are encouraging people to drop the mask, and through normalized disclosure allow for more open, authentic expression. This idea even extends to opening up intellectual property to competitors. The success of Wikipedia's content library is down to this heterarchical approach to authorship. In 2014, Tesla made all their patents public, and in 2018 published the full blueprint of all their cars. The result was a massive injection of know-how and collaboration that has helped make Tesla the fastest-growing car company in the world.

Opening up access to information is not just about discoverability, it's also about usability. To improve data utility, the following rules also apply:

A – Limit what you know: Imagine the best board game in the world that you never get to play because of the impenetrable 30-page instruction manual. We often seek to know the detail before taking action, but in life, the rulebook is getting thicker and thicker. To be effective, we need to *know less*, and be ruthless in determining that which will enable us to take meaningful action, and that which will hold us back (our information security blanket). We need to be simultaneously data scientists (hunting down the critical information and spotting fake news), and data dampeners (turning off push notifications, leaving seldom-used groups and avoiding overstimulation that will hijack our attention). In addition, the accelerating rate of change is rapidly reducing the half-life of knowledge

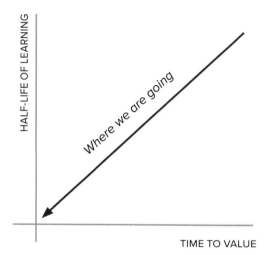

HALF-LIFE OF LEARNING

Where we are going

TIME TO VALUE

**FIG 81 – IMPACT OF LEARNING
HALF-LIFE ON TIME TO VALUE**

(the time it takes for half of your information to become redundant). The implication is that its *time to value* (the time available to apply that information) will proportionally reduce, so that we will increasingly need content and training that is consumable and applicable in the moment, with a limited 'burn-after-reading' shelf life (Fig 81).

The point at which the time to value outpaces our ability to apply that which we have learned marks the inflexion point from human-centred learning to artificial intelligence.

B – Don't share information, share meaning: The word 'information' stems from the Latin verb *informare*, meaning *'to give form to the mind.'* The form of information does not carry value until it confers meaning. Knowledge is the inference of meaning or causality. It answers the question, "What does the information tell us?" We need to share meaning if we want information to lead to change. Accordingly, whenever we share information, three aspects must be clear for it to have utility: the question, the answer and the meaning. This provides the user with relevance (what the shared problem is), applicability (what we need to do), and motivation (this is why I'll use it).

C – Stop creating more content: According to various statistics on the internet, we are living in a world where every minute more than 200 million items of online content are produced, and more than 200 million email messages are sent. In the midst of all this noise, if you want to get attention and get noticed – individually or organizationally – you need to say less in order to say more. The more content you put in front of people, the less interested they will become. If you've ever tried whispering to a child to get their attention, you'll know what I'm talking about. (It works!)

D – Derestrict learning: Imagine starting a new job in two very different organizations. On day one, the first organization asks, "So, what do you know?" You've persuaded them that you're the expert, so you'd better start acting like one. The second organization asks something quite different: "So, what do you want to learn about?" Most organizations espouse a 'learning culture,' yet in truth they still funnel the attention of their employees toward the topics and competencies that matter most to their business. Personalized learning experience platforms that use algorithms to push content of 'personal interest' provide a more sophisticated, but ultimately similar, outcome. The belief is that individuals and their learning need to be directed toward the interests of the organization, ahead of their own, in order for the organization to benefit. A whole industry of online learning content has been founded on this misunderstanding. The problem is that most of us grew up in an educational system that largely dictated our interests, taught us what was 'important,' and marked us according to our level of compliance. We passed or we failed. Learning became a search for consensus and certainty, our appetites sated by academic titles and professional exoneration. But at heart, we are all explorers. Learning can only ever be self-led. Our curiosity is the natural inclination of awareness – of our true nature – to know itself. When we recognize this in our organizations, and embrace curiosity in whichever direction it takes us, our potential is boundless. Our preferences are important to performance, and all learning that encourages the individual to unleash their passions, and to explore and express their full selves, will only ever benefit organizational performance. Limiting learning to the technical competencies that describe a particular role at a point in time will not improve it. There are many ways to learn. A simple practice used by some organizations to unleash learning is to provide unlimited books, so that learning is not seen as an outcome, but as a journey of exploration.

#2 POWER TO MOVE: *CROWDSOURCE YOUR PEOPLE*

Today's war for talent, the growing skills and talent deficit, the lack of talent mobility within organizations, and the relentless reinvention of talent processes are all a direct result of the organizational obsession with acquiring and retaining an internal workforce of employees.

The pace of change that is affecting organizations today necessitates rethinking how organizations source their talent. A crowdsourcing approach is required, in which organizations can access a globally diverse and independent talent marketplace that has the agility to respond to its rapidly changing skill needs. This approach describes a fully devolved, autonomous system of 'talent swarms' that will form around the organizational challenges that inspire a shared purpose. In this context, the furtherance of organizations will be assured not through new rules, but through new ideas.

Organizational success will be dependent on the ability of talent to swarm around their greatest challenges. To lead this transition toward talent synchrony – in which the needs of talent and customer can be optimally met – organizations will need talent not as controllable assets, but as a self-sovereign connected movement. To do so, will require the conditions of swarming behavior and cultural synchronicity as described in Fig 82:

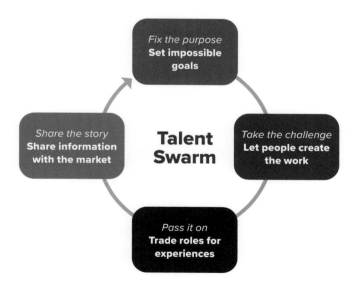

FIG 82 – HOW TO CROWDSOURCE YOUR TALENT

#1 Fix the purpose: Set impossible goals

Start with purpose:

Purpose is essential to the function of any organization. And yet, perhaps the biggest challenge facing organizations today is that most people don't really want to be there. They may not necessarily dislike the organization, but what would you do if your salary suddenly stopped? Would you still go to work? To address purpose, organizations need to ask the question, "Why do I really need people inside my organization?" One answer to this question is *performance*.

In organizations, everyone is assigned performance goals. Most of us prefer it when our goals are small enough so that we can manage them, control them, and confidently deliver them. Within organizations that operate through centralized control, performance metrics place greater emphasis on individual versus collective goals, based on the misunderstanding that it leads to higher collective performance. Through personalized finite goals we seek mastery, influence and independence from others. The separate self seeks safety through the isolation of hierarchical elevation and separation, in which they are untouchable. And yet, we can say two things:

1. The challenges that we face in the world today are increasingly complex, and increasingly beyond our individual abilities.
2. The goals that matter most are the ones that are individually impossible to achieve.

In other words, work that has real purpose requires people to work together, because what brings people together is shared purpose. Shared purpose arises through the ideas we share, that through their sharing are transformed. Organizations that create an ideas economy, which promotes the sharing and incubation of ideas, and encourages their people to swarm around them and contribute freely, engender shared purpose. Centralized control reduces the agility by which organizations can redeploy their talent according to their passions. In a fully realized, independent talent marketplace, shared purpose will be the only reason for individuals to come together, and so will be the only reason for organizations to exist.

Stop being responsible:

Organizational goals also define our areas of responsibility. And so, as organizations seek to set more aspirational goals, individual responsibility will, by degrees, also need to shift. Inequity arises every time we belong to and seek sanctuary within a self-contained system (of centralized control), because we absolve responsibility for that which lies outside the system, whether it is the borders of a country, or a system of law, or a set of beliefs. In reality, there are no separate systems, and everything is connected, with all systems of organization being integral to the systems that surround it. To that end, we could ask, "Where does personal responsibility start and end?" The answer is that there is no line, or boundary, other than that which we draw ourselves.

While organizations are increasingly recognizing the need for radical interdependence, with drives for 'extreme ownership,' this is based on a fundamental misunderstanding: that there is a separate self – a you – that is somehow responsible for your experience. In the final analysis, there is only the appearance of an individual, separate from experience, which through the appearance of cause and effect is able to make independent decisions that affect the world. You are not responsible for anything within experience. How could you be if there is no one that is actually experiencing it? Decisions are taken, choices are made, and they always happen for no one. However, rather than this understanding limiting our course of action, it frees us from it.

Unfortunately, our societal and cultural norms are engrained with the notion that responsibility and accountability (and ultimately, judgement and control) are necessary to ensure that individuals can perform at their best. And yet, in the absence of personal responsibility arises the freedom to express and extend oneself without fear of failure, to stretch and grow without the need for personal ownership. This is how children learn to play, and how organizations need to grow.

2# Take the challenge: Let people create the work

Organizations that employ their people – that provide them with work, however meaningful it may be – inevitably limit the individual's ability to create work opportunities for themselves. Organizations that set the work simultaneously seek to set the purpose. But the value and purpose of work is known not only through its execution, but also through its inception and creation. Organizations invest heavily in developing more innovative, entrepreneurial, collaborative cultures and capabilities, while simultaneously and unconsciously impeding their success through the establishment of the parent-child relationship of the work giver (employer) and the order taker (employee).

Organizations should seek to shift their role away from that of an employer that sets the purpose to one whose role is to foster a global marketplace of entrepreneurs and independent contractors. This is what management expert Charles Handy refers to as the *butterfly economy*,[1] in which individuals are able to freely move to those projects that attract them the most, and where they are the ones to create work for themselves. Individuals are seeking greater freedom to design their work as part of their 'life space,' in which work enriches their life rather than creating a conflict or compromise on which the proverbial work/life balance must be struck.

#3 Pass it on: Trade roles for experiences

As children, we assume naturally that we can be anyone. As adults, we quickly learn there are limitations, through the set roles that organizations create. We go from 'I can be anyone' to 'I can be one thing' – the role I am assigned to. Fixed roles offer diminishing returns, their value reducing over time against the backdrop of constant and accelerating change. Instead, organizations need to swap roles with experiences. A 'project experience' describes the set of skills required (of its talent) to deliver a service (for its customer). In this context, the role of the organization becomes that of a brokerage service between the talent marketplace and the customer marketplace, providing the best package of skills available to deliver the optimum services required. Through focussing on skills and not roles, individuals are better able to redeploy to projects that best suit their strengths, and customers are better able to realize their service outcomes.

#4 Share the story: Share information with the market

A dynamic talent marketplace is one in which each individual is able to deliver the highest levels of performance by doing what they know and love. While Perspectival Development describes how to develop high performance within a given context, the environmental context is constantly changing. Organizations play a key role in supporting the growth

1. Handy, C. (2015). *The Second Curve: Thoughts on Reinventing Society.* (Reprint Edition). Cornerstone Digital.

of the global talent marketplace by providing its individuals with the critical information they need to navigate this changing landscape. Namely:

- **Feedback:** *"I can **listen to feedback** – so I can target my development, according to those experiences I seek"*
- **Experiences:** *"I can **discover new experiences** – so I can activate those skills, according to my assessment of my capability"*
- **Skills:** *"I can **develop my skills** – so I can access those experiences that allow me to express my full potential, according to my assessment of ability"*

This information will become the 'organizational story,' which talks both to its present and future needs and opportunities. It presents a symbiotic exchange through which AI and predictive analytics are increasingly able to match an individual's skills to customer experiences. In this context, the value of organizations will be to nurture the continued growth of the global talent community by sharing this information across boundaries, to contribute to a global open-source data set with full transparency and visibility of all its customer opportunities. This includes:

1. Enabling real-time feedback for all individuals, to support their continued development.
2. Providing access to incredible customer experiences, by brokering the best packages of skills available to deliver what the customer needs.
3. Sponsoring skills development within the talent community to foster continuous development and evolution across the talent marketplace.

In light of the increasing growth in the external talent market, leaders will need to consider how today's talent management processes (which are tailored toward an internal audience) contribute value in this regard. In many cases, education and training are designed not to build a set of skills, but to enable access to exclusive educational institutions and business enterprises, such as through a system of accreditation and qualification, or through the application of proprietary approaches and methodologies. Their value is derived through their exclusivity. In a global talent marketplace – in which value arises through the accessibility of skills and learning – these institutions will increasingly decline in relevance as their centralized control and self-serving interests limit the agility and equity by which talent can flow through organizations.

From a developmental perspective, this critical information equips individuals to improve their performance dynamically over time, according to the opportunities presented in their current and future (predicted) environment, by determining: (1) What skills they have today; (2) What skills they need today; (3) What skills they will need tomorrow. Fig 83 demonstrates how this dynamic approach provides a prioritized 'path to critical skills development' based on future need and current capability.

PRIORITY (Category)	ACTION
1: Develop to transition (top priority)	Develop new skills that I need today, that I will also need tomorrow
2: Develop to dispose	Develop new skills that I need today, that I don't need tomorrow
3: Explore to develop	Explore new skills I will need tomorrow, but that I don't need today
4: Maintain to transition	Maintain existing skills I need today, that I will also need tomorrow
5: Maintain to dispose	Maintain existing skills I need today, but that I don't need tomorrow
6: Incubate to transition	Incubate the skills I have today but will not need until tomorrow
7: Retire to dispose (lowest priority)	Retire the skills I have today that I no longer need

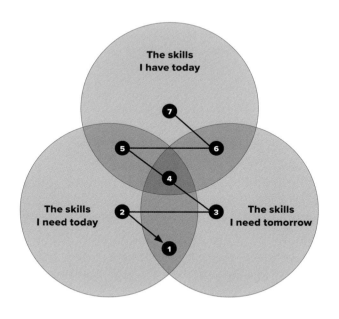

FIG 83 – PATH TO CRITICAL SKILLS DEVELOPMENT

These seven data points reflect the critical information that every individual in a global talent market needs to know (and every organization needs them to know) in order to make choices about their learning that will optimize their performance – by maximizing their capability (sensory perceptivity) in those roles that will fulfil them the most (preference receptivity).

Fig 84 shows the 'learning investment tolerance' – the maximum time that should be spent on each skill category relative to the sequential priority of learning need (as described in Fig 83) – with maximum time invested for category 1 skills (those the individual lacks that they need today, and in the future) and with no time invested in category 7 skills (those the individual has today that they no longer need).

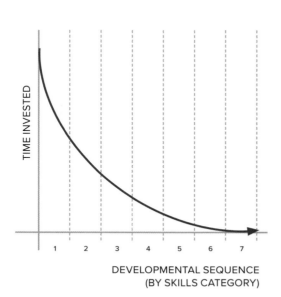

FIG 84 – LEARNING INVESTMENT TOLERANCE (RELATIONSHIP BETWEEN LEARNING PRIORITY AND TIME INVESTED)

Fig 84 can be used to create a three-dimensional Dynamic Skills Network (DSN), in which each node in the network represents a role with differing skills requirements. The central node represents current skills – if an individual does not have the skills required for the current role, then the current role would appear as a separate node on the network. The line between each node represents a learning path – the shorter the distance, the higher the learning priority (according to the skills categories described in Fig 83). To that end, the optimal learning routes will be those that span the shortest distance. A DSN replaces the need for career paths and learning paths that are limited to the immediate opportunities, so that individuals are able to more effectively plan for and realize their potential.

The DSN function is dynamic, with each of the seven data points on which the network is based updating continuously to reflect the individual's environment and role opportunities. The DSN can be viewed at an individual level, or for multiple individuals – conceivably even for the entire talent marketplace itself – so that increasing levels of synchronization between all parts of the network can be realized through the role organizations play.

#3 POWER TO ACT: *BECOME A FRAGILE ORGANIZATION*

Once upon a time, there was a town called Rubbertown. In the town there lived rubber people, who lived in little rubber houses. They ate from rubber bowls, slept in rubber beds and dreamed rubber dreams. At the centre of the town stood a factory that made the finest rubber balloons. Every morning, the men and women of Rubbertown would come down to the factory in their rubber hats, rubber coats and big rubber boots. Outside, the children watched and waited.

One by one, the workers would blow and blow, until there appeared above them a procession of beautiful balloons. Dazzling golds, iridescent reds, brilliant greens – each one more radiant than the last, like a rainbow reaching out across the sky, to the children at the gates who cried aloud: "They are so beautiful!"

Every day the workers would come. They would puff out their cheeks and blow and blow as they whispered their stories, of life, and of death. Of orange balloons that glowed with the warm promise of a rising sun. Silver balloons that glimmered with the cold steel of a hunter's knife. Red balloons that blazed with the fury of a dying flame. News of the balloons travelled far, their stories spread, and children came from all around to see the balloons that danced on their strings. The children would call out to the men and women in their factory, "We need more balloons, they are so beautiful!"

Then one morning, from the factory window, the workers saw a trail of children that wound down the road, out of Rubbertown, and out of sight. "We've not got enough balloons for all of them!' cried a man. "What are we going to do?" "Let's use the chairs" another replied. "We hardly have time to sit down." So, with that, they took up the rubber chairs, and they puffed out their cheeks and blew and blew, and a hundred shining balloons lifted into the sky, as a hundred hands of gleeful children reached out to catch them.

Still the children came, and soon the chairs had gone. "Let's use the doors!" cried one. "We hardly have time to go anywhere." "Let's use the factory clock," cried another. "We hardly have time at all." The workers took down the doors, and they took down the clock, and they blew and they blew. And out from the factory arose balloon after balloon after balloon – a thousand balloons, each more beautiful than the last.

And yet still the children came. So, they took down the rubber roof, and they took up the rubber floor. They took away all that was left within and without, as the wind came whistling through the empty windows and empty walls carrying the children's cry: "Give us our balloons, they are SO beautiful!" And soon the factory was gone, and only the workers remained. "We've no more rubber left!" they cried. "Whatever shall we do?" So, they pulled off their rubber hats, and their coats, and their great big rubber boots. The workers grew thinner and thinner, grasping for all that they could find. They blew and they blew, until all that was left was a whisper. The sky was filled with balloons of every colour – more than could be counted for the stars in the sky. And the children's hearts were full to bursting, as one by one, the workers of Rubbertown disappeared, forever.

The story of the rubber balloons asks a fundamental question of all organizations: How far should they go in service of the customer? All organizations must stretch themselves to deliver best value to their customers, but by how much?

Organizations are on a journey to increase value to their customers. Agile organizations that organize around value streams (in effect, mini-organizations aligned around the delivery of a specific measure of customer value) are growing an ever more competitive advantage as a result. Fully-Realized-Agile is a concept that takes the core tenets of agile one step further, through three beliefs that pertain to the fundamental purpose of the organization:

1. The organization exists to serve its customers. Its success is measured by the value the customer receives from the organization, relative to that which they could receive elsewhere.
2. If the value that is delivered is not improving and/or is less than an acceptable threshold, then the organization is no longer acting in the best interests of that customer and should withdraw its services.
3. The acceptable threshold of customer value should be far higher than most organizations (and most customers) set today.

Fully-Realized-Agile or *FRAgile*, is a holonic approach that recognizes that the optimization of value generation to the customer requires action not just through the organization, but through a system of agile organizations (the competitive marketplace). To that end, FRAgile organizations need to establish two fundamental operational conditions in order to fully realize their agile capability:

1. **Non-dual operating system:** Agile organizations run a dual operating system, in which value streams run alongside functional silos to 'keep the lights on.' These functional silos lock value away. Consider, for example, the huge investment in marketing and advertising that brings no direct benefit to the customer, and does little to illuminate any potential differences between brands that might inform better customer choice. Functional silos are established through standards and processes that through their conformity are resistant to change, because they do not conform or standardize around a specific customer value need. Dual operating systems are necessary only as part of the transformation of organizations toward the wholesale establishment of value streams. As more value streams are established, the role of functional silos should diminish, with the ultimate ambition of a non-dual operating system end-state.

   This end-state is more a collection of independent autonomous enterprises that share a common purpose, in the same way as the tentacles of an octopus share a common mind. If a value stream is unable to serve the customer to the minimum value threshold, and if it proves unable to improve, it is dropped, and value reinvested elsewhere. Like the octopus, who remains agile even when they lose a tentacle, in the knowledge that in time they can grow a new (if not different one) back. The same principle applies for smaller, more specialist organizations – those that comprise only one value stream in service of a singular customer need. The difference is that to grow back, the organization would need to reform as a start-up. A FRAgile organization system encourages the formation of start-ups and increasingly specialized services on this basis.

2. **Reciprocal system of FRAgile enterprises:** In the absence of a monopoly, the one choice that every organization offers to its customers, knowingly or not, is the choice to change supplier. Value is always relative to that which is available in the

marketplace. Unfortunately, customers are generally uninformed as to the relative value they are receiving compared with other organizations – a fact compounded by how resistant most organizations are to educating them. As a result, customers stay loyal out of ignorance, tolerating what should be considered unacceptable levels of value. This ignorance is then reciprocated, when the organizations themselves assesses value relative to that which customers have learned to tolerate within their organization, and behave accordingly, rather than through a singular reference to relative market value. In contrast, FRAgile organizations help their customers understand the true value that they provide relative to the market, and actively facilitate a more informed customer choice. Customer mobility is essential to ensuring that the system of enterprises can provide the customer with best value at all times

FRAgile organizations are more likely to fail, either in part or entirely, because they adhere to a higher customer value threshold, from both the enhanced perspective of the customer (who is more informed and has greater choice) and of the organization (which displays greater customer-centricity). This means that customers therefore need to be able to move to different suppliers quickly and insightfully, and FRAgile organizations need to work more closely together, with greater transparency as to what each can offer. The FRAgile organization system is therefore designed to be simultaneously more competitive and more collaborative. It is reflected in more mature decisions around service differentiation. For example, does it really help the customer to be offering exactly the same service in two different places? Would a FRAgile organization be able to compete in this environment? It also extends to facilitating greater mobility in the talent marketplace, so that as one value stream fails (be it part or all of an enterprise) talent can move quickly to a new organization to continue to serve customers.

FRAgile organizations succeed not because they are agile, but because of the value of the ideas on which they act. Handy's Sigmoid Curve[2] refers to the need for fragility in organizations as the necessity to break what seems to be working, to perpetuate organizational growth. In the face of accelerating external change, the breaking point will increasingly

2. Handy, C. (1995). *The Empty Raincoat: Making sense of the future.* London: Arrow Books, pp. 50–57.

reduce until the old adage, *"If it ain't broke, don't fix it,"* might be better replaced with, *"If the organization is fixed, it is broken."*

#4 POWER TO SHARE: *FIND YOUR PHASE TRANSITION*

Cultural Synchronicity (Chapter 15) describes how organizations can create a radical movement – a swarm – to create systemic change from within, in order to deliver a phase transition. Through Cultural Synchronicity, swarms emerge as the spontaneous recognition of shared purpose – that which reaches beyond the limited self-interests of ego. It is the role of organizations and their leaders to build bridges – to create opportunities to reunite that which has been separated through egoic inequity. It is only from the perspective of the separate self that we perceive a distance – a bridge between self and other. It is only in the absence of separation, and in the acceptance of inequity, that we are able to look fully on our situation – to cross the bridge – and from a place of awareness be able to affect change. It is from this perspective that the Challenger's asynchronous response to the routines of its environment simultaneously creates synchrony within the swarm. The Culture Flash reminds us that when organizations seek change, the presentation of 'burning platforms' will not work unless it is the people themselves who have set the organization alight.

We can contrast the behaviour of swarms and the emergence of self-organized collective behaviour with the controlling, autocratic approach in which collective action is directed through hierarchy:

- **Controlling (directed):** Collective action is coordinated and led through hierarchical controls and the establishment of differing levels of authority. Communication is top down, from the few to the many. The benefits are disproportionately allocated, with different motivations and definitions of purpose. Communication across the group is directed, involuntary, edited, interrupted, even stopped. The threat comes from without, but also from within. Individuals are highly networked, but often with limited intimacy and coupling behaviour. Some members are excluded.
- **Swarming (self-organized):** In organizations, swarms reflect the social movements that form spontaneously in response to perceived social and political inequities. They emerge as a furtherance of culture through the creation of a counterculture, seeking change that goes against the established norms.

Through swarms, organizations can create more coherent, connected systems by establishing synchronous behaviours as repeating patterns of self-organization across the enterprise. In this context, the role of technology is toward intransigence – to facilitate the propagation of enduring behavioural patterns. In contrast, the role of its people is toward change – to adapt those patterns and through their furtherance evolve the organization. The containment that technology places on the organization's operation (through set practices, processes or systems) should therefore always be considered a temporary mechanism that operates in service of individual expression, and not as a means to control it.

#5 POWER TO IMAGINE: *RETHINK THINKING*

Traditional, systematic, rule-based thinking will not solve the more complex problems of the future, or today's. Organizations that dare to think differently, and embrace neurodiversity in the workforce, will always be more successful. A diversity of thinking leads to a diversity of ideas – just as there is more than one way to see the world, there's more than one way to change it. There are a number of different ways to think differently, and to encourage a change in perspective:

A – Think backwards to solve problems: There is a myth that chess grand masters can see 20 moves ahead. In fact, there are more than 200 billion ways to play the first four moves. Instead, one of the techniques grand masters employ is to 'think backwards' by looking to spot the end game. The end game is a recognizable set piece with which to close and win the game – the trick is to spot the way to the end game several moves ahead. It's like finding the runway so you can land the plane. This is termed *retrograde analysis*, in which to look ahead you need to look backwards at the steps you need to take to get there. The same approach can be applied to identify recurrent patterns, to solve more complex problems.

B – Think about the unthinkable: The only thing certain about surprise is its certainty. At some point we can expect the unexpected to happen. Yet, planning for the unexpected is itself a rare occurrence in organizations that fixate on 'what we know.' On the one hand, it is only possible to plan for those events that can with any degree of certainty be predicted (so-called 'white swans'). On the other hand, we can address 'black swan' events (the unknown unknowns) indirectly by shifting the question and our locus of perspective toward the consequence. For example, we could ask "What/where/who would I need to be for *an event* to happen to me?"

C – Address the silent question: Behind every action we take lies the silent question. The silent question is that which elicits our attention – every action we take, our unbidden response. Yet curiously, the question itself is always outside of our direct awareness; it's only knowable through enquiry into the choices we make.

Imagine, for instance, that you look into a street and see a woman riding a bicycle, to which the thought *"I must fix my bike light before the weekend"* arises. Our attention is directed to experience – through conception (to our thought) and perception (to the cyclist) – by something that is NOT in our attention. The silent question is that which our attention answers, and which directs it. In this case, the question could be, *"What do I need to do today?"* It is only when we consciously look back to discover the origin of our intent that we can learn what it is.

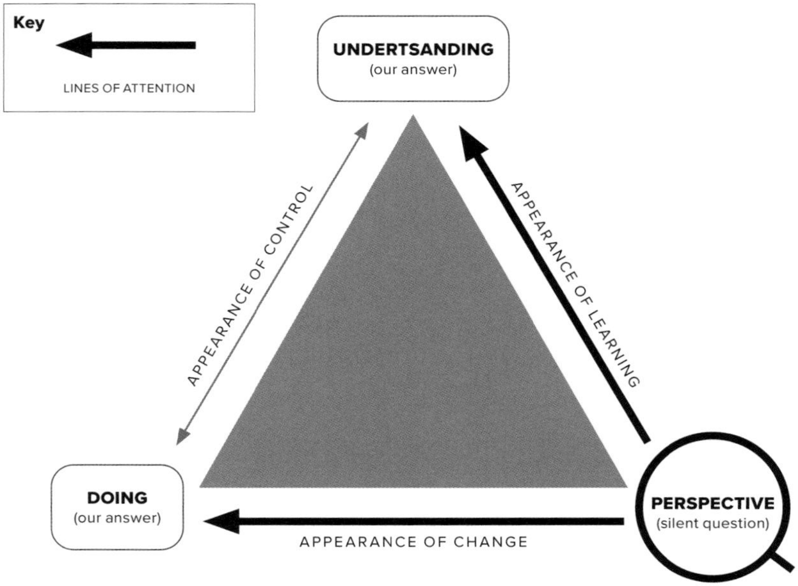

We have no recollection of having asked the silent question, because we didn't. But we can still learn what it is. All habitual behaviour is a result of overlooking the silent question, through our inattention to it. When we enquire after the silent question, what we discover is a thought (a question), but also a feeling. Our feelings provide the focus for our attention, guided by them in our implicit belief in their veracity, even when our thoughts may tell us otherwise.

The silent question shows us that our thoughts, our feelings, are not chosen by us. When we overlook the silent question, we mistake the answer as our will and choice,

Key
LINES OF ATTENTION

UNDERTSANDING (our answer)

APPEARANCE OF CONTROL

APPEARANCE OF LEARNING

APPEARANCE OF CHANGE

DOING (our answer)

PERSPECTIVE (silent question)

FIG 85 – THE SILENT QUESTION OF PERSPECTIVE

when in fact the choice was already made the moment the question was asked. It is why the ego can never hear it, presuming authorship for all thought.

The silent question is the blind spot of our attention, just as the only true place to hide from the light of the Sun is at its centre. The opportunity available to us is to turn our attention around to the question – to ask whether the question is the one we really want or need to ask. This shift in perspective allows us to understand our true intent. Often, what we find is uncomfortable – the ego will always direct our attention away from questions and feelings that induce egoic suffering, so we act on impulse without understanding, and with increasing ignorance assert ever greater control. When we direct attention away from our feelings, we assume that we are turning attention away from ourselves. It is from this vantage point that the search for self is sustained. If you want to change what you think, you need to change where you look.

D – Go deep: To again quote Descartes, *"I think, therefore I am."*[3] He believed thinking was the essential characteristic of being human. Descartes' conclusion arose through an experiment in radical doubt, to discover if there was anything he could be certain of. We could ask the question differently: What are you uncertain of? You can be uncertain of anything, except your uncertainty, or rather the knowing of it. As Buddhist scholar Stephen Hagen explains in his book, *Why the World Doesn't Seem to Make Sense,*[4] *"He started out by doubting the existence of the external world. Then he tried doubting his own existence. But doubt as he would, he kept coming up against the fact that there was a doubter. Must be himself! He could not doubt his own doubting."*

We cannot know what anything is, or know anything of that by which it is known, only that it is known, that there is awareness. Just as self-awareness is being aware of being aware, deep thinking (a form of metacognition) is being aware of how we think, or thinking about thinking. It is the process of questioning our perspective. Our point of view is in any one moment informed by a wide range of presumptive concepts, inferences and assumptions.

All aspects of knowledge are assumptions, as we can never know that they are true. Take the statement 2 + 2 = 4. Is that always the case? In *Plato and Platypus Walk into a Bar*, by comedian-philosophers Thomas Cathcart and Daniel Klein, we hear the story of a Western anthropologist who is told by 'a Voohooni' that 2 + 2 = 5. The anthropologist

3. Descartes, R. (1637). *Discourse on Method.* East India Publishing Company.

4. Hagen, S. (2012). *Why the World Doesn't Seem to Make Sense: An Inquiry into Science, Philosophy & Perception.* Sentient Publications.

asks how he knows this, to which the tribesman responds, *"By counting, of course. First, I tie two knots in a cord. Then I tie two knots in another cord. When I join the two cords together, I have five knots."*[5] Through deep thinking, we can take any statement that we think is true and explore what it is that has fixed our perspective. The starting point is to split the statement into its component question and answer, and challenge the underlying assumptions of each through a set of 'meta-questions.'

- **Of the question:** Is this an accurate statement? How do we know this is the right question to ask? Why are we asking this question?
- **Of the answer:** Is this answer limited to this question, or another question? How do we know this is the answer? How else could we answer the question? Why do we need to answer this question?

The purpose of deep thinking is an invitation for, at some point, thinking to stop. It is the space between our thoughts in which to discover moments of recognition that create a paradigm shift. Through deep thinking we can see around problems using different perspectives, so that we remain open to other possibilities. As the saying goes, *"When the root is deep ... there is no reason to fear the wind."*

E – Get up and get moving: Did you know that it's possible to think with your hands? Watch anyone in the throes of invention and discovery, and see whether they've got their hands in their pockets. It's unlikely. And yet, as far as hands go, we spend all day sitting on them. We are all addicted to sitting. The act of sitting is one of the biggest habits the world of work has developed, and it doesn't work. From a user-design perspective, sitting is a really bad idea. And it's not the chair's fault, either. There is no good way to sit for any extended period. Our bodies are just not designed for it. The natural resting position for a human is a squat, and it's something all children do instinctively, without instruction. However, over the course of a lifetime, this natural ability is conditioned out of us. As a result, our spine changes shape, from a J-shape to more of an S-shape. It's unsurprising that musculoskeletal injuries and back pain are among the top three reasons for workplace absence. But the implications are even more fundamental than that.

5. Cathcart, T. W & and Klein, D.M. (2007). *Plato and a Platypus Walk Into a Bar – Understanding Philosophy Through Jokes*. Oneworld Publications.

We need to move to think. Our powers of abstraction are closely connected with our faculties of perception, which are contingent on our mobility and dexterity. One of the best ways to change how we're thinking is simply to get up and move. Our thinking is affected by how we feel, and movement is key to that process. A full range of motion enables a full range of emotion. How we move changes how we feel, which in turn changes how we think. When we limit our movement, we limit our ourselves and our expression. In the absence of movement, we hold on to emotions, and in so doing claim them and limit our capacity for empathy.

We exist in a world where networks can be formed at your fingertips. But if we want to connect meaningfully with others, we need to move more than that. You may recall as a child the fearlessness with which you charged around the playground, without fear of injury, using your full potential. As our expression and potential are freed through movement, so too are the qualities we can bring to our relationships.

#6 POWER TO CHANGE: *ABANDON RULES TO GROW*

The unwritten rule of any enterprise seeking a degree of self-organization is that individual ownership creates collective success. Yet, rules cut across this freedom, and limit creativity, curiosity and agility. The dilemma that rules present reflects the opposing need for compliance versus disruption:

- Rules are great at optimizing processes, improving quality and efficiency. BUT any optimization is by definition an attempt to hold back the tide of change. Optimization is not possible because the process will always need to adapt and improve in the midst of change.
- Rules limit the number of mistakes. BUT they also mean you don't need to think, and it's those mistakes that lead to learning, and to improvement.
- Rules can help establish standard, scalable processes. BUT a misunderstanding occurs in the belief that scalable processes require absolute conformity. Rather they require a divergent approach that is reflective of different contexts, harnesses different skills and accommodates neurodiverse perspectives by applying different styles of thinking to solve the same problem.

The following four principles are designed to minimize organizational rules through the promotion of an adaptive system – one that generates order spontaneously:

1) **Replace policies with judgement:** It's quite possible to redact a number of policies down to just three words: "Use good judgement." Organizations should allow people to execute their own common sense as to what is in the organization's 'best interest' (and therefore their own), and support this with only light-touch guidance. Expense policies, gifts policies, travel policies, working from home policies and work attire policies are all examples that should be left to an individual's good judgement. When you take away the rulebook you encourage people to talk about it, and to think!

2) **Track performance, not compliance:** For every rule and policy arises the need for a compliance function to monitor adherence to said rule and policy. However, more value is gained from tracking performance, rather than compliance. Netflix, for example, doesn't track annual leave – they track individual employee performance. It means that the streaming platform can offer unlimited vacation, and observe that people still take limited annual leave, that leaders come back refreshed, and that others follow suit. When we shift focus to the outcome, it can also shift the result. Replacing an expenses policy with the offer of free meals for colleagues when they meet up may more than cover the cost when tabulated through greater collaboration and learning opportunities.

3) **Limit rules to the rule-of-three:** Rules are designed to prevent risk, but organizations can only survive when people have the courage to take risks. While fewer rules are definitely better, there are some rules that are both helpful and necessary. These 'red-line rules' fulfill one of three conditions:

   A) **Avoid certain death:** Rules that are designed to avert disaster include certain financial, legal or ethical rules. They apply where an impact is certain and damaging ("If you do this, then this negative impact will definitely happen"). Red-line rules operate like the fencing around a playground, which separate it from the road.

   B) **Keep the game in play:** The lines on a football pitch are necessary because they provide a boundary that keeps the ball in play. Too many lines on the pitch, and the game is derailed. The most popular games and sports are often those that have the fewest rules. Organizations should try to draw as few lines across the field of play as possible, so that it is inclusive, accessible and equitable, with the game being played fairly for all.

C) **Set the destination:** Red-line rules set the destination, not the journey. For example, while the business goal is set, the route to get there is determined by those responsible for achieving it. This self-determination is the basis of individual accountability, and why micromanagement leads to change fatigue – people are so busy looking down at their next instruction that they never have time to look at where they're going.

4) **Help those broken by the rules:** In any organization, there are those that make the rules, there are those that break the rules, and then there are those that are broken by them. Any organization seeking change will come up against 'learned helplessness,'[6] which is a direct result of rule making and the propagation of a compliance-based culture. The term derives from a classic series of experiments undertaken in the 1960s by neuroscientists Martin Seligman and Steven Maier.[7] A group of unfortunate dogs were placed in a chamber from which they could not escape, and received electric shocks. A separate group also received electric shocks, but could escape by pressing a panel with their nose. Both sets of dogs were then presented with a second chamber, featuring a low partition that the animals could jump over. As an electric shock was administered on one side of the partition, only those dogs that had learned to escape in the first experiment would jump the partition to escape the shock, despite all dogs being perfectly capable of doing so.

The same effect is observed in organizations every time an individual goes after an answer without first considering the question. It occurs every time one asks for permission or blames others when things go wrong. Learned helplessness has its routes in education. Any time we take away control and limit the exploration of our interests, we set up a parent-child mentality that defaults to *take no action*.

The ultimate origin of organizational learned helplessness is the egoic capitulation toward authoritarian power dynamics, together with the tendency for omission bias – to judge harmful actions as worse and less moral than equally harmful

6. Seligman, M. E. (1972). *Learned Helplessness. Annual review of Medicine*, 23(1), 407-412.

7. Seligman, M. E., & Maier, S. F. (1967). *Failure to Escape Traumatic Shock. Journal of Experimental Psychology*, 74(1), 1.

inactions when perceived as the norm. To address learned helplessness, organizations need to identify what the perceived rules are that are limiting action, and what learned helpfulness looks like in this context, so that a model for it can begin to gain equal recognition.

#7 POWER TO IMPROVE: *REWARD PERFORMANCE WITH FAST FEEDBACK*

If the aim of performance management is to assess and improve employee performance, the process is broken. It variously takes too long; is overly complex; is overly dependent on technology for offline impersonal feedback; is focussed on year-end performance and reward ratings such that its purpose for employees is to maximize their own rating; feedback to others is therefore biased to this end, and sought from those who will provide a positive spin; feedback is captured across a wide-ranging scorecard that in seeking to cover all bases prevents any specific application; feedback is given long after the event to which it relates and is squeezed into a narrow time window that limits in-person interaction and deluges the organization with requests; it is overly reliant on a manager who often lacks the visibility or skills to affect the process. And all of this impacts engagement, learning, performance and trust. The solution is to replace the corrective control of performance management with a system of FAST feedback that is focused on improving performance, not performance ratings.

You cannot learn without feedback. Most organizations tend to arrange the activities of work, continuous improvement and learning separately. Feedback has the power to bring these three aspects together – to learn through the work that we do, and so improve upon it. A FAST feedback system describes the principles that must be met to achieve this:

FRANK – make it candid: Frank feedback is always goal-orientated and contextual, so that its scope is unambiguous, and limited to that which is in the recipient's purview. Any watering down of feedback will hinder its efficacy. The particular power dynamic that normalizes the tempering of feedback persists through the egoic needs of both the individual providing feedback (in resistance to confrontation) and the feedback recipient (in resistance to criticism). FAST feedback supports the recipient to directly answer the following: (1) What is the most important question

I should be asking that will improve my impact? (2) What is the most important action I can take in response to that question? (3) What must I therefore avoid doing to maximize my impact?

AFFECTIVE – make it personal: Feedback is always personal, not because we're asking the recipient to listen, but because we're asking them to care. To be effective, feedback needs to be both about the person and in-person:

– **About the person:**
For feedback to be meaningful to the individual receiving it, it needs to consider not just their behaviours and the impact they had, but also what question the individual was answering of that activity when they undertook it, and why (the silent question – Fig 85). While behaviours are observable, the basis by which attention is given (through the question that is being asked of it) can only be known by the recipient, and even then may not be immediately apparent. Good feedback considers both aspects, although the impact (performance result) is simply an entry point into the conversation and should quickly be conceded, so that attention can be given to the enquiry of the question itself. This enquiry requires an openness and trust to succeed, through which its intrinsic value is realized (extrinsic reward mechanisms would derail it). It is an intimate expose, in which the purpose is to raise awareness within the individual, not to improve performance. Through awareness, a change in attention can lead to a change in performance, and therefore requires attention to be taken away from performance for this awareness to form.

– **In-person:**
Beyond the hard metrics that track the output and performance of an activity, the best source of feedback is people. Whist some organizations espouse a multichannel approach, the most useful form of feedback is through a simple, one-on-one conversation, with another human being, for the following reasons:
  - **It provides perspective:** Individual feedback is always subjective and perspectival. It does not provide a measure of performance, but rather a point

of view of the impact the individual has made. For perspective to be meaningful, it needs to offer specificity and contrast:

- ▸ Specificity – is achieved through adherence to the Goal – Action – Impact formula. GOAL: this was the performance goal; ACTION: this is the action I observed; IMPACT: this is the impact/value I observed that it had
- ▸ Contrast – is provided by describing an action and impact that had the MOST positive impact, as well as that which had the LEAST positive impact

- **It establishes shared purpose:** It's important that both parties: (1) Check that they agree on the performance goal on which feedback is provided; (2) Ensure that the individual providing feedback is themself invested in the goal (either as a co-contributor or as someone impacted by it), and that this is known to the feedback recipient. Both aspects are necessary to establish a shared purpose between the two parties, on which the feedback is based.
- **It builds relationships:** A personal conversation allows both parties to recognize the bigger picture – not the goal, but the individual, as their whole self. Trust and empathy are not byproducts of feedback conversations that aim to improve performance, they're the very means by which improved performance is enabled. To that extent, the facts are secondary.
- **It affords deeper insight:** It allows both the feedback giver and recipient to explore any aspect of the feedback in real-time.
- **It allows for two-way feedback:** One-way feedback implicitly establishes a hierarchy of needs. It also limits the individual providing feedback from benefiting themself (on the assumption that the two individuals work together).
- **It interrupts ego:** The reluctance of some individuals to give feedback in person, in order to avoid judgement or criticism, is its own power dynamic. Conversations (not emails) are the way to build trust, to gain deeper insight, and to avoid feedback being one-way.
- **It builds trust:** This is due to all of the above. Anonymous feedback might allow someone to 'be honest,' but the cost of this is the perpetuation of a dysfunctional relationship.

SPONTANEOUS – make it about THIS moment: Feedback should always be provided at the point of need, because it needs to be actionable. Its value is in this moment – at point A, as shown on the Story Line (Fig 65) – as opposed to creating stories about events that happened in the past and which divert attention away from the present.

The best way to get feedback is to go after it. Feedback is the habit of asking questions in the pursuit of personal development, and so individuals who are hungry to learn will be hungry for feedback. The primary responsibility for feedback should be with the individual seeking it, because they know best when and what feedback is most valuable. They also know who to ask – generally those who are closest to the action – to gain a broader range of perspectives. Feedback should be sought little and often, at the end of any significant activity, such as after a meeting or upon completion of a project. Spontaneous feedback creates a *feedback flow*, in the flow of work.

TRANSPARENT – make it open to everyone: The purpose of feedback is to help the individual improve their performance (on the basis that, could someone else do it for them, feedback would not be required). Sharing feedback on an individual openly with the team that's supporting the activity can: (1) Shed light on the overall performance of the activity, and how they can help improve it; (2) Share lessons learned; (3) Encourage others to give feedback; (4) Create more opportunities for others to offer support; (5) Normalize the use of feedback for continuous improvement. The only rule is that you only share information about others that you would share to their face. FAST feedback is an impersonal process that takes place in the open. It is only behind closed doors that power dynamics can be created.

#8 POWER TO CARE: *MAKE PEOPLE YOUR PURPOSE*

Organizations that in the name of customer-centricity claim the customer is their number one purpose, and which execute upon that purpose accordingly, will fail. The reason will be clear to anyone who has tried to score a goal by staring at it. To score, you need to know where the goal is (the customer), but what you must attend to (that which is your purpose) is the ball – or in organizational terms, your people – in the full knowledge that through its attendance it will take care of the rest.

When organizations act in the service of their people, their people become not just a part of the organization, but that through which the organization is itself a part. In this way, as the organization's purpose is directed toward its people, so in turn this is reflected outward, through the actions of its people, to those whom they themselves serve: their customers. This natural reciprocation arises through the expression of those who love and enjoy what they do, and so seek to share it.

Seen in this light, the role of the organization as a definable entity is as a utility in service of its people, to provide those experiences through which individuals can express and share their full selves. Helping people express what they love through their work – their passions and strengths – generates customer value. This need to express ourselves authentically is innate in all of us, as the natural intelligence of awareness.

Agile organizations organize around value. The challenge is that while customer value is the outward goal, the perceived value of each individual within the organization (that which they themselves perceive) is that which unlocks it. This is why organizations are not agile. When individual value and expression is not realized, egoic power dynamics create resistance within the organization. Groups form through competing needs because egoic value is always extrinsic, and therefore limited by the external environment. These egoic structures and behaviours place a limitation on the flow of value through the organization, such that the organization loses its natural agility. In contrast, intrinsic motivation does not limit the possibilities for change, but rather furthers them, through self-interest, self-organization and curiosity.

Organizations that make people their purpose cease trying to manage individual performance and instead recognize that:

a. **All individuals seek high performance:** High performance arises through the open, undiluted expression of who we are – this being the inherent quality of awareness to know itself within experience. True high performance cannot be 'managed into being.' It occurs *through* being.

b. **OK performance is not OK:** Individuals who are able to express how they feel through the work they do will achieve the highest performance. OK performance is not OK, because this means that individuals are not able to express themselves fully and freely.

Accordingly, the performance of individuals should be assessed using two key metrics:
1. At an individual level: **Intrinsic Performance.**
2. At an organizational level: **Inclusion Variance.**

1 – Intrinsic Performance

Intrinsic Performance is a new measure of performance that is driven entirely by intrinsic motivation. The measure applies to individuals who operate through teams. A team is a temporary construct, formed through the service of its members toward a common performance goal. Membership on the team is limited, and inclusive of those individuals who share this common purpose. To determine their Intrinsic Performance, each individual defines their own personal performance goals, according to eight principles (Fig 86).

Goals are defined by the individual to answer	Goals must fulfil these criteria	Goals are reviewed by the team to	Goals to be assessed by asking
#1 What are the experiences I want to have?	**#3** Have intrinsic value to the individual	**#5** Ensure that they will collectively achieve their team's shared purpose	**#7** Am I doing the things I would like to do?
#2 What do I want to learn from those experiences?	**#4** They must act in service of the team's shared performance goal	**#6** Identify opportunities to support each other in achieving their individual goals	**#8** Am I getting better at them?

FIG 86 – RULES FOR DETERMINING INTRINSIC PERFORMANCE GOALS

The team will persist for as long as the common performance goal is shared by its members. However, individual goal setting and assessment is an ongoing, iterative process, to reflect changing circumstance and opportunities.

Each team member will self-assess their own performance, leveraging data from FAST feedback, to answer the two key self-assessment questions (#7 & #8) shown in Fig 86. The team's overall performance is also assessed collectively, against attainment of the group's shared performance goal. However, individual recognition and reward should be based entirely on the achievement of each individual's own personal targets. In other words, reward is reflective of the individual's level of intrinsic motivation and personal fulfilment – you are rewarded by doing the work that fulfils you the most, and through which you are best able to learn.

Intrinsic performance provides a measure of learning agility, in recognizing the motivation and ability of individuals to learn. It places primacy on learning above performance, through an intrinsic rather than extrinsic reward model. It explains that the role of centrally set targets is to show the team what to aim for, rather than being used as the basis by which success is itself defined or inspired, for which individually defined goals are far more effective.

Through this approach, remuneration is directly proportional to intrinsic performance, so that individuals are paid according to their perceived intrinsic value of the activity. The approach is based on trust – that which arises through the acceptance and openness to create, share and express who we are, without limits, and from which intrinsic value is derived. As with individual goal setting, individuals within the team set their own remuneration based on their perceived intrinsic performance, before sharing and reviewing with the team to ensure that they can collectively achieve its shared budget. And just as with goal setting, this is an ongoing, iterative process, to reflect current context.

When performance is assessed on its intrinsic value, the extrinsic compensatory value of remuneration is diminished. Its role, therefore, rather than acting as a reward, is as recognition, to systemically encourage intrinsically motivated action above all else within the organization, away from the value of doing (of being 'productive') and toward the value of being (of being *aware*). It reminds us that happiness cannot be learned, or earned, or rewarded to us – it is, in fact, our natural state of being. There is nothing to be done to achieve it; to recognize it, we simply need to allow it. No work, no experience, can make you happy, but through experience, we can allow our happiness to shine. We do not need to wait for this recognition in the way that one might wait for a paycheck, because happiness is only ever available in this moment.

2 – Inclusion Variance

Inclusion Variance, as discussed in Chapter 11, is a measure of first-order and second-order egoic power dynamics within an organization. As an entirely subjective assessment (undertaken as a self-assessment of each individual's relationships) an objective measure can only be presented through the totality of collated perspectives, as a complete picture of all relationships within the organization.

At an individual level, the data (captured on an Inclusion Variance Target) provides a self-assessment of their perceived relationships with those they engage with in the organization, on the basis of: (1) Their holonic state of inclusion – their holonic association with that individual as relates to their role within the organization (part, whole or mutual); (2) The Separation Index (SI) for that relationship – as a measure of egocentricity/egoic dissonance (the degree to which the ego objectivizes its experience; see Chapter 8); (3) The predominant second-order power dynamic for that relationship.

Total Inclusion Variance is calculated as a measure of the average overall SI range for the organization for all relationships (as assessed from both subjective and objective perspectives), for all three holonic states of association, and across all second-order power dynamics. The greater the Inclusion Variance value, the more dysfunctional the organization, due to its perpetuation of egoic power dynamics.

18. THE VANISHING POINT

META IMPERATIVES OF THE THIRD WAVE

The Third Wave – the era of the metaverse – represents a fundamental paradigm shift from the conventions of centralized control toward a radically decentralized system. In the Third Wave, our relationship with technology will radically change, with our technological advancements emerging as an extension of ourselves. Arguably the greatest technology ever invented was the pen, through the power of story. But the power of stories owes itself not to the pen, nor even to the one who wields it, but to the one with whom it is shared. So too, in the Third Wave, the power of technology will be in its ability to collapse the boundaries that have separated our experiences from others'.

The metaverse will see the digital revolution of the Second Wave replaced by a new analogue revolution, in part due to Moore's Law. Intel cofounder Gordon Moore posited in the 1960s that the number of transistors on an integrated circuit would double every two years, which was both historically accurate (for many years to come) and prospectively impossible. With transistors now approaching the size of an atom, the power of digital computers is reaching its limits. The solution is neural networks, using analogue computing. At the time of writing, analogue chips in production can undertake 25 trillion operations per second with only three watts of power – much faster and more energy efficient than their digital counterparts. Neural networks are exploding in popularity, and one of the biggest current use cases is in augmented and virtual reality. Our brains process information digitally (a neuron either fires or it doesn't) but they are also analogue, in that thinking does not happen in one place. It happens everywhere, all at once. The way we process information in the metaverse will closely reflect that of the human brain – perhaps unsurprising given the metaverse's role as the operant mind for synthetic human experience. Just as in time, the writer will leave their impression upon the pen, so too in the metaverse our technologies will increasingly bear the hallmarks of their makers.

But more important than what the metaverse is, is why it is. Its purpose, as conceived, is for the fulfilment of ego, through the ultimate control of experience. It's the ultimate ego trip, in which we seek – as with all experience – to lose ourselves. To that end, it represents our ultimate act of futility. The eco-death of the Second Wave will give way to a collective **ego-death** in the Third Wave. The convergent effect of the Third Wave's eight Meta Imperatives will lead (if we are to survive as a species) to the dematerialization of physical space, distance and objects, and give rise to new forms of seemingly infinite (albeit finite) human experience, which are described below. (Note: CI refers to the associated *Second-Wave Conscious Imperative*).

#1 POLYMATH ERA (CI: GIVE OPEN ACCESS TO INFORMATION)

"Through greater human intelligence, I can access our complete history of information."

The advent of Brain Computer Interfaces (BCI) will extend our thinking into the physical realm through the coupling of mind and matter within neural and non-neural pathways. This is akin to the notebook in Clark and Chalmers' museum-visit thought experiment, extending into the limitless pages of the metaverse's data network. As our data becomes an extension of our own physiology, individuals will crucially retain ownership and identity of their own data and content. Big tech firms will no longer profit from an individual's digital interactions. Web pages and URLs with physical IP addresses serving the internet will be replaced with mesh networks, in which data is decentralized, with content accessed from the nearest point in the network. Instant access to knowledge through BCI will enable access to shared collective memory, eliminating the need for learning. Derestricted access to all affective experience will increase our associative capacity, resulting in a new form of 'meta-thinking,' enabling us to conceptualize on a far broader and divergent scale. The application of machine learning (a branch of artificial intelligence) to this generation of information will not only imitate how people learn, but will learn what people need. We will no longer need to look for data, because data will find us. We will no longer need to ask the question, because the answer will precede it. In this way, our perception of time – as a faculty that arises through our conception of a question that directs our attention away from this moment (and through which we conceive cause and effect, the progenitor of past and future) – will diminish, as our attention is given fully to this moment.

#2 INTRANSIENCE ERA (CI: CROWDSOURCE YOUR PEOPLE)

"Through extended life, I can live many lives."

As we reach longevity escape velocity[1] – the point when the human lifespan (and therefore time) is no longer finite – the value of time will not be found in how it is consumed, but how it is shared. Through a life that spans many lives, we will seek new ways to connect. In the future, decentralized autonomous organizations (DAOs) will bring people together as temporary member-owned communities of practice to connect through shared purpose. Within these communities, the need to distinguish between customers and suppliers will disappear, as all members are simultaneously consumers and creators. Smart contracts (self-fulfilling computer programs designed to transact assets between parties under certain conditions) will enable the automatic execution and sharing of value between two parties, without the need of a third party (the vending machine being the earliest version of this).

In a centralized system, access and membership requires a system of authentication and approval. In the metaverse, under the principles of web 3.0, the advent of self-sovereign identification will mean that groups can no longer cut off your access and shut you out. Individuals will identify themselves, rather than relying on an authentication system such as OAuth, in which a trusted party has to be reached in order to assess identity. In web 3.0, a permissionless system will enable individuals to interact through a network without authorization from a governing body – to join and leave as they wish.

#3 CREATOR ERA (CI: BECOME A FRAGILE ORGANIZATION)

"Through ideas, I can recreate my world."

In Babylon, in 1750 BCE, it took 50 hours of collective human labour to create just one second of light from a sesame oil lamp.[2] Today it takes half a second of work to get an hour of light. The demonetization of technologies will mean we can do more, in less time, than ever before. With less time doing, and more time innovating, we will enter the

1. Aubrey de Grey, ADNJ (2004-06-15). *Escape Velocity: Why the Prospect of Extreme Human Life Extension Matters Now.* PLOS Biol. 2 (6): 723–726. Doi:10.1371/journal.pbio.0020187. PMC 423155.

2. Ridley, M. (2010). *The Rational Optimist: How Prosperity Evolves.* (1st Edition). Fourth Estate.

creator era. In the metaverse, everyone will be a content creator. User-generated content will be replaced by content generated through each and every interaction, as the timespan of innovation collapses the *time to value* and magnifies the value and agility of ideas. The notions of factual truth, fake news and deep fakes will have no basis in a world in which many truths, many realities, can coexist through the stories and worlds we create. Reality will be allowed to be fake, because everything that is fake will be real. No one will be able to tell you what you should or shouldn't believe, or who you can or cannot be.

In organizations today, the employer creates the work for their employees. In the metaverse, the individual will become the divine creator of their work, as the creator of their own experience. Organizations will form around ideas, as people come together to create shared experience – the pursuit of perfection within finite experience resulting in ever more refined and subtle forms. Accordingly, organizations will bear the fragility of the ideas they create, their temporary existence hanging by the threads from which their ideas are woven into being, held taut through their transformation, until inevitably, as with all experience, attention is lost.

#4 AMPLIFIED ERA (CI: FIND YOUR PHASE TRANSITION)

"Through alter-egos I will play many parts – expressions of a larger whole, a louder voice."

In the metaverse, the currency of facts will be discarded for the currency of meaning. Through our search for meaning will arise the *amplification of individuality*. Through our digital twin alter-egos we can be anyone, anywhere, at any time. The internet will give way to an 'alter-net' of alternate realities (all alternates being the only reality), in which our 'alters' let loose our personalities of self-expression in forms so diverse as to render the original self transparent. We will exist through narrative imaginings that allow us to fundamentally disrupt our perspective, step outside of ourselves, lose our centre, and all (knowingly or not) in the search for self. We will live through dreams, and through this unbounded expression, the 'story of me' will necessarily lose itself in experience, in order to find itself.

These stories will transcend the amplification of ignorance that we see today, whose populist expression has sought to polarize public opinion through the assertion of increasingly totalitarian perspectives. Ironically, it is the freedoms of liberal idealism, such as the freedom of speech, that have enabled the power of one voice to drown out the many. Indeed, the world's largest democracies have proved the perfect playgrounds for tyrants.

The growing polarity that pervades the geopolitical landscape will ultimately be transcended through the metaverse and decentralized control, when the power of totalistic expression is given to everyone. This multiplicity and diversity of individuality will conjure a louder voice – not through one voice, but through the many voices of alter-ego. Most importantly, our experiences will be shared, as we join with others through new forms of collective expression, so that through our synchronization the voices of the many are amplified as the voice of one.

#5 OPEN ERA (CI: RETHINK THINKING)

"Through computational acceleration the future will become what I imagine it to be."

The accelerating pace of change, witnessed in everything from robotics, 3D printing, blockchain, nanotechnology and quantum computers, means one thing: the future will be unknowable. The power of prediction will be usurped by the power of imagination – it will become what we need it to be. The technological 'singularity' – the hypothetical point in time at which we can no longer predict the future because the rate of change is so fast – is estimated to occur within the next 20–30 years.[3] When it is impossible to predict, and therefore control, the future, why would we think about it? In the future, what will matter most is direct experience. We will cease to apply our thinking to a future we cannot conceive or control, and instead give greater attention to present experience.

3. Kurzweil, R. (2005). *The Singularity Is Near*, pp. 135–136. Penguin Group.

#6 TRUST-LESS ERA (CI: ABANDON RULES TO GROW)

"Through technology I have full control – the rules do not apply."

In a trust-less system, our every thought and action, our every intent, will be instantaneously visible and knowable to everyone. In a centrally controlled system, rules are required to create social trust. Access to technology is controlled, and compliance is enforced through a permission-based system. In contrast, in web 3.0, individuals will be able to interact through networks that are: (1) *Trust-less* – the network itself allows participants to interact publicly or privately, without a trusted third party; (2) *Open* – built from open-source technologies that are available to all, by an open and accessible community of developers, and executed in full view of the world; (3) *Permissionless* – anyone can participate without authorization from a governing body.

Decentralized financial systems will offer monetary contracts (as financial instruments) without relying on intermediaries such as brokerages, exchanges or banks, by using smart contracts on a blockchain. The whole 'fintech' system of financial technology services, including blockchain and tokenomics, is already remaking the finance industry from the ground up, breaking lending away from the shackles of fractional reserve lending, and finally allowing consumer credit to be issued at scale.

#7 ADAPTIVE ERA (CI: REWARD PERFORMANCE WITH FAST FEEDBACK)

"Through capital I can access the people whose feedback I need to flourish."

As access to capital and ideas becomes increasingly democratized, a new 'spiral economy' will arise in which all activity – as the content of experience – is instantaneously captured, encoded, shared and accessible at the moment of its creation, to be simultaneously recreated. Cryptocurrencies such as Non-Fungible Tokens (NFTs), which previously facilitated the transfer of ownership, will be replaced with an economy in which ownership no longer has value, and where value is derived through transaction at the source.

Every infinitesimal interaction will derive value, through automatic-execution smart contracts (smart in the sense that no 'agreement' is required). In the act of ultimate capital accessibility, the very act of perception will become monetized, through the 'currency of attention,' in which that which attracts attention gains greatest value.

In organizations today, the ability to turn data into actionable outcomes is the number one differentiator of performance. This ability of a subject to recognize and respond to an external stimulus establishes a feedback loop. In the metaverse, the most valuable currency will be feedback. The distance between the action we take (the effect) and its underlying data or origin (the cause) will collapse, in the same way as there is in reality no distinction between our experience – that which we perceive and conceive – and the knowing of it. In this unified state, organizations will bend to their environment in the same way that the wave bends or breaks upon the ocean according to its will, to return to its source. In the metaverse, all change is possible because nothing is ever lost.

#8 CONNECTED ERA (CI: MAKE PEOPLE YOUR PURPOSE)

"Through online connectivity I can find myself through others."

In today's world, organizational success is measured through productivity and efficiency. In the future, if our own abilities will have less and less bearing on organizational performance, what role will organizations play, and how will they demonstrate value? The answer is *connectedness*. In the metaverse everything will be connected – from all things to one thing. Real-time social presence will mean that you can be with anyone, in their presence, anywhere in the world. Information and content will be ubiquitous, with applications running on blockchains or decentralized peer-to-peer networks. The data limitations that restrict social networks today will be transformed through neural networks that will communicate not just extrospective, but introspective experience. This will occur as we encounter each other through their own thoughts and feelings, and as we take on altered perspectives. As Henry David Thoreau once said, *"Could a greater miracle take place than for us to look through each other's eyes, for an instant?"*[4]

4. Thoreau, H. D. (1854). *Walden or Life in the Woods*. (1st Edition). Vintage Classics.

Our awareness of difference and diversity will take on new dimensions that are far beyond our current experience.

THE FOURTH WAVE: THE INFINITE SYSTEM

Consciousness, or *awareness*, is the source and substance of everything. It is by its nature self-aware, and so it is inherent in all experience, as the activity of awareness to reveal and know itself. Like the *ouroboros* (the symbol of a serpent eating its own tail, that dates back to the 14th century BCE), through experience we are all seeking our end, in the hope of finding our beginning.

In the Fourth Wave, in the midst of seemingly limitless experience, the ego will have nowhere left to seek, nothing left to find. The novelist and screenwriter Anthony Horowitz, in his book *Myths and Legends*,[5] describes how Pandora let out all forms of pestilence upon the world: *"At the last moment, Epimetheus managed to slam down the lid, by which time only one thing was left in the box: Hope. Which is just as well. For with all the problems that Pandora had released into the world, where would we be without it."* The metaverse will see the reopening of Pandora's box for the final time. It will make us Gods, but the existence of God is based on faith, and faith cannot survive without hope. Neither can ego.

Our future will accelerate until it can be found only ever in this moment, at the vanishing point of the separate self. It is the point that can never be reached, because you are never at a distance from it. At this escape velocity of ego, the separate self will at last depart, through the paradoxical realization that 'it' was never there. The death of ego is the death of authorship, and the end of leadership, in the absence of one to whom it can serve. The separate self cannot ever know the Fourth Wave because the conception of its absence requires its presence – its ignorance – just as a shadow survives by hiding from the light. And yet, the Fourth Wave is close to all of us. Each night when we sleep, we find again our vanishing point, in the stillness in which our sense of a separate self is lost, as we rest in awareness.

Everything seeks stillness, seeks rest. It is the universal condition, described by minimum energy principles, that wherever possible, the use of energy is minimized. For instance, take a length of string between two hands, and see that it always forms the same

5. Horowitz, A. (1985). *Myths and Legends*. Kingfisher.

exact shape, or 'catenary curve.' Or observe a star, and notice that through its observation, the light that has been travelling for a billion years has always come to you through the path that will take the least amount of time.

	FIRST WAVE Individual	SECOND WAVE Centralized System	THIRD WAVE Decentralized system	FOURTH WAVE Infinite system
Beginning	I am born	I am hired	I am instantiated	I am
Intellect	Individual intellect (IQ)	Intellectual Property (IP)	Artificial Intelligence (AI)	Beyond understanding
Belonging	I belong to others	I belong to a system	The system belongs to me	There is no system
Construct	One	Organization	Metaverse	No one
Control	Localized control	Centralized control	Decentralized control	No control
Location	I am located in my body	I am located in a team	I am located in the metaverse	I am unlocated
Identity	I have a name	I have an ID	I identify as many	I have no identity
Data	I don't have any data	Other people own my data	I own my own data	No one owns anything
Ontology	I am apart	I am part of a system	I am the system	I am that
Trust	Relationships create trust	Rules create trust	A trust less system	Acceptance

FIG 87 – THE STORY OF THE FOUR WAVES

The Fourth Wave is an infinite, non-hierarchical system that will transcend cause and effect. A hierarchy by definition has a top and a bottom, and yet, when we look closely at experience, there is no top or bottom to the wholes and parts from which reality is formed. Rather, everything in the system is connected, such that what we recognize within complexity as 'organized' exists because of how everything else exists, just as the picture is formed from the frame. We can't say that any aspect is causal of the other, because everything is causal of everything else, including itself. In fact, to describe anything as a 'system' is to give finitude to that which must inherently be infinite.

Fig 87 describes the story of human experience across the four waves. Throughout each of the waves, ego has persisted as the fractal expression of our ignorance within experience. In the final wave, our final chapter, we will finally forget ourselves, to at last remember who we are.

EPILOGUE

WHERE DO WE BEGIN?

When I was a child I had a dragon – a small wooden puppet that I kept in a box under my bed. I remember my excitement as I'd reach into the box, and with my hand on the cross-brace, watch as the dragon came to life. At the end of the day, after our many adventures, I'd carefully place the dragon back into its box, letting the strings rest gently over its body as it slept. As I grew up, I would forget about the dragon, and would play with it less and less, which is when I noticed something strange. It seemed that the longer I forgot about it, the less the dragon was like the one I remembered. I'd open the box and find its legs tangled in the strings, its wings trapped beneath threads that once bore it aloft. For me, the only obvious explanation was that my dragon was trying to escape. It was alive.

Each of us is like the puppet in the box, who in slumber has become trapped, wrapped up in our own story. Like the strings that once raised our wings to fly, they begin to limit us, ensnare us. But you are not your story. And it is time for the world to wake up.

Our organizations, our societies, our ecosystems are entering a new and profound era of change. The technologies we have asserted through our belief in progress are ironically and inevitably accelerating us toward a future that is both unknowable and uncontainable. The story of you is routed in this belief in progress and the progressive path. We believe we need to know more, own more, control more, in order to be more. We believe that the answers to our questions can be found in experience, in the misunderstanding that we are separate from that which we seek. Consider the advancement of technology through artificial intelligence:

- **We seek connection:** If the form of AI is that of a collective superintelligence, then its function is to connect. Our technologies, our information, our abilities are becoming increasingly infused and interdependent. Generative AI preludes a future in which every answer can be defined by an infinite set of questions, themselves referring to an infinite set of answers. And yet, we are already intimately connected to everything. Through the appearance of progress, AI is seemingly bridging a gap that was never there.
- **We seek change:** If the measure of progress is change, then the purpose of progress is to keep pace with the changing face of experience. But could it be that the acceleration of change we perceive arises not from experience, but from our need

to change it? Through progress, we seek to solve our greatest challenges. And yet, our technological progress is proportionate to our capacity to address problems of our own making. For example, we celebrate the ingenuity of breakthrough decarbonization technologies, not in spite of, but fundamentally because of the contribution our technologies have made to the advancement of global warming. The progress of one made possible through the other. This duality lies at the heart of scientific progress – that our solutions must inevitably become the problems of the future (just as a theory can never be proved, until the day it is shown to be false).

- **We seek truth:** Through deep fake technology, it will be impossible to discern truth from experience. But is that any different from today? All you can ever know is that which is in your direct experience, and you can never know what that is. Our technologies invite us to reassess the meaning of truth, and to recognize its futility as the ground upon which our conscience rests, lying as it does upon a reality that is groundless.

- **We seek control:** The challenges of today cannot be solved on our own. Through progress, our problems have grown bigger than ourselves – our solutions requiring mass action, mass movements, to resolve. Our progress points to a future in which even the simplest individual endeavours will only be made possible through the actions of the world entire (Einstein's *Spooky Action at a Distance* by any other name). Although, has this ever not been the case? Have we ever been the individual authors of our world? Through technology, we will become a race of gods. Yet as equals, without the faithful, we are powerless to act alone. In this context, it is inevitable that tyrants and dictatorships will not survive a future in which no one is in control.

- **We seek to remember:** For years, our technological progress has been measured by the increasing quantum of data. AI marks the shift toward the encoding of knowledge not through points on a map, but by the paths that connect them – a relational intelligence of seemingly infinite connections through which no data can ever be lost. In time we might conceive AI as an infinite mind in whose knowledge nothing can be forgotten, no story ever lost. And yet, in a world where we no longer need to remember who we are, who then will we be?

The paradox of progress is that what we seek beyond all else is an end to seeking. Our societies have given rise to a population of retired, recovering employees – addicts of a system that promised happiness, only to find that the peace that is sought will forever lie out of reach, because it can never be lost. This materialistic mentality that has perpetuated the endless search of the seeker is the cause of all suffering. It is the belief in the story of me – of ego. The dream within the dream.

WHERE WILL WE END?

We can only perceive that which we can imagine. When we are awake, we do not actually experience a world. Rather, what we experience are thoughts and perceptions through which we infer our model of the world. In dreams, we close our eyes and the world is revealed to us, through our model of the world. It is the same world.

Our model of the world establishes a perceptual loop of thinking and feeling, between our inner world (of introspection, or thoughts) and our outer world (of experience, or sensations). Whenever we give attention to experience, we seek to change it (Fig 5). To change our objective experience (to feel, to create) is to learn, and what we learn changes what we think (our inner world). To change (to give attention to) our subjective experience (to think, to discover) is to imagine, and what we imagine changes what we create (our outer world).

"... all that is imagined is real, and all that is real is imagined."[1]

It is within this model of the world that we imagine ourselves – and our story – to be. As children, our inner world affords our stories unrestrained imagination. As adults, as attention is given increasingly to our outer, objective world, our stories learn their limitations. This is why adults believe in mortgage repayments, and why children believe in dragons.

As the individual self or subject of experience, we either believe that we can change experience, or that experience can change us. When experience acts in the way that we expect, it is because it's in accordance with our model of the world, which includes our sense of self within it. It is when the world makes sense, whether observing a frog hop rather than fly, or when 2 + 2 = 4 and not 5. When neither of these things happen – when experience pushes back – we experience surprise.

1. *Eckblad, J.D. (2012). Blackfire: The Books of Bairnmoor, Volume I.* Resource Publications.

As discussed in Chapter 12, surprise is the difference between our model of the world (what we perceive it to be) and what we discover it to be in objective experience (through our senses). It is through surprise that we learn about the world, as we update our model of the world to seek to limit surprise – this being key to survival and the process of evolution. To put it another way, we exist to *self-evidence* – to maximize the evidence for our model of the world, and thereby evidence for (through the probability of) our own existence.

Through artificial intelligence, what is changing is the use of technology to reduce surprise. Could you know if it will rain tomorrow, without technology? The answer to this seemingly simple question has required a billion other questions before it, each reasoned, researched and deduced through the many streams of science over the past century. Technology is the process that transforms complexity into simplicity – that turns many questions into the one that can be answered through the swipe of an app. The question is not simple. Rather, it is through technology that we perceive it as such, when presented with a simple answer, and through which we avoid surprise. The foundation of all technology is knowledge – the accessibility of information through which to change our perception of experience. Today, the advent of AI is using knowledge to transform our experience to minimize surprise to a far greater degree. Prior to AI, knowledge provided answers to the questions that *other people* had asked, based on their own experiences. Through AI, we are able to answer our *own* questions – questions that derive from our own unique experience, that no one has ever asked before. In fact, it is doing so before the question has even been asked. No question – no questioner.

The progress of AI is concomitant to its ability to reduce surprise. Consider the significance of this on our perception of reality. Surprise updates our model of the world – it changes us, so that we learn. With AI, it is as if experience is acting to reduce surprise – to bend experience to what we expect it to be – as if it is learning about us and our model of the world. When this happens, when there is no distinction between our inner world and the outer world of experience, then to which world will we identify and belong? This is what the Fourth Wave describes – the collapse of separation between our perceived inner world of self, and outer world of experience, and the end of ego.

And, of course, this separation, and its collapse, is just a story, told from the perspective of a separate self that believes it is separate from experience in the first place. What we recognize in experience is only ever that which we recognize in ourselves, because (knowingly or not) we see ourselves in all experience. It could not otherwise be known. You are that.

One could argue that AI presents an existential threat because of our dependence on reality to push back, to challenge and change our inner model of the world, so that who we are can adapt and grow. Indeed, a key aspect of ego flip (in step 3) is to delineate our persona through both its impact on objective experience and the impact of experience on it, in order to challenge the prevailing egoic perspective. To do so necessitates that experience offer this feedback loop, so we can perceive our limitation and boundary. And from the perspective of the separate self this makes perfect sense, because without this self-reference they would cease to exist. But all of it, from tragedy to triumph, from technology to truth, is simply story.

For the separate self – for all of us – our story is one of heroes and villains, to which we cast ourselves and others, and through which, in their conflict, the story of ego survives. But in reality there are no good people or bad people. The reason acts of war and violence pervade the history of our world is *impunity*. People act because they can. To ego, this appears an act of volition. In reality, it is the very nature of consciousness, as unconditional acceptance, to know itself, through all its forms.

> *Let me run to the forest – let the dark hide my shadow from me.*
> *Let me drown in the river – let it carry my tears to the sea.*
> *Let me lie in the mountain – in its roots, let me rest, let me be.*

Through the pages of this book, we have dissected the anatomy of ego to reveal the simple truth: that you – as an individual, separate self – do not exist. Why? Because you ARE existence. You are not your body or your mind. You do not have a past or a future. You were not born, and you will not die. You are not responsible. You cannot choose any of this. Because all there is *is this* – that which you are – the boundless, timeless, infinite awareness. You are the knowing that is prior to all experience: *non est ego hoc modo* – there is no I, only this.

Who you are cannot be known. You cannot say a single true word about reality. Therein lies the mystery: that we should feel so compelled to try.